W9-BVV-428

The Union Forever

The Union Forever

Lincoln, Grant, and the Civil War

JOHN Y. SIMON

Edited and with an introduction by
Glenn W. LaFantasie
for the Ulysses S. Grant Association
and the
Institute for Civil War Studies,
Western Kentucky University

Foreword by
Harold Holzer and Frank J. Williams

UNIVERSITY PRESS OF KENTUCKY

Editorial and Sales Offices: The University Press of Kentucky
663 South Limestone Street, Lexington, Kentucky 40508-4008
www.kentuckypress.com

16 15 14 13 12   5 4 3 2 1

Library of Congress Cataloging-in-Publication Data

Simon, John Y.
  The union forever : Lincoln, Grant, and the Civil War / John Y. Simon ;
edited by Glenn W. LaFantasie for the Ulysses S. Grant Association and the
Institute for Civil War Studies, Western Kentucky University ; foreword by
Harold Holzer and Frank J. Williams
      p. cm.
  Includes bibliographical references and index.
  ISBN 978-0-8131-3444-4 (hardcover : alk. paper)
  1. Lincoln, Abraham, 1809-1865—Military leadership. 2. Grant, Ulysses
S. (Ulysses Simpson), 1822-1885—Military leadership. 3. Command of
troops—History—19th century. 4. United States—History—Civil War,
1861-1865—Campaigns. 5. United States—Politics and government—
1861-1865. I. LaFantasie, Glenn W. II. Title.
  E457.2.S57 2012
  973.7'41—dc23   2011046136

This book is printed on acid-free paper meeting the requirements of the American
National Standard for Permanence in Paper for Printed Library Materials.

Manufactured in the United States of America.

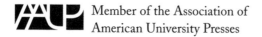 Member of the Association of
American University Presses

To Harriet Furst Simon

Contents

Foreword

Preserving and publishing important scholarship is a tradition among both historians and the presses that so usefully keep their works in print. There is nothing unusual about collecting and issuing the best or least accessible of a great scholar's works. This book is one such example. The results provide new generations of readers crucial access to lasting ideas that stand the test of time. What is most unusual—unique perhaps—occurs when such collections are designed not only as resources but as tributes. That is the case with this book. This volume not only presents predictably fine scholarly works by a brilliant historian but pays affectionate tribute to the man who wrote them. And it is altogether fitting and proper that we so honor John Y. Simon with the publication of his essays.

In a long and productive career as a historian and editor, not only did John Y. Simon demonstrate a keen eye, a fine mind, and a dazzling talent, but he consistently showed loyalty to friends and fellow scholars. Abraham Lincoln said, "The better part of one's life consists of his friendships." Those who knew John Y., and who undoubtedly miss him as much as we do, would no doubt agree that those words might well have been written about the original irrepressible talent we so sadly lost much too soon.

A year before George Bernard Shaw died, he was asked by a journalist to name a famous person—a statesman, artist, philosopher, or writer—whom he missed the most. Sorrowfully, Shaw replied, "The man I miss the most is the man I could have been." We who knew and admired him miss John Y. Simon precisely *because* he became all that he could be. The words of the great twentieth-century Spanish philosopher José Ortega y Gasset also come to mind: "The person of excellence is the one who demands a great deal of himself. The vulgar person is the one who demands nothing of himself." John Y. Simon, who gave his all for his profession and his colleagues, was by this or any other measure truly a person of excellence.

But those who knew him understood that John Y. could also be stubborn and willful. Fortunately, John's willfulness was always directed for the good—of his school, of his beloved Grant Papers project, of his profession, of his colleagues, and of course of his wonderful family.

The people we admire most and longest—those whose successes inspire us most—are not quickly fading celebrities with astronomical incomes. They are true geniuses like John Y. Simon (and the man he wrote about, Ulysses S. Grant).

Simon's and Grant's dedication and determination were long lasting. The most important thing in their lives was their faith in what they truly believed was good and worthwhile and their ability to believe in believing. They had a sense of commitment that was closely guarded, for they knew that without it, they would be doomed to despair.

John Y. Simon and Ulysses S. Grant both had courage. To have this kind of courage, one needs to be clear and self-confident in one's beliefs. One learns to trust one's own judgment, and while one makes mistakes, they are not the errors born of self-doubt. John Y. and Grant were steady, reliable, and persuasive. They believed they could accomplish whatever they promised themselves and their friends. They usually did.

Unlike Grant, John Y. boasted an unforgettable sense of humor. His dry and often acerbic wit will be remembered and cherished by the students and friends who laughed along with him at his brilliant ripostes. Was ever a scholar so brilliantly clever?

John Y. Simon's thirty-one volumes of *The Papers of Ulysses S. Grant* represent a milestone in documentary history. The Lincoln Forum awarded him its highest honor, the Richard N. Current Award of Achievement. The jury that presented the work's editor with the Lincoln Prize in 2004 declared: "It is inconceivable that any historian would write on the Civil War without having these volumes at hand. John Y. Simon has been an ambassador to the academic and public world, demonstrating the quality of Civil War scholarship."

The same can be said about the deftly lucid essays contained in this volume. While he spent almost his entire career immersed in the words of an American hero—Ulysses S. Grant—he was also comfortable, indeed highly insightful and original, as this collection will demonstrate, in treating such corollary subjects as Abraham Lincoln, Mary Lincoln, Ann Rutledge, and the Civil War.

He remained in demand, too, as a consultant to other editorial projects, including *The Papers of Jefferson Davis* and *The Legal Papers of Abraham Lincoln*. John was always there to help, and the word "no" was never part of his vocabulary. As such, he headed the Association for Documentary Editing and the Illinois Association for Advancement of History and served on countless advisory boards. It was no accident that he was universally acclaimed as "the dean of American documentary editors." He set the bar, created the template, and left the reading public richer for the result.

Despite work to be completed on a supplemental volume to the *Grant Papers*, a super index, an annotated edition of the *Memoirs of Ulysses S. Grant*, and a digitized edition of the *Papers*, John Y. Simon lived to see the Grant Papers project to its conclusion, just as Grant lived until his memoirs were completed. Both fought tenaciously in life for their legacy in death.

And how did John Y. Simon want to be remembered? First and foremost, as the editor of the *Grant Papers*, of course. But something of his legacy shines forth from this volume, too—from his piercing and authoritative writing—and of course from his life's work as a colleague and friend that we remember and honor.

We were—we are—truly grateful to call him an inspiration, an example, but above all a friend.

Frank J. Williams
President
The Ulysses S. Grant
   Association

Harold Holzer
Member, Board of Directors
The Ulysses S. Grant
   Association

Editorial Note

In preparing these essays for republication, I have tried to standardize some minor editorial concerns for consistency's sake. For example, I have silently corrected typographical errors and editorial errors of spelling and punctuation. I've also regularized punctuation, such as the use of ellipses. References to inclusive dates have been rendered consistently as in, for example, 1854–1862, instead of 1854–62. Months and years have also been standardized throughout the text as in, say, May 1848 instead of May, 1848. The possessive plural is always given as in, for instance, Thomas's rather than Thomas'. Commas are used in every instance to set off each particular in a series, such as in Lincoln, Grant, and Sherman. Some other minor grammatical changes have been made, mostly for the sake of clarity and to conform to the preferred style of the University Press of Kentucky. In the bibliographical notes, volume numbers appear in arabic rather than in roman numerals. Other minor editorial matters, such as making sure that an officer's full rank is given at the first mention of his name, have been silently effected. I have regularized abbreviations used in the source citations; in most cases, I have followed the abbreviations Professor Simon employed most frequently in his writings or the annotations found in the *Grant Papers*. As the reader will note, some of the essays have source notes and others do not; in that regard, the essays have been reprinted as originally published.

Inevitably, there is some overlap in these essays and some repetition, particularly in the repeated use of a few quotations Professor Simon seems to have favored. Yet this repetition does not detract from the original scholarly contribution that may be found in each of the separate essays.

—GWL

Introduction

Glenn W. LaFantasie

John Y. Simon was a gentleman and a scholar. He would have disliked my use of a cliché to describe him, but I can think of no one who fits the phrase better than he did. He would have relished, however, the fact that the phrase originated with Robert Burns in a whimsical poem about dogs. Burns was one of Abraham Lincoln's favorite poets. Ulysses S. Grant liked Burns as well and was once overheard quoting the lines, "Man's inhumanity to man / makes countless thousands mourn."[1] I don't know if John had a fondness for the Scotsman's poetry, but it hardly matters. John was the epitome of a scholar who, in all aspects of his life, was a gentleman as well.

In his time, he was also the foremost expert on Ulysses S. Grant and a leading Lincoln scholar. John traveled comfortably in the different spheres of Grant and Lincoln studies, moving between them with felicity and grace and brilliantly tying them together, as the final two essays in this collection demonstrate so well. As a gentleman, John was a modest scholar. He did not brag about his achievements or boast about the high place he occupied among the nation's top Civil War historians. But any historian who works on Grant knows the debt he owes to John Y. Simon, not only for making Grant's voluminous papers readily available, and doing so with annotations that are trenchant and learned, but also for putting the general and his role in winning the Civil War in a perspective that has enabled scholars and students to understand the man on his own terms, by means of his own words. It sounds like an easy thing to do. Every historical editor knows it is not—that, more often than not, documents do not speak for themselves. John knew how to publish Grant's documents in such a way as to retain the general's voice while also elucidating the context and meaning of every sentence, every word. In the case of Lincoln, John earned his immense reputation by writing nimble and astute essays—the best of them published here

1

in one place for the first time—about the man, the president, and the commander in chief. Quality, not quantity, explains why John was so highly regarded among Lincoln specialists. His scholarship on Lincoln revealed how readily John could look into Honest Abe's eyes and see all the way down to his soul. When John wrote about Grant or Lincoln, or about the two of them together, he said more in his essays than some historians have said in the space of whole books. His sparkling essays, his formidable talents as a documentary editor, his broad and deep knowledge of the Civil War—these are what defined his stature as a historian and, more particularly, what distinguished him as an expert on Lincoln and Grant. Perhaps it also had something to do with the fact that John, like Lincoln and Grant, sprang (as the Lincoln 1860 campaign song put it) "out of the wilderness, down in Illinois."[2]

I first met John in the summer of 1979 at the Institute for the Editing of Historical Documents, more affectionately known to its participants as "Camp Edit," held at the Wisconsin Historical Society (at that time known by the more dignified name of the State Historical Society of Wisconsin) in Madison and sponsored by the National Historical Publications and Records Commission (NHPRC), a unit of the National Archives. As a young historian about to embark on the formidable project of editing the correspondence of Roger Williams, the founder of Rhode Island, I attended the institute to find out how one goes about putting historical documents into print. John was a member of the institute's faculty, and I recall his lucid explanation of how to select manuscripts from a large corpus of documents, like the Grant papers, without printing random jottings and every grocery list. He dealt with the topic in typical fashion: his presentation was thorough, intelligent, and hilarious.

My first encounter with John was probably similar to that of everyone who ever met him: his presence filled the room, his huge voice fit his physical features, and his bombasts—often purposely designed and timed to shock or to titillate—revealed at once that here was a man who took his work, but not himself, very seriously. John's advice about the canons of selection in documentary editions was judicious: "Editors," he said, "must fall back upon their own sense of significance in determining what to print. Recognizing that this is a creative and subjective judgment does not lessen the obligation to provide the fullest documentation with the available resources." But he also cautioned, wisely, that editors "should try to avoid being trapped by method and acknowledge a greater responsibility to the documents than to their own procedures."

The best part of John's presentation, however, was his description of Clarence Carter, a historical editor of an earlier generation who had become known for his "raffish behavior," which included excessive drinking and pinching waitresses well into his seventies.[3]

Most of the time, John's humor was a straightforward expression of his enthusiasm for his family, life, history, teaching, and the Chicago Cubs—not necessarily in that order. Actually, I never knew that John was a Cubs fan (several of our mutual colleagues have lately asked incredulously, "How could you *not* have known that?"). Amazingly, it never came up in any of our conversations over three decades. Perhaps he instinctively knew that as a New Englander I was surely a Red Sox fan, that misery doesn't always love company, and that it would be best for us to avoid the subject of baseball altogether (my misery lasted until the 2004 World Series; John's for a lifetime). I think he loved history more than baseball, family more than history, but all of his many loves were tightly intertwined into a Simonian knot.

A banker's son, John Younker Simon was born on June 25, 1933, in Highland Park, Illinois. As a teenager, he worked as a stock boy in the legendary Abraham Lincoln Book Shop in Chicago, where he became a close friend of the owner, Ralph Newman, who founded the store, in part, to provide books needed by Carl Sandburg to finish his Lincoln biography and Lloyd Lewis to start his Grant biography. In the shop, John got to meet such luminaries as Bruce Catton, Benjamin P. Thomas, and Nancy Davis (the future Mrs. Ronald Reagan). For John, working in the shop was a "daily adventure." Newman, who was a founder of the Chicago Civil War Round Table, the first such organization in the nation, complained about the large number of cronies who hung out in the shop just to socialize. "I ought to sell drinks and give books away," John quoted Newman as saying. His fondness for Newman sparkled in an address John delivered at the bookman's memorial service in 1998. Newman, said John, "was an American original, a self-made man, and a public relations master."[4]

After high school, John headed east and attended Swarthmore College, where he majored in history and earned a bachelor of arts degree in 1955. About nine hundred undergraduates attended the college in the mid-1950s, when Solomon Asch, who would gain world renown in the field of Gestalt psychology, was conducting his famous experiments on peer pressure and conformity in society. John, who rarely walked in lockstep, followed his own path from the Philadelphia suburbs to

Harvard University, where he began working on a master of arts degree in history, which he received in 1956, and a doctor of philosophy degree in history, which he earned five years later. For three of his years at Harvard, he served as a teaching fellow.

His dissertation adviser was Paul H. Buck, a Harvard legend who had served as a professor, dean of faculty, provost, endowed professor, and director of libraries, besides winning the Pulitzer Prize in 1938 for his book *The Road to Reunion*. Buck once said that "the scholar . . . proceeds from what he knows, and what he knows is the result of painstaking accumulation of data," and this statement serves as an apt description of how John Simon went about researching his dissertation, "Congress under Lincoln, 1861–1863," which prepared him well for his future career as a Civil War historian; indeed, John became well known as a historian who was unfailingly thorough as a researcher—a scholarly trademark that owed much to Paul Buck's influence.[5] While at Harvard, John met Harriet Furst, the Goucher College graduate whom he married in 1956. For both, it was a love story that exceeded the fabled bonds of affection between Ulysses S. Grant and Julia Dent. As John worked on his degree, Harriet taught elementary school in Quincy, Massachusetts. Their two children were born at Boston's Beth Israel Hospital: Philip in 1957 and Ellen in 1960.

In the late summer of 1960, the Simon family moved to Columbus, Ohio, where John began teaching at Ohio State. Two years later, John's former boss Ralph Newman was instrumental in putting together a plan to collect, edit, and publish the papers of Ulysses S. Grant in celebration of the Civil War Centennial. The centennial commissions of three states—Illinois, New York, and Ohio—agreed to sponsor the project, which would be housed at the Ohio Historical Society. Together the state commissions created the Ulysses S. Grant Association (USGA) with a not-for-profit corporate charter from the state of Illinois. An editorial board, chaired by Allan Nevins and including Newman among its members, was established, and the board selected John to serve as executive director of the USGA and editor of the Grant Papers volumes. Ralph Newman cosigned the bank note that gave the project its initial funding. Work began on September 1, 1962, on what was slated to be a fifteen-volume edition; over the years, the project grew to double that size as hundreds of thousands of Grant documents came to light. John took a leave from his faculty position at Ohio State to throw himself into what would become a labor of love spanning more than four decades. He believed that destiny worked to bring him into Grant's orbit. "I'd always been interested both in documents and in the period in which Grant lived," he told a reporter in 2004. "I've always thought that if I had been born earlier, I would have edited the Lincoln papers, but they were done by the time I grew up. I sort of fell into the prospect of doing the Grant papers, but it was a logical one."[6]

When the initial funding for support of the Grant Papers ran out after the centennial, Newman and John arranged to move the project to a new home at Southern Illinois University (SIU), where the president, Delyte W. Morris, expected, quite rightly, that the undertaking would enhance the university's scholarly reputation. The Grant Papers relocated to Carbondale in 1964. As well as serving as editor of the Grant Papers and executive director of the Ulysses S. Grant Association, John taught in the Department of History, first as an associate professor and, after 1971, as a full professor. In addition to SIU's support, the project received significant grants over the years from the National Endowment for the Humanities (NEH) and the NHPRC.

At SIU, John flourished, not only as an editor but also as a teacher. He quickly drew students to his lecture courses and seminars; history majors and graduate students learned rapidly that any course with Simon would always include substance and sarcasm, truth and laughter. His students praised him for making the past come alive, for talking about historical figures as though he knew them personally, warts and all. John consistently displayed his talent for telling a good story and telling it well. In that respect, he was much like Lincoln, whom he deeply admired. Instinctively, John knew how to share an anecdote without burying the lead or flubbing the punch line. Although I never attended one of his classes, I did get to see and hear John in action at various conferences, including early meetings of the Association for Documentary Editing. During one memorable session in 1981, John praised the benefits of microfilm by noting that the medium was "first dramatized as an instrument of historical revisionism by Whittaker Chambers." In the same talk, John assumed the pose of a philosopher: "Socrates taught us that the unexamined life was not worth living; we have learned since that the examined life is frequently quite unpleasant."[7]

As a teacher and mentor, he always made time for questions and relished those moments when students stopped by his office to ask about specific points raised in his classes or just to say hello. Often they sought him out for advice. Those who did so benefited from his prudent counsel. Both graduate and undergraduate students fondly remember that he always seemed to have a joke or a smile. Put off by pretentious or dour faculty members, they appreciated his sense of humor, his open-mindedness, and his ability to inspire them to greater heights. What's more, John taught his students how to focus their energy on analysis and the use of clear speaking and writing to express themselves. He reached students beyond the Carbondale campus by offering courses on interactive television. His lectures so delighted his students that they sometimes burst into applause when he had finished. None of this went to his head. John was an exceptional professor, but his feet were always firmly planted on the ground.

With the publication of the first volume of the Grant Papers in 1967, John established his reputation as a historical editor par excellence. Reviews of that first volume—like the reviews of every volume he saw through press—received lavish, but not unwarranted, praise from historians. "This collection, when complete, will be definitive," wrote R. J. Havlik in the *Library Journal,* "and will help to assure General Grant his proper place in history."[8] Hal Bridges wrote in the *American Historical Review* that "the editing is clear, informative, and unpedantic" and that historians would approve "the intelligent editing" and declare "'well begun' to all concerned with this fine project."[9] Reviewing volume 2, which was published in 1970, Warren W. Hassler Jr. remarked in the *Journal of Southern History* that "if succeeding volumes in this series continue to show the high standards of workmanship and scope thus far demonstrated, they should undoubtedly add to our insights into the complex character of the seemingly simple and obvious little general who would eventually be hailed as the Hero of Appomattox."[10] Indeed, John—who surrounded himself with an able staff—ensured that there would be no slippage in quality in all the volumes that the project produced. Herbert Mitgang hailed the "immaculate editorship" he found in volumes 13 and 14.[11] In a review of volumes 25 and 26, Michael Les Benedict extolled them as "a rich resource for the study of Reconstruction and related issues" and called them "an extremely valuable resource for researchers." As for the edition as a whole, Benedict urged that "every research library with an interest in American history should have a set."[12]

Small wonder, then, that in 2004 John received a Lincoln Prize for Special Achievement as editor of the Grant Papers. There were other awards and prizes, too, including a Distinguished Service Award (1983) and a Julian P. Boyd Award (1998) from the Association for

Documentary Editing; an Award of Merit from the Illinois State Historical Society (1970); the Harry S. Truman Award from the Kansas City Civil War Round Table (1972); the Delta Award from the Friends of Morris Library at SIU (1976); the Moncado Prize Award from the American Military Institute (1982); the Founders Award from the Confederate Memorial Literary Society (1983); an honorary Doctor of Humane Letters from Lincoln College (1983); the Nevins-Freeman Award from the Chicago Civil War Round Table (1985); and the Ninth Annual Richard Nelson Current Award of Achievement from the Lincoln Forum (2004).

As these awards attest, John was fastidious as an editor, but he made what he did look effortless. In personal style, he was more Oscar Madison than Felix Unger. But when it came to precision and artfulness, John was the consummate editor and historian. "The work we do is sometimes a mystery to the public," he admitted to a reporter in 2004. Congressmen, he said, were among those who simply could not understand why Grant's papers needed to be edited in the first place. "We don't want those documents edited," they would say to him whenever he appeared before a congressional committee to urge increased funding for documentary projects from the NHPRC or the NEH. "We want them published just the way they were written." John would then patiently explain to them that documentary editors shared that goal, but there was a great deal more to publishing historical documents than just transcribing them from manuscripts and getting them onto printed pages. "What we do, we hope," said John, "is like an art restorer who's concerned about presenting the original painting just as it was created. But that's not always easy, and there are [editorial] questions that come up along the way." He gave a common and useful example: "Crossed-out words: do we drop or include them? We've always included anything that was crossed out in the original document, because it does give some clue as to what people were thinking."[13]

In documentary editing circles, John was revered as a project director willing to go to extremes to ensure the accuracy of the volumes he put together. At meetings of the Association for Documentary Editing, his peers discussed in hushed, awestruck tones the proofreading standards of the Grant series: two independent teams of proofreaders, working on two sets of galleys or page proofs. He and Harriet worked together at home in the evenings, Harriet reading the typed manuscript aloud while John marked corrections on the page proofs. Then their corrections would be compared with the other team's findings. Everyone associated with the project was involved in proofreading, each person casting a diligent eye to catch every mistake, any inadvertent divergence from the original document. John often shared his insights about documentary editing, as well as nuts-and-bolts advice on editorial methodology, at the annual meetings of the Association for Documentary Editing, an organization he and Harriet (an experienced documentary editor of the John Dewey Papers project at SIU) helped found in 1978.

Despite his great professional success, there were personal disappointments and tragic setbacks in his life that John managed to overcome. In 1976, he suffered a heart attack; nine years later, he underwent bypass surgery. In 1995, his son, Philip, died, and John and Harriet were bent low under the weight of heartache and despair. Advancements in heart technology, however, benefited his health: he received a defibrillator implant in 2003, and it markedly improved his quality of life and his productivity on the job. He also struggled with a broken foot—on two different occasions, in fact—so that he sometimes walked with a cane and even used a scooter to get around. Joys and sorrows offset each other: his daughter, Ellen Roundtree, married and gave birth to two beautiful girls. John relished the role of a jovial and devoted grandfather, a role that became all the more important when Ellen's husband, Lester, died of leukemia in 1999. John spent every minute that he could at family gatherings and less formal playtimes with his granddaughters. While he continued to have health problems as he grew older, he refused to give up one of his great pleasures—cigarette smoking. Some of us fondly remember that the smoke often encircled his head like a wreath, reminiscent of Clement Moore's St. Nicholas. I once urged him to quit smoking, as I had done. He told me, cheerfully but pointedly, to mind my own business.

Besides being an expert on Grant, John also developed exceptionally strong credentials as a Lincoln scholar. The time spent in Ralph Newman's bookshop seemed to instill in him an insightful understanding of Lincoln, inside and out. In 1995, he and other established Lincoln scholars founded the Lincoln Forum, a national group dedicated to enhancing the memory and preserving the legacy of Abraham Lincoln. Some, but not all, of his fine research and writing on Lincoln is included in this volume. Among his most notable and celebrated works on Lincoln is his tour de force on the relationship between Lincoln and Ann Rutledge, an essay that persuaded Lincoln experts to reexamine the old legends in light of the convincing evidence John offered that showed the likelihood—despite all the efforts by numerous historians to debunk or discount it as myth—that they had become romantically involved during Lincoln's time in New Salem. Unsurprisingly, John also focused his interpretive talents on analyzing the crucial relationship between Lincoln and Grant, the two historical figures he admired most. Those incisive essays are also included in this volume, along with a cornucopia of articles on a broad range of topics concerning the sixteenth president and his general in chief. As one discerns easily from reading John's essays, he very much liked Lincoln and Grant, although he did not shy away from noting their faults or admitting their mistakes. While his talents as a historical editor made him weigh and use documentary sources with great care, it is evident that John approached Lincoln and Grant not so much as an editor but as a biographer, asking questions of these men and the sources they left behind in order to gain a better understanding of who they were, what made them tick, and why they did what they did.

John Simon's scholarship on Grant and Lincoln made a significant contribution to the historiography of the Civil War and to the literature about the Union cause and its leadership. Collecting his essays on these two Northern leaders reveals—much more emphatically than the separate publication of them did over the span of his career—how formidable a Civil War historian John Y. Simon actually was. As one reads the essays published here, one after another, it's apparent that Simon brought insightful analysis to his study of these two great men and expressed his perspicacity in clear and sometimes sparkling prose. In part 1 of this volume, the essays reveal some of the inner dimensions of Lincoln—what went on in his head and heart; how he handled relationships with family (especially his father); a likely sweetheart (Ann Rutledge); his annoyingly passive generals (particularly Henry W. Halleck); and African Americans who stood at the very center of the conflict over slavery and the fight for freedom that became, because of Lincoln's Emancipation Proclamation, the great goal of the Union war effort. As for Lincoln's father, Simon effectively revised prevailing opinions about the man as a shiftless good-for-nothing, a portrait that derived from William Herndon's uncomplimentary assumptions about him. While other historians have also worked to develop a more realistic picture of Thomas Lincoln and to plumb the depths of the complex relationship between the father and his famous son, Simon helped point the way by arguing that our understanding of Lincoln's greatness does not require a belittling of his father. In a similar fashion, John led the vanguard of a new generation of historians willing to reconsider the veracity of the accounts, based on testimony taken by William Herndon after Lincoln's death, that described Lincoln's romantic involvement with Ann Rutledge while he lived in New Salem. While he acknowledged that Herndon "soared beyond the evidence," he concluded that historians had unfairly discounted the Rutledge story, which, in his opinion, showed conclusively that the "available evidence overwhelmingly indicates that Lincoln so loved Ann that her death plunged him into severe depression."[14] Consequently, most Lincoln biographers now accept that Lincoln and Rutledge shared a special relationship with one another, even if the precise details of their liaison may never be fully known.

Among the essays collected for this volume, Simon also offers a startlingly forthright assessment of the Confederacy's ill-fated decision to open fire on Fort Sumter. In many respects, his interpretation anticipated the rising tendency among Civil War historians to emphasize the importance of the Union cause over the now heavily documented implications of the South's Lost Cause. His argument squarely condemns Jefferson Davis for starting the war—a view that explicitly counters those historians (and neo-Confederates) who lay blame for the war at Lincoln's feet. In another intricately crafted essay, Simon reveals how Lincoln artfully blended the causes of Union and emancipation together by pragmatically understanding that the North could not possibly win the war without destroying slavery as it also sought to restore the Union. Here, too, John's emphasis on how deeply Lincoln cared about the Union opened the door for other historians to limn the contours of Lincoln's devotion to a perpetual Union, his intense nationalism, and his practical approach to the problem of ridding the nation of slavery. Simon enjoyed probing the complexities of Lincoln's thought and actions— particularly how the two became intertwined and variously expressed by the sixteenth president. In his essays on Lincoln's dealings with Major General Henry W. Halleck and his famous pessimistic memorandum of August 23, 1864, which recognized the possibility that he might lose the presidential election that year, Simon explores the many layers of complexity that help to bedevil our understanding of Lincoln, despite all that we know about him. What were the implications of Lincoln's despair in the late summer of 1864? Simon asks. Unlike many Lincoln biographers, he does not feel compelled to supply definitive answers to the many questions he raises about Lincoln as the president faced the trials of his reelection campaign. In considering Halleck's passivity as a field general and even as an administrator in Washington, Simon provides the intriguing explanation that Lincoln kept him in the War Department because Halleck's own lack of assertiveness allowed the president to dominate Union military policy. Long before "memory" studies of the Civil War came to dominate the scholarly literature as they have during the first decade of the twenty-first century, John wrote about the role that Ward Hill Lamon and Dennis Hanks played in shaping Lincoln's image after his death while also commenting on how, in their estimation, Andrew Johnson's Reconstruction policies mirrored Lincoln's own intentions for reuniting the nation. Simon deftly points out the flimsy basis upon which both men asserted their contentions of knowing Lincoln's "personal sentiments."[15]

John Simon's incisive analysis continues to shine in his essays on Grant in part 2. In fact, John was in the forefront of a thorough reassessment of Grant, including his experiences as a Civil War general and as president, that has now, over the past thirty years, resulted in a historical consensus that holds Grant in high esteem for his military prowess and that no longer denounces him as an incompetent president, especially in light of Grant's forceful stand in favor of African American civil rights during his two terms in the White House. Increasingly, Grant has regained the admiration that he possessed among the American people at the time of his death in 1885. In no small measure, the reassessment that has led to Grant's resurrection as a highly regarded historical figure is due to Simon's own herculean efforts to make Grant's papers accessible to a broad audience of specialists and Civil War enthusiasts. But John also charted the course toward Grant's rehabilitation with the essays reprinted here—writings that not only put Grant in a favorable light but that also reveal the man in his fullest dimensions, warts and all. A good number of other historians and writers have followed Simon's lead and offered admiring portraits of Grant, general and president, often using John's superb *Grant Papers* volumes and his essays as a starting point but also, in some cases, moving the reconsideration of Grant far beyond John's own analysis and conclusions (the works of Brooks D. Simpson, Jean Edward Smith, and Joan Waugh come immediately to mind).[16] In short, John Simon removed the tarnish from Grant's reputation so that other historians of the late twentieth century (and beyond) could examine him from new angles and with fresh perspectives.

Take, for example, Simon's evaluation of Grant on the occasion of the one hundredth anniversary of his death. His overview of Grant's life—and his significance as a historical figure—underscores how public perceptions of him had faded since his death, when the American press and people heaped praise on their fallen leader. In "The Paradox of Ulysses S. Grant," Simon looks more closely at how Grant's historical reputation declined after 1900, but concludes that William Tecumseh Sherman got it wrong when he declared that Grant was a "mystery" to him and to most Americans. By scrutinizing Grant's words and deeds, says Simon, the enigma melts away, and "the real man" emerges.[17] John's touching essay on the relationship between Grant and his wife, Julia Dent, tells an engaging love story that looks beyond the man's persona and offers us a window into his intimate world. Simon, however, does not rule out the role of good luck in having moved Grant's career forward, especially as a result of the support he received during the war (but not afterward) from Congressman Elihu B. Washburne of Illinois or the consequences of bad judgment in the case of Grant's "obnoxious order" that banished Jewish sutlers from the Union lines in December 1862. Both of the essays addressing these subjects offer snapshots of a complex, even flawed, man who nearly forgot to mention his most vigorous congressional sponsor in his *Memoirs* and who neglected to say anything at all about General Orders No. 11 in that same book. A more recognizable Grant may be found in Simon's adoring, but not hagiographical, account of the general's dealings with Lee at the surrender of the Army of Northern Virginia on April 9, 1865, at Appomattox. In this sweeping summary of Grant's military career, Simon uproots several myths, including, most provocatively, the unfair criticism of Grant as a butcher or as a general bent on throwing his own men into a meat grinder only for the sake of annihilating his enemy.

John's scholarship also refined our understanding of the complexities that defined Lincoln's relationship with Grant. The two essays reprinted in part 3 have been chosen because they reveal in fine detail the nature of the relationship between Lincoln as commander in chief and Grant as general in chief and how, as the war ground on, Lincoln learned to manage his generals, particularly Grant, who, unlike other Union generals, fully and unquestionably accepted the constitutional premise that civilian authority, namely Lincoln as commander in chief, held the supreme command, even if Grant, from time to time, found Lincoln's orders wrongheaded or unnecessarily labor intensive. More intensely than any other Grant biographer has done, Simon argues that Lincoln asserted more and more scrutiny—and even more control— over Grant in 1864 and 1865 than traditional accounts would have us believe; nevertheless, Grant obeyed the commander in chief's orders, even when he did not necessarily agree with them, just as every good soldier should do. John's interpretation of the relationship between Lincoln and Grant also tells a great deal about how these two men defined their roles—singly and in concert with one another—as they learned what needed to be done to win the war.

One is tempted to say, based only on the essays republished here, that John understood Grant more deeply, more intimately, than he did Lincoln, but that conclusion cannot sustain itself in light of his ready command of Lincoln's words and his profound appreciation for Lincoln's efforts to save the Union. In "Lincoln's Despair," John asks: "Does anyone really know Lincoln? Can anyone follow his thought to the point of predicting his policy? This wondrously unique statesman continually frustrates such efforts."[18] Similarly, in an interview with the Civil War Forum in 2000, John said about Grant: "I've never thought that I understood the man fully, and for that reason I've never become tired of him. . . . Grant's a very real person, and one with many dimensions to him. There's still more to learn and I'm eager to do it."[19] But these essays may lead readers to a very different verdict: John knew more about Lincoln and Grant—and the Civil War in general—than even some of their greatest biographers. No doubt he did not believe he had entirely figured them out. But he comprehended them as living historical figures, not amorphous ghosts, and he had the formidable ability to tell his readers—clearly, concisely, and engagingly—what he knew about them.

John's sense of humor comes through in these essays, but so does his seriousness as a historian. Indeed, it was John's commitment to taking Lincoln and Grant seriously as men, rather than as icons, that enabled him to write so persuasively about each of them and about how they got along together. Like most historians, John could at times overreach himself, as some readers might believe he does when he dismisses out of hand the stories that linked Grant's departure from the antebellum army with his drinking problem. Nevertheless, John believed that Grant should be taken at face value, and in the case of rumors about his struggles with alcohol, he tried to steer his readers—and researchers who consulted the published *Grant Papers*—toward reliable and verifiable sources that confirmed the general's sober competency notwithstanding the vicious murmurs from his enemies.

As for Lincoln, John's approach was refreshingly pragmatic and perspicacious. He warned, for instance, against placing too much importance on the words accepted as Lincoln's. This was especially important in cases, like the famous Lyceum Address of 1838, whose text survives only in widely varying newspaper accounts, not in holograph documents. He emphasized, too, that Lincoln's thoughts often took time to mature, citing evidence of some choppy, extemporaneous comments that the president made in July 1863 that he later refined into the eloquence of the Gettysburg Address. John also dismissed the musings of psychobiographers, arguing that they committed the mistake of discussing Lincoln's unrecorded thoughts and feelings with very little to go on. The result, he said, generally turned out to be wild "flights of fancy."[20]

Despite John's admission that he still had things to learn about Lincoln and Grant, even after spending nearly a lifetime studying both men, these essays demonstrate his impressive command of sources and his aptitude for fathoming these Civil War giants as if he had known them personally, as if he had sat in the room where Lincoln pondered the momentous issue of emancipation or crouched beside Grant as he sat whittling a stick on the edge of a battlefield. Saying that John brought these great men to life is not enough; he certainly did that, but he also led his readers into the recesses of their minds and souls. After reading the essays collected here, we emerge from the experience believing that we have met Mr. Lincoln and General Grant more than just in passing, and in so doing we have learned, as a dividend, a great deal about John Simon, our historical interlocutor.

Still, in important ways, John was unlike the two Civil War leaders he studied. Lincoln was self-taught and, one could say, self-wrought. Grant was more bookish than many suppose, but neither of these Union men was as learned and as studious as John Simon. Yet John did share with Lincoln a considerable wit and a formidable ability to tell stories, and like Grant, he showed an iron determination to get the job done, whether in his classroom or in putting a volume of the Grant Papers to bed by dotting the last "i" and crossing the final "t." John had infinitely more patience than Grant ever displayed, either as a general or as president, and while neither man would suffer fools gladly, John rarely uttered an unkind word about anyone—except perhaps for a Civil War journalist named Edward Crapsey, of whom John said it was hard to believe "that anyone would have such an ugly name."[21] More often, John was typically self-effacing rather than condemning of others. Once, during a radio interview, John was reminded that he was "a Harvard man." "Guilty," he pleaded, but then quickly added that he had attended the school so long ago, "I think Increase Mather was still around."[22] In print, John was always kind and fair—and honest. He once said this in a book review: "Quirky and unsophisticated, unevenly researched, this book both charms and exasperates."[23]

His curmudgeonly manner and wicked wit made him irresistible to video documentary producers, and John spent a good deal of time in his later years as a historian before the cameras. On the Civil War lecture circuit, he was a popular and entertaining speaker. Audiences loved his irreverent comments, his boisterous delivery, and his puns and witticisms. John did not tell jokes per se; he simply was *always* funny, in and out of the classroom, in front of or behind the podium. When I told him that I had been named to an endowed chair at Western Kentucky University, he replied dryly, "I wish someone would give *me* a chair" (he was temporarily getting around with a cane at the time, but his comment was surely a double entendre). Loving the limelight, John was enthralled by every opportunity that came his way to appear on television or on the radio. He once told an interviewer: "There are no sweeter words in the English language than 'I saw you on television.'"[24] Yet, at the same time, he was unpretentious, modest, and occasionally shy to a fault. I once came upon him sitting alone on the fringes of a big party at one of the major historians' conferences where we often reconnected in person. This was a rare chance to talk quietly with him, and I asked him why he—a solid Midwesterner—had gone to Harvard for his PhD. "Oh, it was the place to go," he said, "and they were nice enough to let me in."

Unlike Grant, John failed to finish his last project, which, ironically enough, was to edit the authoritative edition of Grant's last project, his acclaimed *Memoirs*. Luckily, that task is now in the extremely able hands of John F. Marszalek, and the project's files have been relocated to the new base for the USGA at Mississippi State University. I can imagine Ulysses S. Grant and John Y. Simon chuckling over this delightful irony—Grant once took Mississippi, but now Mississippi has captured Grant.

Of course, the published *Grant Papers* stands as John Simon's great legacy—a monument that rivals, and in many ways surpasses, the impressive edifice of Grant's Tomb or the heroic Grant Memorial on the Mall in front of the U.S. Capitol. But John did not work to leave a legacy or a monument. He worked to make history—particularly the legacies of Lincoln and Grant—better understood and better appreciated. He succeeded marvelously—and, no doubt, well beyond his own expectations.

He's gone from us now, and I miss him. Editing his essays for publication helped to bring me close to him again, even for a short time. As I read each line, each word, John's thunderous basso voice came back to me. Those who knew him personally will have a hard time reading these essays without hearing those booming Simonian tones on every page. And, like his great scholarly contributions to the study of Grant, Lincoln, and the Civil War, that voice was a striking and even arresting one.

At one point in rereading these essays, I came upon a phrase that made me reach for the phone so that I could share my thought with John, before I lost its strand. My hand touched the receiver, but reality struck before I picked it up. It was a wrenching experience, even more heartrending than attending the poignant memorial service held for him on the SIU campus a few weeks after he died. For that brief moment, reaching for the phone, I was lost, and I was sad.

I'm still sad. I hope that this book, in some small measure, returns at least a few of the many favors John did for me—and for so many other students, young historians, and aspiring historical editors. I am confident that it will reveal the remarkable depth and breadth of John's scholarship on Lincoln and Grant. But I can't stop wishing that I could hear just one more time that monumental voice on the other end of the line.

Part 1

Abraham Lincoln

1

House Divided

Lincoln and His Father

Psychological analysis constitutes the current frontier in the study of Abraham Lincoln. In a wildly speculative book, *Patricide in the House Divided: A Psychological Interpretation of Lincoln and His Age,* George B. Forgie explained the coming of the Civil War in terms of the post-heroic generation's mixture of admiration and resentment of the Revolutionary generation. The mighty achievements of the founding fathers seemingly inhibited their heirs until a national crisis, partially provoked by Lincoln, provided Lincoln's opportunity to assume heroic stature. Although Lincoln held center stage in Forgie's drama, his father received scant attention; instead, George Washington filled the role of father and Stephen A. Douglas that of wicked brother.[1] In *Abraham Lincoln: The Quest for Immortality,* Dwight G. Anderson argued similarly but less coherently that Lincoln's "project of becoming 'God' worked itself out in both a private and a public context, against both his natural father and his political father [Washington], with the result that a personal death anxiety became transformed into a symbolic immortality both for himself and for the nation."[2] Expanding on Forgie's views, Anderson explained that "by aligning his personal resentments against constitutional fathers with the injustice of Negro slavery, Lincoln discovered in the Declaration of Independence a means of liberation for both himself and the slave."[3] Such high-flown theorizing has provoked disbelief, bewilderment, and scorn from many scholars.[4] Both Forgie and Anderson placed Lincoln in a complex psychodrama, casting major political figures in familial roles while slighting the humble members of Lincoln's own family. These theories have roots in the painful relationship between Lincoln and his father, a topic that deserves more attention. At the very least, an exploration of the cause, nature, and consequences of such an estrangement should precede any effort to discover its manifestation in political metaphor.

Around 1850, as Lincoln and William H. Herndon rode in a buggy toward the courthouse in Menard County, Illinois, Lincoln spoke of his mother, praising her for his own best qualities of mind and character, crediting in turn the unknown Virginia gentleman who had fathered her. "God bless my mother," he concluded, "all that I am or ever hope to be I owe to her."[5] Thereby, indirectly, he passed judgment upon his own father, a man for whom he never had a single recorded word of praise.

In order to emphasize and dramatize Lincoln's ascent to greatness, some early biographers, led by Herndon, Lincoln's former law partner turned biographer, exaggerated the "stagnant, putrid pool"[6] from which he rose, in the process characterizing his father, Thomas, as shiftless, inept, dull, and ignorant. Questioning surviving Kentucky pioneers, Herndon found some who doubted that Thomas could have fathered the president—or anyone else for that matter. These accounts and other recollections afford a valuable glimpse of self-serving memories, provincial superstitions, and backwoods meanness, but provide little reliable information about the real Thomas Lincoln. Robert Todd Lincoln, conscious of his role as guardian of the family honor as well as its papers, may have censored and certainly influenced the treatment of his grandfather in what he hoped might become the standard biography of his father.[7] Despite these efforts, Woodrow Wilson wrote that Lincoln "came of the most unpromising stock on the continent, the 'poor white trash' of the South."[8] John T. Morse gave an unflattering view of Lincoln's parents and sneered at Lincoln biographers who had "drawn fanciful pictures of a pious frugal household, of a gallant frontiersman endowed with a long catalogue of noble qualities, and of a mother like a Madonna in the wilderness."[9] The rehabilitation of Thomas Lincoln required substituting fact for fancy.

Following Herndon's lead, those who wrote about Lincoln often mingled biography and genealogy in order to seek seeds of greatness in his family. Those who rejected illegitimate forebears felt obligated to praise his parents. William E. Barton, after demolishing arguments that someone other than Thomas had fathered Abraham, concluded that Thomas "was not a great man. But he was great enough to be father of a man of outstanding greatness. . . . We can not afford to hold in light regard the man who gave the world so great a son."[10] Belief in the genetic transmission of greatness infected the Lincoln literature with acrimony and nonsense.

The search for a documented Thomas Lincoln, leading Louis A. Warren to county courthouses, church records, and other contemporary documents, revealed a man more nearly typical of his time: a man who owned horses and livestock, paid his share of taxes, assembled cash and credit to acquire farmland, served the county when necessary, and maintained his standing in the local Baptist church.[11] Based upon records rather than recollections, a portrait of Thomas as sturdy pillar of a frontier community rather than shiftless drifter provides more solid ground for interpretation. Yet neither portrait alone will illuminate the tangled relationship of father and son. The importance of Thomas Lincoln lies less in who he was than in what his son thought about him.

Although the *Collected Works of Abraham Lincoln* fills nine substantial volumes, the son wrote remarkably little about his father. That little deserves careful attention. In responding to a Massachusetts man named Solomon Lincoln, interested in genealogy, Lincoln stated: "Owing to my father being left an orphan at the age of six years, in poverty, and in a new country, he became a wholly uneducated man; which I suppose is the reason why I know so little of our family history."[12] In 1859 and again in 1860, when called upon for biographical information for campaign purposes, Lincoln wrote that his father "grew up[,] litterally without education."[13] In 1860, Lincoln elaborated: "He never did more in the way of writing than to bunglingly sign his own name."[14] The word "bunglingly" was gratuitous, and Lincoln neglected to mention that his father could read a little.[15]

Lincoln wrote: "My parents were both born in Virginia, of undistinguished families—second families, perhaps I should say."[16] Subsequent genealogical research, partisan and passionate, has accomplished little toward eroding that blunt and candid statement. Its significance lies in the equation between the two families because documentary evidence puts the Lincolns a cut above the Hankses; for example, most Lincolns but few Hankses could write their names.[17] Desperate endeavors to provide Nancy Hanks with a proper father came too late since Lincoln apparently believed that his mother was born out of wedlock. In one autobiography, he wrote of her as "of a family of the name of Hanks," but provided a full name on other occasions.[18] As a boy he lived amid an extended family of his mother's relatives, a confusing flock of Hankses and Sparrows. One of his closest boyhood associates, cousin Dennis

Hanks, who later claimed, endearingly, to have "learned him his letters," was illegitimate.[19]

In contrast, the Lincolns can now be traced to Samuel Lincoln, who settled at Hingham, Massachusetts, in 1637 and whose descendants pushed south and west, some amassing considerable landholdings. When Abraham Lincoln, Thomas's father, was killed by an Indian in 1784, he owned more than five thousand acres in Kentucky.[20] The early death of his father left six-year-old Thomas "a wandering laboring boy,"[21] and later gave his son the impression that he came from an "undistinguished" family.[22] In his first political statement, Lincoln declared that he "was born and have ever remained in the most humble walks of life. I have no wealthy or popular relations to recommend me."[23] Such antecedents benefited any Whig candidate, as Lincoln noted in calling attention to Henry Clay's "undistinguished parents."[24] Asked about his relationship to the prominent Lincoln family of Massachusetts, Lincoln replied, not entirely facetiously, that "he could not say that he ever had an ancestor older than his father."[25]

Just as grandfather Abraham had gone from Virginia into Kentucky in 1780 in search of larger landholdings and greater economic opportunity, other pioneers pushing westward expected to better their fortunes. By the time grandson Abraham was born in 1809, his father owned the birthplace farm, 348½ acres on Nolin Creek, paid for in cash, and may have owned additional farmland elsewhere and real estate in Elizabethtown. In addition to farming, he augmented his income by working as a carpenter. While still a young man, Thomas had reached the height of his prosperity.

The Lincolns moved to Indiana in 1816; according to Abraham, "This removal was partly on account of slavery; but chiefly on account of the difficulty of land titles in Ky."[26] Thomas Lincoln had encountered lawsuits over his title to three different farms in Kentucky, suggesting adequate cause to move to Indiana, where federal surveying promised greater security in landholding. Under similar circumstances, even Daniel Boone left Kentucky. The role of slavery is more difficult to assess; only Abraham's statement and the membership of the Lincolns in a church opposed to slavery support this explanation, but Abraham's statement may be discounted since it reinforced and justified his political position.[27]

Thomas's life in Indiana, less solidly documented than that in Kentucky, indicates economic decline. The man who once purchased a hat in Elizabethtown for one pound, sixteen shillings,[28] now seems to have struggled to keep his head above water. Whether or not the Lincolns spent the first winter in Indiana in a three-sided cabin, a "half-faced camp," with a fire burning on the open south side, is in dispute,[29] as is the quality of the eighteen-by-twenty-foot cabin that replaced it. In what amounted to an "unbroken forest,"[30] Thomas selected land about one mile from the nearest source of water.[31] Lincoln remembered "pretty pinching times . . . at first . . . but presently we got reasonably comfortable."[32] After fourteen years in Indiana, Thomas sold to a neighbor the eighty acres he owned, for which he had paid $160, along with an additional twenty acres and all his improvements, for $125.[33]

Lincoln remembered that he held an ax in his hands much of the time, "less, of course, in plowing and harvesting seasons."[34] Neither the schools available in the region nor his father's resources satisfied young Abe's hunger for education. When his father endorsed a note for a friend who defaulted, Abe had to leave school to work for a neighbor.[35] Divergent reminiscences obscure the issue of whether the father did all he could to further his son's education or instead criticized him for reading instead of working. In his autobiography, Lincoln noted that "after he was twentythree, and had separated from his father, he studied English grammar."[36] Years later, Thomas was quoted as complaining, "I suppose that Abe is still fooling hisself with eddication. I tried to stop it, but he has got that fool idea in his head, and it can't be got out."[37] Dennis Hanks recalled that Abe "was lazy—a very lazy man. He was always reading, Scribbling, writing, ciphering, writing Poetry."[38] Indeed, Abe was a "stubborn reader, his father having sometimes to slash him for neglecting his work by reading."[39] A neighbor for whom Abe worked complained that he "was always reading and thinking. . . . Lincoln said to me one day that his father taught him to work but never learned him to love it."[40] When Abe spoke out of turn to a passing stranger, Thomas cuffed him,[41] and he also interrupted Abe's earliest speeches, which distracted others from their farm chores.[42] Wondering whether "Abe Loved his farther Very well or Not," Hanks concluded, "I Dont think he Did."[43]

When Lincoln was nine years old, his mother died. Of her character, even her appearance, nothing reliable is known, and the impact of her death on her son remains matter for speculation. A few years later, in 1822, Thomas Lincoln helped to build the nearby Pigeon Creek Baptist Church, using his carpentry skills on the door and window frames and constructing a pulpit as well. He and his new wife joined the church, which he served as trustee and committee member, and he once attended a church conference as a representative. Thomas "was one of the five or six most important men" in the congregation.[44] When taken to church by his parents, Abe would later repeat the sermon nearly verbatim, mimicking the preacher.[45] Lincoln never joined that or any other church.

At the age of eight, Lincoln shot a turkey and afterward never "pulled a trigger on any larger game."[46] His father had moved the family to a region difficult to farm but teeming with animals, where hunting furnished a large proportion of the family food. Like many pioneers, Thomas preferred to hunt, considering farming fit for women and children. As Abe grew, his dislike of hunting created another division between father and son.

In 1819, Lincoln's stepmother, Sarah Bush Johnston, brought her three children into the Lincoln cabin: two daughters and John D. Johnston, about one year younger than Abe.[47] According to the son-in-law of Dennis Hanks, who drew on family traditions, Thomas treated Abe "rather unkindly than otherwise, always appeared to think more of his stepson John D. Johnston than he did of his own son Abraham."[48] By all accounts, John seems to have been a conventional pioneer youngster. Reminiscing about Abe and John, Sarah Lincoln recalled that "both were good boys, but I must say, both now being dead, that Abe was the best boy I ever saw or ever expect to see."[49] "He and his step-brother never quarreled but once."[50] Somehow Sarah seems to have given Abe the support and encouragement he should have received from his natural parent.

In 1821, one of Lincoln's two stepsisters married, as did both the other stepsister and his sister Sarah in 1826. Abe and John were the only remaining children in the Lincoln cabin. Lincoln remembered that he and Johnston "were raised together—slept together—and loved each other like brothers."[51] In seven letters to Johnston (1848–1851), Lincoln indicated repeatedly how close the two had once been and used the word "brother" in every letter; in Lincoln's 1860 autobiography Johnston appeared as his "stepmother's son."[52] As boys, however, they cooperated in a cruel prank that killed Thomas Lincoln's pet dog and jointly operated a distillery.[53] Johnston and Lincoln stood together in a family feud with the Grigsbys, a quarrel originating in Lincoln's belief that his sister Sarah had died in childbirth through the neglect of her husband, Aaron Grigsby.[54] Lincoln wrote nasty satirical verse about the Grigsbys, but it was Johnston who received a thrashing in a fistfight with William Grigsby.[55] Later, when challenged to fight by the muscular stepbrother, the Grigsbys backed down. A neighbor recalled that "when the Lincolns were getting ready to leave [Indiana], Abraham and his stepbrother . . . came over to our house to swap a horse for a yoke of oxen. John did all the talking. If any one had been asked that day which would make the greatest success in life I think the answer would have been John Johnston."[56]

Eleanor Gridley, canvassing Coles County, Illinois, in 1891 in search of Lincoln relics and reminiscences, talked to a grandson of Mrs. Lincoln.

> Grandmarm said "that Abe wasn't considered nigh so smart as Uncle John D. Johnston, who could talk well, dress well, and go about the neighborhood of an evening." Nuther wus he [Abe] much of hand to go among the gals 'cept to corn shuckin', and as John D. Johnston, grandmarm's son, wus right peart, she told him onct that John would cut him out with the gals; but Abe said "that didn't bother him any," and so the folks kept thinking that John wus the smartest of the two, 'cause he [Abe] wus allers sittin' in the house at night porin' over his books, quiet and sad like, and John could talk right smart like. At last John began to quit larnin', but Abe kept right on. . . . Grandmarm said "that Uncle Abe wus allers asked to all the shuckin' bees and he wus the fust one chosen, 'cause they knowed his side war shore to win, and allers after the bee wus over he had to rastle with some of the boys, or he'd tell some of his cur'us stories that wus so funny they'd make a hog laugh."[57]

Much the same impression of the differences between the two came from Mrs. Samuel Chowning.

> In the spring of 1833 when I wus then a girl of only sixteen years Grandpap Lincoln as usual "sugared off," and John D. Johnston invited the young folks to come over some evening, when Abe Lincoln wus up to the old home. John D. Johnston sent us word that Brother Abe had come and we made up a little party. Well, John D. and Abe Lincoln took me across the

river in a canoe. John had promised us young folks some taffy and purty soon he said to Grandpap Lincoln, "I want some taffy for the girls." You know John D. Johnston was mighty good lookin' and awful takin' and we knowed he'd get some taffy for us. We girls didn't care much about Abraham Lincoln, though, for he wus so quiet and awkward and so awful homely, and he never made up to the girls anyhow, so none of 'em cared about asking any favors of him.[58]

Young Lincoln, often described as uninterested in girls,[59] may have been making the best of circumstances, a supposition reinforced by some of his early letters. In Springfield, in 1837, Lincoln reported: "I have been spoken to by but one woman since I've been here, and should not have been by her, if she could have avoided it."[60] As to marriage, "I can never be satisfied with any one who would be block-head enough to have me."[61] Lincoln considered himself homely and frequently described himself as humble. If young Lincoln cared whether girls liked him, his humiliation must have increased when his stepbrother "cut him out with the gals."

In 1830, the Lincoln-Hanks clan, a party of thirteen, left Indiana for Macon County, Illinois, where Abe helped to fell trees and split rails for fencing, then settled into the cabin for the horrendous winter that followed. That spring, Lincoln went on Denton Offut's flatboat to New Orleans, then returned to his parents, who had moved to Coles County, for a brief visit before beginning work in Offut's store in New Salem. Lincoln had come of age and was leaving his parents permanently. Johnston, who had gone with Abe to New Orleans, may have tagged along to New Salem; the two were messmates during the Black Hawk War, after which Lincoln went back to New Salem, Johnston to Coles County, where he lived with or near the Lincolns for twenty years.

Thomas lived for twenty years after Abe left, years in which his son was elected to the state legislature, became a lawyer, married, started a family, and served a term in Congress. Father and son had little contact. Lincoln rarely visited his parents, no Lincoln or Hanks relatives attended the Springfield wedding[62] or (with one exception) ever visited the Lincoln house, and the older Lincolns never met Mary Lincoln or saw their grandchildren. Beyond references by Abraham to Thomas in family letters and in autobiographical and genealogical accounts, Lincoln wrote about his father only one other time. On February 25, 1842, in a letter to his close friend Joshua Speed, commenting on Speed's doubts that he had done the right thing by marrying, Lincoln noted that "my old Father used to have a saying that 'If you make a bad bargain, *hug* it the tighter.'"[63]

The only Lincoln relative who visited Springfield was Harriet, daughter of Dennis Hanks, who lived with the Lincolns in 1844 and 1845 while attending school. According to Herndon, Mary Lincoln treated Harriet like a servant; for her part, Harriet recalled Mary as a "Stingy" woman who "loved to put on *Style*."[64] In 1851, John D. Johnston tried to place his thirteen-year-old son Abraham in the Lincoln home to enable him to get an education; Lincoln was sympathetic, but Mary vetoed the proposal.[65] In writing to Johnston, Lincoln misspelled the name of the son as "Abram," as if to deny that the boy had been named in his honor. Mary contributed to building barriers between Lincoln and his family, but there is little reason to believe that her husband forcefully objected.

Just when Lincoln turned twenty-one and asserted his independence, his father turned fifty-two, with his career as carpenter behind him and his living dependent on farmwork difficult for a man of any age. Unsurprisingly, his fortunes steadily declined. Equally unsurprising under such circumstances, he looked more and more to a son for assistance; John D. Johnston was the only son available.

Herndon wrote that Johnston "was an indolent and shiftless man, a man that was 'born tired,' and yet he was an exceedingly clever man, generous, and very hospitable."[66] Oddly enough, Herndon and others described Thomas Lincoln in similar fashion. One visitor called him the "cleverest homespun man I ever saw—could tell more good anecdotes than 'Abe.'"[67] Just as Thomas appeared most promising as a young man, so too did Johnston.

> John D. Johnston is remembered by the early settlers of Coles County, Ill., as a foppishly dressed young constable, who made his nice clothes conspicuous in the vicinity of the abandoned town site of Richmond, three miles southwest of Mattoon. John Cunningham, one of the older residents of Coles County, says of him: "He was the Beau Brummel of Goose Nest Prairie, and would sport the best clothes to be had, regardless of whether they were ever paid or not.... The term shiftless fitted him in respect to his having no particular occupation. He was

always prepared to make a pleasing address, and was smart for a young man of those days, but without other education than that acquired by contact with others. Some persons thought him a brighter man than the immortal Lincoln. Had Johnston lived in this age, he would have filled the niche of the dude to perfection."[68]

Another old neighbor remembered Johnston as "profligate and dissipated."[69]

Because Lincoln so rarely visited his parents, who were illiterate, he usually communicated with them through Johnston; as Thomas Lincoln aged, he depended more on Johnston for assistance in managing his business affairs. To ensure that his father would never be landless, Lincoln bought forty acres for two hundred dollars from Thomas in 1841, deeded the land to him for life, and promised it to Johnston for the same sum thereafter.[70] In 1848, Lincoln answered jointly a request from his father for twenty dollars and from Johnston for eighty dollars. Thomas got his money, necessary to save his land from sale to satisfy a judgment, but not without a gentle scolding about his carelessness in financial matters. Johnston received nothing, although Lincoln mentioned having sent him money previously. Lincoln asserted that Johnston's need arose "by some defect in your *conduct.* . . . You *are* an *idler.* I doubt whether since I saw you, you have done a good whole day's work, in any one day."[71] Lincoln then offered to match, dollar for dollar, all the money Johnston could earn in Coles County for the next four or five months. The letter closed "Affectionately Your brother," but it was probably too late to repair the damage. In corresponding with his Coles County relative, Lincoln used a condescending and sanctimonious tone absent elsewhere.

Johnston had, moreover, led Lincoln's father into business deals and land transactions that sometimes ended in the courts.[72] Johnston's idleness, financial distress, and early death apparently stemmed from heavy drinking.[73] Dennis Hanks had the last word on Lincoln and Johnston: "I think Abe done more for John than he deserved. John thought that Abe did not do enough for the old people. They became enemies a while on this ground. I don't want to tell all the things that I know: it would not look well in history. I say this: Abe treated John well. . . . A kinder harted man never was in Coles County, Ill nor an honester man. I dont say this because he was my brother in law: I say it, noing it. John did not love to work any of the best. I plaged him for not working."[74]

Over the years, Thomas changed from a rising young Kentucky farmer to the pathetic failure of Goosenest Prairie, becoming troublesome and embarrassing to his son. Money sent to Thomas might just as well have been sent to Johnston, whose finances were intermingled with those of his stepfather and whose hold over the old man gave him access to all his resources. Lincoln's continued ownership of the homestead guaranteed that his parents would not show up destitute in Springfield and that political opponents could not capitalize on their poverty.

In the last decade of his father's life, Lincoln assigned some Coles County legal fees to Thomas to collect, adding up to no great sum. When Thomas tried to sell one for fifteen dollars, he was unable to do so.[75] In 1845, when Lincoln left a thirty-five-dollar fee for Thomas to collect in Charleston, Johnston signed his stepfather's name to the receipts.[76] Even accepting reminiscences that Lincoln gave his parents ten or fifteen dollars every time he visited them, the total of Lincoln's support remains small. Despite Lincoln's concern for his stepmother's welfare after his father's death, she received no documented gifts of cash prior to 1864.

As a young man, Lincoln acquired debts from his New Salem store venture—he called it the national debt—that he paid off steadily for many years. Although the Lincolns lived simply in Springfield, by the late 1840s they could afford a servant, and Lincoln's income from the law for that decade is estimated at $1,500 to $2,000 yearly at a time when the governor could live comfortably on $1,200.[77] Lincoln could have given his parents more money than he did. Except for meager handouts when he visited his parents, Lincoln probably ceased his support about 1848, just when his finances improved.

In May 1849, Lincoln heard from cousin Dennis Hanks's son-in-law and Johnston that Thomas was desperately ill and "anxious to See you before He dies & I am told that His Cries for you for the last few days are truly Heart-Rendering. . . . He craves to see you all the time . . . his only Child that is of his own flush & blood."[78] Thomas soon recovered, perhaps before his son could respond. In early 1851, Thomas again fell ill. On January 12, 1851, Lincoln answered two letters from Johnston and one from the daughter of Dennis Hanks, all through a single letter to Johnston. Lincoln wrote belatedly, he explained, "no[t because] I have forgotten them, or been uninterested about them—but because it appeared to me I could write nothing which could do any good." "My business is such that I could hardly leave home now," he added, "if it were not, as it is, that my own wife is sick-abed. (It is a case of baby-sickness, and I suppose is not dangerous.)" The third Lincoln son, William Wallace Lincoln, had been born on December 21, 1850; there is no reason to believe that Mary Lincoln had an especially difficult recovery. Using his wife's illness as an excuse, then adding that it was not a serious matter, might well entitle him to be called "Honest Abe." Worse followed: "I sincerely hope Father may yet recover his health; but at all events tell him to remember to call upon, and confide in, our great, and good, and merciful Maker; who will not turn away from him in any extremity. He notes the fall of a sparrow, and numbers the hairs of our heads; and He will not forget the dying man, who puts his trust in Him. Say to him that if we could meet now, it is doubtful whether it would not be more painful than pleasant; but that if it be his lot to go now, he will soon have a joyous [meeting] with many loved ones gone before; and where [the rest] of us, through the help of God, hope ere-long [to join] them."[79]

These words of religious consolation, sometimes quoted out of context as evidence of genuine concern and compassion, might well be read more perceptively as indicating alienation. After all, Thomas had a Bible and people to read it to him; what he lacked was a visit from his only surviving child. In selecting for his biblical text "the fall of a sparrow," Lincoln evoked one of his mother's maiden names and perhaps some of the gossip concerning her character. While danger exists, of course, of reading too much into this letter, recently characterized as "morally . . . dubious and hypocritical,"[80] certain aspects exist on the surface: Lincoln did not immediately answer two letters from Johnston about the impending death of his father; he offered two weak excuses for not visiting the dying man and wondered whether a visit "would not be more painful than pleasant"; and he urged his father to call upon God, "who will not turn away from him in any extremity," rather than his son, who did turn away.

Thomas died five days after the date of Lincoln's letter to Johnston. Lincoln did not attend the funeral, and there is no clear evidence that he visited his Coles County relatives during the next decade. "I saw him every year or two," Sarah Lincoln said in 1865, not specifying whether the visits continued after her husband's death.[81] Lincoln probably did not see his father's grave until January 31, 1861, when he visited his stepmother for the last time.

The death of Thomas Lincoln in 1851 apparently closed a sad

chapter in his son's life. Abraham continued to take an interest in the welfare of his stepmother. During the following summer he relinquished to Johnston without requesting payment the eighty acres he inherited from his father, presumably because Johnston promised to take care of Sarah Lincoln.[82] In November, however, learning about Johnston's plans to sell his land and move to Missouri, Lincoln wrote Johnston a series of stinging letters: "If you intend to go to work, there is no better place than right where you are; if you do not intend to go to work, you can not get along any where. Squirming & crawling about from place to place can do no good. . . . Part with the land you have, and my life upon it, you will never after, own a spot big enough to bury you in."[83] Lincoln then urged Johnston not to misunderstand the letter, not written "in any unkindness." Lincoln wrote it, he stated, to get Johnston "to *face* the truth—which truth is, you are destitute because you have *idled* away all your time."[84]

In writing to Johnston, Lincoln complained vehemently that current plans for selling the Lincoln land would bring two hundred dollars to his stepmother, which, invested at 8 percent, would yield sixteen dollars per year. Lincoln objected because Johnston planned to take one hundred dollars for himself; left with Mrs. Lincoln, her income would rise to twenty-four dollars yearly. "I can not, to oblige any living person, consent that she shall be put on an allowance of sixteen dollars a year."[85]

In 1852, Johnston, by now adept at manipulating his relatives, did get away to Arkansas with cash from the sale of land and more from the sale of land owned by his second wife, and by the summer of 1852 wrote a boastful letter about his prospects.[86] Little more than one year later he was back in Coles County and penniless; a few months later he was dead at the age of forty-four, leaving personal property valued at $55.90[87] and, probably, as Lincoln had predicted, owning no land to be buried in.

In a letter to Johnston of November 1851, Lincoln had added "A word for Mother" urging her to live with her granddaughter (the former Harriet Hanks) and her granddaughter's husband, Augustus H. Chapman.[88] Following Thomas's death, Mrs. Lincoln lived with friends and relatives, though apparently she spent the most time in the Lincoln cabin on Goosenest Prairie. Accounting for her whereabouts in the 1850s presents difficulties; the impression arises that nobody in Springfield knew or much cared where she lived.

On April 5, 1864, Dennis Hanks wrote to Lincoln to acknowledge his "Little Check for 50.00." When he "shoed it to mother She cried Like a Child." Hanks added: "She is Mity Childish heep of truble to us."[89] His opinion of Lincoln's generosity appeared in the phrase "Little Check," and if such checks had arrived more frequently they might have evoked fewer tears. Another relative wrote that Dennis kept the money anyway, never took care of Mrs. Lincoln, and "threatened to put her on the county."[90] Hanks became an appropriate successor to Johnston as caretaker of Lincoln's parents.

By all accounts, Thomas's grave remained inadequately marked; reminiscent accounts of Lincoln in 1861 whittling the initials "T. L." on a board and sticking it into the ground hardly enhance the image of filial devotion.[91] Lincoln may have intended to provide a tombstone, but the evidence comes from a letter written by Mary Lincoln to Lincoln's stepmother in late 1867: "My husband a few weeks before his death mentioned to me, that he intended *that* summer, paying proper respect to *his* father's grave, by a head & foot stone, with his name, age && and I propose very soon carrying out his intentions. It was not from want of affection for his father, as you are well aware, that it was not done, but *his* time was so greatly occupied always."[92] Mary Lincoln followed her husband's lead by neglecting the grave, which remained unmarked until 1880, when a local effort to raise money for a monument attracted the attention of Robert Todd Lincoln, who then made a generous contribution.[93] Robert also helped to provide a tombstone for Nancy Hanks Lincoln, another grave his father had intended to mark.[94]

Was Mary Lincoln merely polite and tactful in writing of her husband's intention to mark his father's grave? Possibly; yet it is doubtful that Lincoln could have put his father entirely out of his mind. The fourth Lincoln son, born on April 4, 1853, was named for his grandfather, although Abraham never mentioned it. Johnston had named his firstborn for Thomas in 1837.

Biographers discussing Lincoln's coolness toward his father have frequently followed Herndon's lead by explaining the problem in terms of Thomas Lincoln's failings. Herndon knew Lincoln well, but admitted that "there was something about his origin he never cared to dwell upon."[95] After Lincoln's death, Herndon spent years dwelling upon what Lincoln concealed, often at the expense of members of the Lincoln family. Oddly enough, when Herndon first published the letter Lincoln wrote as his father was dying, Herndon thought that he had established Lincoln's belief in immortality, and Herndon's foremost disciple claimed that the letter "forever dispels the imputation that [Lincoln] was callous or indifferent to the needs of his father."[96]

In order to understand the relationship between father and son, no denigration of Thomas is necessary. "Happiness was the end of life with him," John Hanks concluded; "a man who took the world easy," wrote Dennis Hanks, who knew "No Better Man than Old Tom Lincoln."[97] Abe's ambitions exceeded his father's expectations and could not be fulfilled under his father's roof. If young Abe had been neglected or mistreated by his father, the explanation may depend more upon Thomas's poverty than his ill-will. Far more important is the matter of Thomas's favoritism toward his stepson. When Abe left the family cabin, Johnston did fill the role of dutiful son, however defectively. Lincoln's early closeness to his stepbrother indicates that rivalry either did not exist when they lived together or existed within manageable limits.

Lincoln's word "painful" in dismissing a visit to his dying father may be the best word for their relationship in the last years of Thomas's life. Such a relationship must have had roots in Lincoln's childhood but deteriorated so dramatically over time that in 1851 Lincoln neglected his filial duties to visit his dying father, to attend his funeral, and to mark his grave. According to Mary Lincoln, the last of these obligations remained on his mind in 1865. He was, after all, still the only member of the family able to afford a decent stone.

To what extent this painful relationship with his father influenced his career cannot be accurately ascertained; any venture toward answering the question must be speculative. Unlike speculations that put Lincoln in the midst of a political psychodrama, however, these arise from Lincoln's relationship with a figure of great personal significance in his life.

From 1854 through 1860, virtually all Lincoln's public speaking involved discussion of the extension of slavery into the territories. He repeatedly invoked "our Revolutionary fathers" and insisted that nothing could resolve the issue other than "a return to the policy of the fathers."[98]

For what he believed would be the most important speech of his life, he chose the biblical metaphor of the house divided and repeated the phrase throughout the 1858 campaign against Douglas. Urged by political associates to drop the house-divided metaphor as extreme and inaccurate, Lincoln stood his ground, suggesting that the words held special meaning for him.[99] In the debates, Douglas repeatedly attacked the house-divided doctrine, asserting that the division had existed for eighty-two years without causing collapse before Lincoln and the Republicans insisted on uniformity.[100] In defense, Lincoln repeatedly quoted the entire passage in his speech, in which he provided a qualified context for his metaphor.[101]

Lincoln's battle against the house divided led eventually to the war for the Union, and again he portrayed the central issue in familial terms. For secessionists, he charged, "the Union, as a family relation, would not be anything like a regular marriage at all, but rather a sort of free-love arrangement, to be maintained on what that sect calls passionate attraction."[102] In his inaugural address, he used the image of divorce, declaring it impossible because "physically speaking, we cannot separate."[103] His task, he said less formally, was to "keep house." "The present moment finds me at the White House," he told Ohio troops in 1864, "yet there is as good a chance for your children as there was for my father's."[104]

Examples could be multiplied, but with misleading effect if they paint a portrait of Lincoln obsessed with fathers and families. The significance of metaphor should be kept within bounds. Explanations of Lincoln's politics that emphasize family conflict assume that resulting tensions were unrecognized or unconscious.[105] On the contrary, Lincoln's words and acts demonstrate his awareness of family estrangement, nowhere more clearly than in letters to his onetime brother. A campaign visit to Indiana in 1844 took Lincoln to the site where his "mother and only sister were buried" and inspired him to write poetry still incomplete many months later: "My childhood's home I see again, / And sadden with the view; / And still, as memory crowds my brain, / There's pleasure in it too."[106] Lincoln's pain represented private sorrow rather than unconscious motivation.

The "chequered past" arose again in poetic form during the Civil War when Lincoln wrote to a noted actor of his admiration for the soliloquy of Claudius in *Hamlet* beginning "O my offence is rank."[107] The offense: "a brother's murder." Lincoln recited this soliloquy from memory in 1864, then recited the opening lines of *Richard III* in which Richard, proclaiming his ugliness, resolves to plot against his brother.[108] On several occasions, Lincoln spoke of Shakespearian plays, scenes, or speeches that held special meaning for him, predominately tragedies involving family conflict and the death of kings, legitimacy, and usurpation.[109] Lincoln had studied some of the plays "perhaps as frequently as any unprofessional reader."[110] To interpret Lincoln's interest in Shakespeare solely in terms of public figures and events of the Civil War is to ignore Lincoln's painful relationships with his own father and brother, unresolved at the time of their deaths, and to forget that Lincoln began to read Shakespeare intently as a boy in Indiana and continued to do so in Illinois. Wartime events expanded the meaning of these dramas of family conflict for Lincoln without eliminating their original personal and emotional connections.

The first house divided is the cabin in Indiana to which Thomas brought his second wife and her three children. Abe's new mother treated him with exemplary kindness, and his stepbrother became his closest friend; nonetheless alienation developed between father and son. In later years, as Johnston became closely involved with Thomas's affairs and more like him in character and conduct, Lincoln wrote him stinging letters of rebuke, and Lincoln's letter written as his father lay dying reflected old antagonisms. Such powerful emotions did not dissipate after Thomas's death in 1851 or Johnston's death in 1854 but reappeared as metaphor in Lincoln's utterances during the controversy over the extension of slavery and accompanied him from Springfield to Washington. Family relationships so strongly shaped his life and thought that it is impossible to understand this melancholy man without knowing the unhappy boy.

2

Abraham Lincoln and
Ann Rutledge

The romance of Abraham Lincoln and Ann Rutledge inspires both poetry and polemics. Sometimes identified as the crucial event in young
Lincoln's life, spurring him to greatness, the romance has more often
recently been dismissed as legend; indeed, references to an Ann Rutledge legend or myth often create public confusion about her actual
existence. In his psychological portrait of Lincoln, Charles B. Strozier
concludes a brief paragraph, "Ann Rutledge may have been Lincoln's
first love and her death may have prompted a severe depression on his
part. But since there is no single thread of good evidence on the subject,
the episode must be passed over quickly."[1] Strozier's haste, and that of
other contemporary Lincoln scholars uneasy in the presence of Ann
Rutledge, suggests the propriety of a reexamination of the evidence and
its treatment by biographers.

For more than thirty years after her death, Ann Rutledge's name
was unmentioned in any prominent public setting until William H.
Herndon, Lincoln's former law partner, lectured in Springfield, Illinois,
on November 16, 1866, on "A. Lincoln—Miss Ann Rutledge, New
Salem—Pioneering, and the Poem called Immortality—or 'Oh! Why
Should the Spirit of Mortal be Proud.'" In Herndon's account, Lincoln
first became well acquainted with Ann in 1833, when he boarded at
her father's tavern. She was engaged to John McNamar, a prosperous
merchant who had left New Salem and never returned during her lifetime. In McNamar's absence, Ann fell in love with Lincoln; promised
to marry him after McNamar released her; and then, engaged to two
men simultaneously, fell ill of fever. Lincoln visited her on her deathbed,
and "his heart, sad and broken, was buried" in her grave. He neither
ate nor slept, and "his mind wandered from its throne." Nursed back

to health by Mr. and Mrs. Bowling Green, Lincoln "*never* addressed another woman, in my opinion, 'yours affectionately;' and generally and characteristically abstained from the use of the word '*love.*'"[2] Herndon concluded by reciting the lugubrious poem that Lincoln had memorized when Ann died.

Printed immediately as a broadside, Herndon's lecture attracted newspaper attention, much of it skeptical.[3] Herndon's rambling and badly organized discourse digressed at length on the character of pioneers and the scenery of New Salem, while the sketchy story of Ann Rutledge rested chiefly on assertion. The facts, said Herndon, were "fragmentary," and he had not "told the whole story; nay, not the half of it. . . . I am forced to keep something back from necessity, which shall, in due time, assume a more permanent form."[4] Presumably, would-be Lincoln biographer Herndon resisted giving away free the heart of his projected book, but lawyer Herndon should have recognized the weakness of his case.

Herndon further compromised the case for Ann Rutledge by coupling it with an assault upon Mary Todd Lincoln. In 1837, after Herndon had waltzed with Mary at their first meeting and complimented her as gliding with the "ease of a serpent," Mary took offense and never forgave Herndon, excluding him from her home during his seventeen years as Lincoln's law partner. Uncouth and socially inept, too frequently drunk, and an active abolitionist, Herndon was the sort Mary loathed, and she never dissembled her contempt for her husband's closest associate. Just how much Mary's snubs hurt Herndon became clear when he embellished the Ann Rutledge lecture with the conjecture that Lincoln had never loved another woman.

Mary's oldest son, Robert Todd Lincoln, who heard of the lecture almost immediately, wrote that Herndon was "making an ass of himself" and went to Springfield to try to persuade him to desist.[5] Mary called Herndon a "miserable man" taken into Lincoln's office "out of pity," where he proved a "hopeless inebriate" and "only a drudge." That "dirty dog" might well beware the vengeance of Mary's friends. Since her husband had assured her that "he had cared for no one but myself," Mary intended to "remain firm in my conviction—that *Ann Rutledge, is a myth.*"[6] Her statement, if believable, proves only that Lincoln had never dared tell his wife about his unquestionable courtship of Mary Owens. Mary Lincoln's sputterings show that Herndon's arrow hit the target but prove nothing about Ann Rutledge.

Herndon had grossly mishandled a major incident in the Lincoln story. He had used Ann Rutledge for an irrelevant and baseless attack on Mary Lincoln which provoked counterattacks by her defenders; he had mingled the evidence with speculation; he had insulted Lincoln's memory by exaggerating his grief to the point of madness and had even fabricated a soliloquy in which Lincoln ranted in Shakespearian tones. By insisting that Ann died of emotional conflict rather than typhoid, Herndon substituted melodrama for medicine. Neither Herndon's reputation nor that of Ann Rutledge ever recovered from this series of blunders.

Opposition from the Lincoln family strengthened Herndon's resolve to portray the real Lincoln; yet somehow he could not organize his thoughts into a biography. Abandoning futile efforts, he finally sold his notes and papers in 1869 to Ward Hill Lamon, another former legal associate of Lincoln, who in turn hired a ghostwriter. The result, credited to Lamon, combined the research of Herndon and the writing of Chauncey F. Black, son of a member of President James Buchanan's cabinet. Within it appeared the Ann Rutledge story, based upon material gathered by Herndon before he lectured, supplemented by further information elicited by the lecture.

For the first time, the account appeared buttressed by evidence. Many residents of New Salem recalled Ann's attractive appearance and traits; fewer offered substantial testimony concerning her involvement with Lincoln. As a ghostwriter narrating a story already challenged, Black quoted extensively from testimony gathered by Herndon. Black concluded that "the story of Ann Rutledge . . . is as well proved as the fact of Mr. Lincoln's election to the Presidency," a defensive statement unlikely to provide reassurance.[7] When Herndon himself narrated the story in his 1889 biography of Lincoln, he also relied on witnesses.

In his biography and correspondence, Herndon treated the romance as a Rosetta stone to interpret Lincoln: (1) Ann's death turned Lincoln away from religion, inspiring some agnostic writing at the time and a lifelong aversion to organized religion; (2) Ann's death turned Lincoln away from love, and his eventual marriage proved one of convenience only; (3) Ann's death turned Lincoln into a melancholy man who never could enjoy true happiness or contentment; and (4) Ann's death turned Lincoln away from domesticity and toward greatness by shifting his ambitions from private to public matters. Herndon's mythic and controversial Lincoln, rising from crude origins to greatness by strength as well as virtue, never achieved the popularity of a Lincoln possessing innate moral grandeur; yet Herndon's passion for truth was undeniable. He had given Ann Rutledge a permanent place in the Lincoln saga and had added romance to the vanished village of New Salem.

William Randolph Hearst bought the barren acreage of New Salem in 1906 and gave it to the Old Salem Chautauqua Association of Petersburg, which began the work of erecting cabins on the original sites before conveying the property to the state of Illinois, which continued reconstruction in the 1930s.[8] The crude cabins of New Salem State Park contrasted with the Victorian parlors of the Lincoln house in Springfield, as did the women whose spirits dominated the two sites. In Oakland Cemetery, a few miles from New Salem, lie the remains of Ann Rutledge, exhumed in 1890 from the Old Concord Burial Ground by an avaricious undertaker financially interested in the cemetery.[9] In 1921, the undertaker's cheap stone was supplemented by a granite monument engraved with the lyric of Edgar Lee Masters:[10] "I am Ann Rutledge who sleep beneath these weeds, Beloved of Abraham Lincoln, Wedded to him, not through union, But through separation. Bloom forever, O Republic, From the dust of my bosom!"

The rebuilding of New Salem forced historians to confront Ann Rutledge again. Biographers wary of placing too much emphasis on Ann's lasting impact challenged historical novelists who embellished Lincoln's tragic romance. In the 1920s, William E. Barton, whose tireless research had even led him to the bedside of ninety-three-year-old Sarah Rutledge Saunders, eighty-seven years after her sister Ann's death, wrote that "Abraham Lincoln and Ann truly loved each other," even though he deplored the "mushy lies" told about them.[11] Paul M. Angle, however, dismissed the romance as merely "traditional," lacking contemporary records, based upon testimony by interested parties assembled by Herndon, no "impartial investigator."[12] Carl Sandburg, of course, portrayed a Lincoln so helplessly in love that "a trembling took his body and dark waves ran through him sometimes when she spoke so simple a thing as, 'The corn is getting high, isn't it?'"[13] "The corn is getting high, indeed!" snorted Edmund Wilson.[14] In 1928, the *Atlantic Monthly* began publishing a series of articles based upon sensational discoveries that included purported letters from Lincoln to Ann, and the exposure by Angle of all the documents as forgeries worked against scholarly belief in the authenticity of the romance.[15] Because attractive female characters enhanced motion pictures, no version of young

Lincoln neglected Ann. Both *Young Mr. Lincoln,* a 1939 film starring Henry Fonda, and *Abe Lincoln in Illinois,* a 1940 film starring Raymond Massey, dramatized the romance as pivotal in Lincoln's life.

The Ann Rutledge canon was augmented in 1944 by the rediscovery of an 1862 article by John Hill, a Democrat contemptuous of Lincoln, in the *Menard Axis,* a county newspaper so obscure that the article had previously gone unremarked. The son of New Salem merchant Samuel Hill, partner of McNamar, and rival for Ann's affections, Hill wrote scornfully of young Lincoln as a "love-sick swain."

> He chanced to meet with a lady, who to him seemed lovely, angelic, and the height of perfection. Forgetful of all things else, he could think or dream of naught but her. His feelings he soon made her acquainted with, and was delighted with a reciprocation. This to him was perfect happiness; and with uneasy anxiety he awaited the arrival of the day when the twain should be made one flesh.—But that day was doomed never to arrive. Disease came upon this lovely beauty, and she sickened and died. The youth had wrapped his heart with her's, and this was more than he could bear. He saw her to her grave, and as the cold clods fell upon the coffin, he sincerely wished that he too had been enclosed within it. Melancholy came upon him; he was changed and sad. His friends detected strange conduct and a flighty immagination.—They placed him under guard for fear of his commiting suicide.—New circumstances changed his thoughts, and at length he partially forgot that which had for a time consumed his mind.[16]

Sent to Herndon in 1865, the article encouraged him to establish the girl's identity, to ruminate on the lasting effect of Lincoln's bereavement, and proved that Herndon had not invented the romance. In the *New York Times,* Lloyd Lewis wrote that the Hill account established that the Ann Rutledge "'Myth' was a fact after all," that Herndon's account was true, an article provoking Louis A. Warren to an indignant reply under the headline: "The Rutledge Ghost Stalks Again." "The Lincoln fraternity," thundered Warren, "for years have known the story to be pure fiction."[17]

Exaggeration of the romance provoked scholarly exasperation in 1945, when J. G. Randall attached an appendix chapter, "Sifting the

Ann Rutledge Evidence," to the first volume of his magisterial *Lincoln the President*. The availability of the surviving Herndon source materials at the Library of Congress had induced Randall to encourage his wife, Ruth, to undertake research on both Mary Lincoln and Ann Rutledge, and his prize graduate student, David Donald, to study Herndon.[18] An early chapter, "The House on Eighth Street," discussed the Lincoln marriage primarily by refuting Herndon's account, and the appendix maintained the attack by challenging every aspect of the Ann Rutledge story.

Virtually all details of the romance depended upon statements and letters collected by Herndon, and the Randalls demonstrated that these were often contradictory. When Herndon persuaded former residents of New Salem to talk about Ann Rutledge, he transcribed their statements, and the Randalls questioned both the leading nature of his inquiries and his accuracy in recording testimony.

What the Randalls call "the Rutledge tradition" began with a document prepared by Ann's brother Robert before Herndon lectured. Robert responded to eight questions from Herndon in a lengthy and careful statement that fills nearly seven printed pages. Only two questions related to Ann, and her story occupied merely 15 percent of Robert's account of Lincoln's life in New Salem.

> In 1830 my sister being then but 17 years of age a stranger calling himself John McNeil came to New-Salem. . . . A friendship grew up between McNeil and Ann which ripened apace and resulted in an engagement to marry—McNeil's real name was McNamar. It seems that his father had failed in business and his son, a very young man had determined to make a fortune, pay off his father's debts and restore him to his former social and financial standing. With this view he left his home clandestinely, and in order to avoid pursuit by his parents changed his name. His conduct was strictly hightoned, honest and moral and his object, whatever any may think of the deception which he practiced in changing his name, entirely praiseworthy[.]
>
> He prospered in business and pending his engagement with Ann, he revealed his true name, returned to Ohio to relieve his parents from their embarrassments, and to bring the family with him to Illinois. On his return to Ohio, several years having elapsed, he found his father in declining health or dead,

and perhaps the circumstances of the family prevented his immediate return to New Salem. At all events he was absent two or three years.

In the mean time Mr Lincoln paid his addresses to Ann, continued his visits and attentions regularly and those resulted in an engagement to marry, conditional to an honorable release from the contract with McNamar. There is no kind of doubt as to the existence of this engagement. David Rutledge urged Ann to consummate it, but she refused until such time as she could see McNamar—inform him of the change in her feelings, and seek an honorable release. Mr Lincoln lived in the village, McNamar did not return and in August 1835 Ann sickened and died. The effect upon Mr Lincoln's mind was terrible; he became plunged in despair, and many of his friends feared that reason would desert her throne. His extraordinary emotions were regarded as strong evidence of the existence of the tenderest relations between himself and the deceased. McNamar however, returned to Illinois in the fall after Ann's death.[19]

Robert believed "that any authentic statements connected with the history of the beloved Abraham Lincoln should belong to the great American people" and trusted Herndon to eliminate anything that might "injuriously affect" living persons.[20] Herndon's misuse of the romance to settle scores with Mary Lincoln and to explore Lincoln's psychology did not invalidate Robert's account. The Rutledge family had the best reasons to know and to remember the details of the romance, and Robert wrote with careful precision.

His only clearly erroneous assertion was that McNamar's family lived in Ohio instead of New York. After proclaiming that Ann was engaged to two men at once and that the conflict caused her death, Herndon pressed for confirmation, and, while politely denying both, Robert fell into the semantic trap of calling Ann's engagement to Lincoln both conditional and unconditional. At best, the Randalls caught him in a technical error. He never, however, altered his basic account, which, unlike Herndon's melodramatic account of Ann's death, received support from surviving witnesses.

Criticized by the Randalls for consulting other family members in addition to providing his personal recollections, Robert had prepared an account that incorporated the testimony of his mother and older brother John, important witnesses otherwise unavailable.[21] John Rutledge's letters reflect unfamiliarity with the pen, and when Mary Ann Rutledge learned in 1860 of campaign charges that Lincoln had not paid his board bill at the Rutledge tavern, she "caused a letter to be written to Mr. Lincoln" answering the accusation.[22] Whether lack of literacy or the blindness she suffered in old age (she died in 1878, aged ninety-one) prevented her from offering direct testimony, Ann's mother, the most valuable living witness of the romance, stood behind Robert's statement.

The Randalls' assertion that Ann was engaged to McNamar at the time of her death also hinged on technicality. McNamar left New Salem in 1832 on what he called "a long business trip to the East"[23] and returned some three years later. He left "for the purpose of assisting my fathers family, my coming west being principally to obtain means."[24] He had, indeed, prospered, yet "at that time I think neither Mr. Lincoln nor myself were in a situation to enter into what Mr. Seward would call 'entangling alliances.'"[25] What the Randalls called "the strangely neglected subject of McNamar's love for Ann" requires reappraisal before their engagement provides evidence against Lincoln's courtship.[26] Others asserted that Ann was already engaged, but McNamar never did.[27]

The Randall study of conflicting evidence omitted the salient point that no knowledgeable witness denied Lincoln's affection for Ann. James Short, a close friend of Lincoln who had employed Ann's mother as housekeeper, wrote that he "did not know of any engagement or tender passages between Mr L and Miss R at the time. But after her death . . . he seemed to be so much affected and grieved so hardly that I then supposed there must have been . . . something of the kind."[28] McNamar, in New York when Ann died, had never heard "that Mr Lincon addressed Miss Ann Rutledge in terms of courtship," and Ann's aunt believed that she would have married McNamar had she lived.[29] Although cited by the Randalls as evidence against the romance, none of the three refuted Lincoln's courtship. Publication of Herndon's lecture and widespread newspaper coverage virtually invited additional testimony. Witnesses had emerged who denied Lincoln's insanity, not his grief, without challenging the romance. After surveying the manuscripts, the Randalls emphasized three witnesses—Herndon consulted a "score or more"—who doubted. Of the exceptions, McNamar held a personal interest in minimizing the romance, and Short had become his brother-in-law.

Dismissing the romance depends upon beginning with Herndon's original account and discrediting his informants as contradictory. Beginning instead with Robert Rutledge's testimony and comparing it with surviving witnesses puts the romance in different perspective. Herndon's stubborn insistence on dual engagements causing Ann's death cannot be sustained; she died of "brain fever," later called typhoid, as did James Rutledge, her father, later in the year.[30] At the time of Ann's death, the Rutledges lived on land owned by McNamar, an indication of their declining fortunes as New Salem declined, and the death of James administered the final blow. Family need might have forced Ann to marry McNamar had she lived—if he would have her—but this issue is irrelevant to her involvement with Lincoln.

Herndon relied upon the recollections of old settlers of the New Salem area, their children, and the Rutledge family because Lincoln apparently never mentioned Ann in Springfield—with one remarkable exception. Isaac Cogdal, a former resident of New Salem, later a lawyer, visited Lincoln in his office during the winter of 1860–1861 and many years later repeated his conversation to Herndon.

> Abe is it true that you fell in love with & courted Ann Rutledge said Cogdall. Lincoln said, "it is true—true indeed I did. I have loved the name of Rutlege to this day. I have kept my mind on their movements ever since & love them dearly." . . . Ab—Is it true—said Cogdall, that you ran a little wild about the matter: I did really—I ran off the track: it was my first. I loved the woman dearly & sacredly: she was a handsome girl—would have made a good loving wife—was natural & quite intellectual, though not highly Educated—I did honestly—& truly love the girl & think often—often of her now.[31]

The Randalls challenged the statement because Herndon transcribed it years after the conversation; Cogdal addressed Lincoln as "Ab[e]"; another informant stated that Lincoln had told Cogdal that Ann was then living in Iowa; and Lincoln, who had a deserved reputation for reticence about his private life, had not mentioned Ann to close friends in Springfield. To the Randalls, "the Cogdal record seems artificial and made to order. It was given out after Lincoln's death; it presents him in an unlikely role; it puts in his mouth uncharacteristic sayings."[32]

What should be taken into account is that while Springfield friends called him "Lincoln," old friends from New Salem days called him "Abe." Ann's mother and brothers were living in Iowa in 1860, perhaps giving rise to a misunderstanding by someone repeating Cogdal's account.[33] Lincoln spoke of Ann because Cogdal asked, something few would have had the knowledge, opportunity, or temerity to do. Lincoln might not have answered before his last winter in Illinois, a time when he visited his father's grave, neglected for a decade, and left Springfield saying, "All the strange, chequered past seems to crowd now upon my mind."[34] Cogdal, who may well have misrecollected Lincoln's words some half-dozen years after the conversation, had no known reason to misrepresent what Lincoln said.

The Randalls' case against Lincoln's grief began with a letter from Mathew S. Marsh of New Salem, written three weeks after Ann's death, mentioning Lincoln as "a very clever fellow and a particular friend of mine," likely to frank the letter, something Lincoln eventually did although contrary to regulations. Marsh mentioned no recent sorrow in Lincoln's life, only that he was "very careless about leaving his office open and unlocked during the day."[35] In addition, Lincoln dated a survey for Marsh one month after Ann's death.

Even more decisive, in the Randalls' view, was the beginning of Lincoln's courtship of Mary Owens one year after Ann's death. Mary Owens takes her place in the Lincoln story through Herndon's insatiable quest for information. Tracked down in Missouri, Mary Owens Vineyard ignored several letters from Herndon before transmitting three letters from Lincoln and information about the courtship. Without what some condemned as Herndon's unseemly curiosity and pestiferous persistence, Mary Owens might also be regarded as a myth or legend. After the affair ended, Lincoln wrote that he had seen Mary Owens in 1833, "thought her inteligent and agreeable, and saw no good objection to plodding life through hand in hand with her."[36] Mary Owens, however, wrote, "As regards Miss Rutledge, I cannot tell you any thing, she having *died* previous to my acquaintance with Mr. Lincoln, and I do not now recollect of ever hearing him mention her name."[37] As the Randalls correctly point out, Lincoln's courtship of Mary Owens beginning one year after Ann's death "fails to harmonize with the popular concept that Lincoln's whole life was influenced by his love for Ann."[38] Nonetheless, the point is irrelevant to Lincoln's relationship with Ann or his emotions when she died.

The Randalls concluded that the romance was "unproved" and "does not belong to a recital of those Lincoln episodes which one presents as unquestioned reality."[39] They chose these words carefully, aware that their investigation cast doubt on Ann as Lincoln's first, great, and only love, not on her existence. Any account of Lincoln's early life dependent solely on the proved and unquestioned must be nearly impossible. The Randalls reclassified the romance as an accusation requiring proof, something of which Lincoln would be held innocent until proved guilty, rather than a biographical incident about which a preponderance of reliable evidence would prevail.

Reversing Herndon's assumption that because Lincoln loved Ann he could not love Mary, the Randalls sought to rehabilitate the Lincoln marriage by discrediting Lincoln's earlier romance. Both cases rested on the shaky assumption that Lincoln could not have loved different women at different times. Herndon had used Ann as a weapon against Mary; now champions of Mary used Ann as a weapon against Herndon.

David Donald's biography of Herndon published in 1948 further damaged belief in the romance by illuminating Herndon's faults and obsessions.[40] After her husband's death, Ruth Randall completed a Mary Lincoln biography notable for its defensive tone about her and scorn of Herndon. Through Ann Rutledge, Herndon "perpetrated a vast hoax," which "takes away Lincoln's real love and substitutes a bogus love." The romance "makes Ann a usurper who robs Lincoln's wife of the thought and consideration normally directed toward the woman who has shared a great man's life." The chapter concluded with Mrs. Randall's unpleasant parody of Masters's poem.[41] In a biographical sketch of Ann for a major reference book, Mrs. Randall used the word "legend" or "legendary" in every paragraph.[42] Essentially, her case against the romance rested on an indictment of Herndon, the prime investigator and disseminator of the story, who was prejudiced against Mary Lincoln and credulous about information that supported his theories.

Indignant about the misuse of the romance in film and fiction, the Randalls and Donald skillfully exposed the shaky underpinnings of any detailed account of the relationship. This commendable correction of the historical record, once valuable, now requires reappraisal, especially as it provoked an overreaction. So thorough was the demolition work that Mary reigned on Eighth Street as a paragon of domesticity, with Herndon barred from the scholar's study as firmly as he was once barred from the Lincoln dinner table. Ann Rutledge was viewed as the creation of Herndon, Lincoln's Parson Weems.

Following the Randall attack, Lincoln scholars distanced themselves from the romance. The editors of Lincoln's *Collected Works* mentioned Ann Rutledge only twice in their notes, identifying John McNamar as "the fiancé of Ann Rutledge, for whom Lincoln's attachment has become legend," and identifying John Hill as one who "rather than Herndon deserves recognition for primary irresponsibility in first publishing stories which have been perpetuated in popular belief."[43] Benjamin P. Thomas concluded that "in the face of affirmative reminiscences, Lincoln students can scarcely declare with certainty that no such romance took place. But most of them regard it as improbable, and reject utterly its supposed enduring influence upon Lincoln."[44] Thomas's argument from consensus is echoed in Mark Neely's *Abraham Lincoln Encyclopedia,* where "the romance is now regarded as unproved and its profound effect on Lincoln's later life as completely disproved."[45] Scholarly authority has made the romance somewhat disreputable. Biographer Stephen Oates daintily sidesteps the romance.

> In later years, some of Lincoln's associates spawned legends about him and Ann, contending that they were romantically involved and that Ann was the only woman he ever loved. In actual fact, Ann was engaged to another man. And though the man left New Salem and eventually broke off the engagement, there is no evidence that Ann and Lincoln ever had anything more than a platonic relationship. And when in time the Rutledges moved to a farm over on Sand Creek, seven miles from New Salem, Lincoln often visited them because he cherished Ann's friendship and respected her father. . . . In August, 1835, news came of a tragedy that gave him a severe case of the "hypo." Ann Rutledge was dead—dead of the "brain fever," at the age of twenty-two. Her coffin resting in the Rutledge farmhouse was reminiscent of the coffins of his sister and the mother he would never talk about. His friend Ann was gone, proof of how transient were human dreams of happiness and lasting life. For all are fated to die in the end. All are fated to die.[46]

There is no evidence whatsoever of a platonic relationship. Ann was young and attractive; McNamar shamefully neglected his fiancée, as everyone around seemed to know. If Lincoln was overwhelmed with grief by a reminder of the finality of death, the problem of finding why Ann's death touched him so deeply remains.

Denying the reality of Lincoln's attachment to Ann while admitting his desperate grief when she died creates an image of Lincoln as subject to unpredictable periods of debilitating depression. Only one comparable depression is known. Descriptions of Lincoln's grief over Ann's death parallel his reaction to the "fatal first of Jany. '41," when his engagement to Mary Todd terminated under circumstances still obscure. Two letters written by Lincoln in January reveal his emotions.

> What I wish now is to speak of our Post-Office. You know I desired Dr. Henry to have that place when you left; I now desire it more than ever. I have, within the last few days, been making a most discreditable exhibition of myself in the way of hypochondriaism and thereby got an impression that Dr. Henry is necessary to my existence. Unless he gets that place he leaves Springfield. You therefore see how much I am interested in the matter. . . . Pardon me for not writing more; I have not sufficient composure to write a long letter.[47]

> For not giving you a general summary of news, you *must* pardon me; it is not in my power to do so. I am now the most miserable man living. If what I feel were equally distributed to the whole human family, there would not be one cheerful face on the earth. Whether I shall ever be better I can not tell; I awfully forebode I shall not. To remain as I am is impossible; I must die or be better, it appears to me. The matter you speak of on my account, you may attend to as you say, unless you shall hear of my condition forbidding it. I say this, because I fear I shall be unable to attend to any bussiness here, and a change of scene might help me. If I could be myself, I would rather remain at home with Judge Logan. I can write no more.[48]

Friends in Springfield noted the depression; once again documentary evidence that Lincoln attended to some business casts doubt on the debilitating nature of his emotions.

Does Lincoln's grief when Ann died mean that he loved her? Oates and others have suggested that her death evoked the loss of the two most important women in his early life: his mother, who died when he was nine, and his sister, Sarah, who died in childbirth at the age of twenty. Arguing so implies that Ann was also an important woman in his life without addressing the central question of their relationship. Similarly, to suggest that the death of a beautiful and unmarried twenty-two-year-old girl conveys enough tragedy to cause grief in the absence of romance evades the issue of Lincoln's depression, so intense that memories lingered for thirty years.

To write that Lincoln "was of course subject to depression through out his life"[49] ignores evidence that despite frequent periods of sadness and melancholy, on only two occasions did friends express concern about his behavior or even hint that he might be suicidal: following the death of Ann Rutledge and after the broken engagement to Mary Todd. In the latter case he wrote the word "hypochondriaism" or "hypo" twice, a word that appears elsewhere only in correspondence with Mary Owens.[50] According to the *Oxford English Dictionary*, "hypo," sometimes mistakenly assumed to be a word Lincoln coined, means morbid depression of spirits and appears in literary works of the period, while doctors used "hypochondriaism" to describe the symptoms of severe depression.

Depression and melancholy differ significantly, the first representing a debilitating and dangerous lack of perspective, the second a rational response to unpleasant thoughts, events, or memories. Throughout Lincoln's career as lawyer and president, observers noted his melancholy, sadness, or rapid changes of mood, without questioning his mental health. Only twice in adult life did he go "off the track."

The central and unsolvable mystery is not Lincoln's affection for Ann, but her feelings for him. The Rutledge family believed that the engagement was to remain secret until McNamar released Ann and Lincoln finished studying law. Outside the family, only Mentor Graham, the New Salem schoolteacher who taught both Lincoln and Ann, claimed to have been told of the engagement by Lincoln and Ann. Even Herndon noted that Graham was "at times nearly non co[m]pus mentis—but good & honest."[51] A stone allegedly discovered at New Salem in 1890, inscribed "A. Lincoln Ann Rutledge were betrothed here July 4 1833," tricked nobody except the Lincoln collector who bought it.[52] The only object sustaining the romance is a tattered copy of Kirkham's *English Grammar*, first mentioned in a Springfield newspaper the day after Lincoln's burial, as once having a flyleaf, later lost, identifying it as Lincoln's property. Robert Rutledge wrote within a few days that the book had been given to his sister Ann.[53]

Young Lincoln, homely and awkward, penniless and badly dressed, ill at ease with women, was an unpromising suitor for the village belle, no matter how neglected by her fiancé. Lincoln's later lack of confidence regarding women argues against his successful courtship of Ann. Successful or not, he could still love her. Uncertainty over the existence of a formal engagement beclouds the importance of the romance in Lincoln's life. He suffered the devastating blow of the death of the woman he loved.

In 1865, Herndon began to seek every detail of the romance recoverable; unfortunately, he then soared beyond the evidence. Herndon's enlargement of the romance, however, might better be viewed as cautionary than as prohibitory. Reliable evidence will not sustain any detailed account of the courtship. Further, any interpretation of the formative influence of Ann's death on Lincoln's thought and career lacks foundation. On the other hand, placing Ann herself and Lincoln's grief in the realm of legend represents a denial of evidence perhaps equally detrimental to understanding the man. A century ago, Lincoln's two former private secretaries, writing what they hoped would become the definitive biography, requiring approval of every word from Robert Lincoln in return for access to his father's papers, admitted that Lincoln was "much attached" to Ann, "and though there does not seem to have been any engagement between them, he was profoundly affected by her death."[54] Such grudging concessions exceed those made more recently by biographers of Lincoln or of Mary Lincoln, and the change of opinion reflects less the influence of new evidence or analysis of existing evidence than the influence of new fashions and concerns.

Although the full story of Lincoln and Ann Rutledge will never be known, the reality of that story appears certain. Historians might wish that Ann's friends and relatives had not waited thirty years to record their reminiscences. They did so then only because Herndon prodded, believing that nothing about one so important as Lincoln was too private for history. This belief, considered unseemly in the years immediately following Lincoln's death while his widow still lived, has modern adherents. Since 1945, labeled myth, legend, and fiction, Ann has faded into disrepute while defenders of Mary Lincoln have created an alternate legend of Lincoln's happy marriage. Ann Rutledge, however, simply will not go away. Available evidence overwhelmingly indicates that Lincoln so loved Ann that her death plunged him into severe depression. More than a century and a half after her death, when significant new evidence cannot be expected, she should take her proper place in Lincoln biography.

3

Abraham Lincoln, Jefferson Davis, and Fort Sumter

When four well-known and respected historians proposed to explain *Why the South Lost the Civil War* a few years ago, they quickly dismissed any explanation based upon a single cause. Ultimately they emphasized the weakness of Southern nationalism, in turn caused by weakness of morale stemming from an internal clash between religion and the institution of slavery.[1] This spiritual malaise owed much, they acknowledged, to military, economic, and political factors. Their chapter entitled "First Blood" opened with the first battle of Bull Run—as Confederate historians they called it First Manassas—forgetting or ignoring a 1957 book by the talented popularizer W. A. Swanberg, *First Blood: The Story of Fort Sumter.*[2]

The circumstances under which Confederate batteries opened fire upon Fort Sumter on April 12, 1861, play no role in the 1986 explanation of *Why the South Lost the Civil War.* I believe that this represents a serious defect in any discussion of Confederate defeat. Surely one reason why the South lost was that war began at the wrong time, in the wrong place, and for the wrong reasons. Worst of all, the South fired the first shot.

The consequences of firing the first shot against a small and relatively defenseless garrison shaped the initial military strength of both North and South. Men who might otherwise have fought for the Confederacy, clung to neutrality, or opposed a Republican war against slavery, resented Confederate bullies firing on the flag. They supported a war for the Union that did not become a war against slavery until so much later that opposition to emancipation gave the Confederacy few substantial advantages and failed to destroy Northern determination to suppress the rebellion.

Confederate firing on Fort Sumter represented Abraham Lincoln's triumph, Jefferson Davis's blunder, and was recognized as such even during the Civil War; Southern writers soon began to blame Lincoln for provoking the South into firing the first shot, an argument that at least had the merit of acknowledging Confederate error.[3]

As a delegate to the Democratic convention in Charleston in June 1860, Benjamin F. Butler of Massachusetts had voted on fifty-seven ballots for Jefferson Davis as nominee for president of the United States. Justifying his course more than thirty years later, Butler pointed to Davis's outstanding antebellum record as soldier and statesman.[4] As two new presidents took office in 1861, Davis held every objective advantage over Lincoln for executive leadership. Educated at Transylvania and West Point, Davis had attended two of the best schools in the nation. Asked to fill out a biographical form, Lincoln answered a query about his education with the single word "defective." Davis had put his military education to effective use during the Mexican War as colonel of the First Mississippi Rifles. Lincoln's service as captain of volunteers in the Black Hawk War of 1832 led him to ridicule his record as "a military hero."[5]

As secretary of war in the Franklin Pierce administration, Davis had administered the complex bureaucracy of his department and had supervised major surveys and explorations connected with a transcontinental railroad. Lincoln's executive experience consisted of senior partnership in a two-man law office so disorganized that he labeled an envelope "When you can't find *it* any where else, look into this."[6] Mississippi twice elected Davis to the U.S. Senate, where he assumed leadership of Southern Democrats after the death of John C. Calhoun. He twice resigned his seat: in 1851 to campaign unsuccessfully for governor of Mississippi and in 1861 to follow his state into secession. Lincoln had twice failed to be elected to the Senate, and his single term in the House of Representatives had ended in 1849. Finally, Davis had been elected president of his new nation by unanimous choice of the state delegations, entering office with respect and admiration throughout the Confederacy, while Lincoln, the recipient of 39.9 percent of the popular vote, lacked similar respect and admiration even within his own cabinet, where Secretary of State William H. Seward intended to practice the statecraft and leadership that he assumed Lincoln could not supply. If Seward, who had discussed policy with Lincoln, had little confidence in his ability, those at a distance had even less reason to expect much from the president. Considering the facts that Lincoln took office without executive experience in the midst of a national crisis caused by the secession of seven states and the establishment of a Confederate government, and that the foremost symbol of national integrity was an indefensible fort in Charleston harbor surrounded by enemy batteries, his inaugural address becomes a remarkable statement of belief and intent. To reassure the South, he repeated an earlier pledge: "I have no purpose, directly or indirectly, to interfere with the institution of slavery in the States where it exists. I believe I have no lawful right to do so, and I have no inclination to do so." Secession he labeled "insurrectionary or revolutionary," and he intended to execute federal laws in every state. "In doing this there needs to be no bloodshed or violence; and there shall be none, unless it be forced upon the national authority. The power confided to me, will be used to hold, occupy, and possess the property and places belonging to the government, and to collect the duties and imposts; but beyond what may be necessary for these objects, there will be no invasion—no using of force against, or among the people anywhere." In closing, Lincoln reiterated and emphasized the point made earlier. "In *your* hands, my dissatisfied fellow countrymen, and not in *mine,* is the momentous issue of civil war. The government will not assail *you.* You can have no conflict, without being yourselves the aggressors. *You* have no oath registered in Heaven to destroy the government, while *I* shall have the most solemn one to 'preserve, protect and defend' it."[7]

Lincoln had concluded his draft of the address with a stern warning. *"You* can forbear the *assault* upon it; *I* can *not* shrink from the *defense* of it. With *you,* and not with *me,* is the solemn question of 'Shall it be peace, or a sword?'"[8] Accepting Seward's suggestion for a more conciliatory close, Lincoln dropped these words from the final version. He substituted: "I am loth to close. We are not enemies, but friends. We must not be enemies. Though passion may have strained, it must not break our bonds of affection. The mystic chords of memory streching from every battle-field, and patriot grave, to every living heart and hearthstone, all over this broad land, will yet swell the chorus of the Union, when again touched, as surely they will be, by the better angels of our nature."[9] These words, some of Lincoln's best remembered and most often quoted, were not his and do not even sound like him. They provided a soft, rhetorical, pleading finale to a message otherwise direct, muscular, and resolute. Inasmuch as they concealed Lincoln's hardheaded and logical approach to men and measures, they struck a false note.

Five weeks later, the Civil War began. Lincoln's Fort Sumter policy during these crucial weeks had received intensive examination for a century before Richard N. Current brought it into sharp focus in 1963 in *Lincoln and the First Shot*, a magisterial explication that requires no emendation or replication now. Before sending a fleet to reprovision Fort Sumter, Lincoln had considered asserting federal authority at Fort Pickens instead of Sumter, and he may have discussed abandoning Sumter if the Virginia convention adjourned without further considering secession—thus trading a fort for a state. But at no time did he deviate from policy he had clearly enunciated in the inaugural address.

Lincoln steered a straight course while that of Seward ran crookedly enough to confuse Confederate leaders about federal intentions. Seward wove a web of speculative possibilities that entangled the Confederate commissioners in Washington, who did not believe that Lincoln would make the ultimate decisions. Hoping to delay and deceive the federal government while the Confederacy strengthened its military preparations, the commissioners and their superiors eventually learned that they themselves had been deceived. They had misjudged a superior strategist. Confusion turned to frustration and finally anger when Lincoln ignored Confederate authorities, sending word of his intention to reprovision Sumter to Governor Francis Pickens of South Carolina instead of to President Davis. Lincoln's refusal to negotiate with or even to acknowledge the existence of the Confederate government enraged Davis into reacting emotionally rather than rationally to news of the federal fleet approaching Fort Sumter.

When news of Lincoln's Fort Sumter decision reached Montgomery on April 8, did the Confederacy have an alternative to commencing a bombardment? Of course it did. Defiance of federal authority had begun with the secession of South Carolina on December 20, 1860, and had continued with the secession of six other states, the seizure of federal property in those states, the formation of a Confederate government, and the assembling of men and means to maintain independence through force. This period of trial separation, which Lincoln hoped might end with Unionists leading secessionists back to allegiance or with negotiations that might yet save the Union, could have continued, and, if Lincoln's hopes proved unrealistic, then Davis might in time gain new support and additional territory. To achieve independence, the South needed unity and determination, something not yet attained in April.

The Confederacy had gained no new state since Texas had seceded on February 1. To Davis and his firmest supporters, the cause appeared self-evident; elsewhere in the South, potential adherents wavered and doubted. If convinced that Lincoln would wage an aggressive war, especially an assault on slavery, these wavering Southerners would be forced to join the Confederate cause. Sworn to maintain the Union, Lincoln might eventually have asserted federal authority at some point less propitious than Fort Sumter. If the federal fleet had succeeded in reprovisioning Fort Sumter, the tiny garrison would have remained only a Union symbol, not a physical threat to Confederate Charleston. Any increase in the size of the garrison by landing additional troops or any additional ammunition or armament would have left the military balance in Charleston harbor unchanged. "The little garrison" at Fort Sumter, wrote Senator Jefferson Davis in January, "presses on nothing but a point of pride."[10]

Little had changed by April except the condition of Confederate pride. Sources enabling historians to reconstruct the deliberations of Davis's cabinet on April 9 are regrettably thin. Many years later, Secretary of State Robert Toombs was quoted as telling Davis that "the firing upon that fort will inaugurate a civil war greater than any the world has yet seen; and I do not feel competent to advise you."[11] As discussion continued, however, Toombs eventually burst out with his true feelings to declare that firing on the fort "is suicide, murder, and will lose us every friend at the North. You will wantonly strike a hornet's nest which extends from mountains to ocean, and legions, now quiet, will swarm out and sting us to death. It is unnecessary it puts us in the wrong; it is fatal."[12] Because the most trenchantly prophetic portion of the statement came from an adulatory biography of Toombs written after his death, historians have doubted its authenticity. As it confirms the recollection of Confederate secretary of war Leroy Walker, present at the cabinet consultation, it deserves credit as the only significant insight into the deliberations.

Warned by Lincoln against aggression, Davis now received similar advice from the ablest member of his cabinet. Only a few days before the cabinet meeting, Davis himself, in writing to Braxton Bragg at Pensacola, stated: "There would be to us an advantage in so placing them that an attack by them would be a necessity but," he immediately added, "that advantage is overbalanced by other considerations."[13] Fort Pickens, then, he informed Bragg, might be considered a "military problem" and its capture desirable. Aware of the disadvantage of firing the first shot, Davis was nonetheless prepared to do so at Pickens. When Toombs uttered his prophetic warning concerning Sumter a few days later, Davis had already weighed and rejected such counsel.

When news of the fall of Sumter reached the Virginia convention, some delegates reacted as Davis had hoped they would. Not so Jubal A. Early. "I must confess that upon this day my heart is bowed down with sorrow, not so much that the flag of my country has been compelled to give way to another; not so much that a gallant friend and comrade of mine in former times has been compelled to yield to the force of overruling numbers, as that I find Virginians ready to rejoice in this event. ... Mr. Chairman, this act has done nothing to advance the cause of the Confederate States. In my humble opinion, it has placed a gulf between them and the people of Virginia. The mass of the people will never be found sanctioning their cause."[14] Early reluctantly acquiesced in Virginia's secession and joined the Confederate army, rising to corps command in the last year of the war. Even after Sumter fell, Colonel Robert E. Lee conferred with General Winfield Scott and Francis P. Blair Sr. about command of Union forces, telling both that he would follow the course of Virginia and take no part in an invasion of the South. After the Virginia convention acted, Lee resigned from the U.S. Army.[15] Not all Virginians possessed such state loyalty.

Davis fired on Fort Sumter with the expectation that the call to arms would unite the South against Northern aggression. The outcome was disappointing, as the onset of war pushed Virginia, North Carolina, Tennessee, and Arkansas into secession, but not Kentucky, Missouri, Maryland, or Delaware. In states that seceded, notably western Virginia—eventually an independent state—and eastern Tennessee, substantial Unionist sentiment was somewhat balanced by Confederate support in states that did not secede. In Northern states, Sumter gave Lincoln the support of Democrats led by Stephen A. Douglas and countered potential defection in the lower Ohio Valley, notably in southern Illinois and southern Indiana. Davis began the war in a way that could not have provided Lincoln greater advantages.

"After four years of arduous service, marked by unsurpassed courage and fortitude," General Robert E. Lee informed his troops, "the Army of Northern Virginia has been compelled to yield to overwhelming numbers and resources."[16] Oddly enough, Lee's explanation of Confederate defeat receives inadequate attention in *Why the South Lost the Civil War*. Instead, the historians argued that Confederates possessed men enough to win the war had they all determined to fight to the death. While other historians endorse the concept of "overwhelming numbers," actual numbers remain unclear. Census figures for 1860 put the number of white males between the ages of eighteen and forty-five in the Confederate states at approximately 1,000,000 and elsewhere in the nation at 4,500,000. Thomas L. Livermore estimated that if enlistments were compressed into three-year terms, the U.S. Army raised 1,556,678 men, Confederates 1,082,119.[17] After reviewing more than twenty-five studies of troop strength, E. B. Long concluded that 2,000,000 Union troops opposed 750,000 Confederates.[18] A comparison of proportions of surviving veterans counted in the 1890 census increases Confederate strength to a range of 850,000 to 900,000 confronting the same 2,000,000 opponents.[19] Certainty on numbers remains elusive, yet the South raised a remarkable army from a limited population. At the beginning of 1862, the Union had a two-to-one advantage in the field; by the end of 1864, this had increased to three-to-one.[20] On its strongest day, the Confederacy had fielded 55 percent of Union strength.

Despite this disparity in troop strength, the South came close to victory. Because the North had to wage war in enemy territory, superior numbers were no luxury but a necessity. The need for added manpower led both to the draft and to the enlistment of blacks; yet even such unforeseen measures did not lead to quick and decisive federal victory, but only to hard-fought battles on the road to Appomattox. In January 1863, by one estimate, to occupy Confederate territory, to protect against cavalry raids, and to maintain railroad lines, the North used 190,000 men—one-third of all its troops in the field—to counter the threat of 43,000 Confederates, one-sixth of its armed force.[21] In other words, the North maintained an occupying force four times the size of its adversary. Throughout the war each side needed every man it could muster.

Alleged Northern aggression at Fort Sumter, consisting of an attempt to feed a few troops in an isolated garrison, loomed as a monstrous affront to Davis at Montgomery but took on an entirely different aspect to a merchant in Kentucky or a farmer in Missouri, both of whom, statistically, were more likely to enlist in the U.S. Army than in the Confederate army. These were the initially uncommitted men that Lee so desperately needed.

Lee, even though so often victorious, has been criticized for so frequently attacking the enemy, thus draining the South of irreplaceable manpower. Even conceding this criticism of Lee, however, we must question why the manpower pool of the South remained so small. Confederate firing on Sumter transformed a potential war of Northern aggression into a war for the Union that diminished Confederate capacity to secure Southern independence. Even the military genius of Lee could not overcome the political blunder of Davis. Lee had to play the cards that Davis dealt. Firing on Sumter was a fatal blow foreshadowing Confederate defeat.

In his message to Congress on April 29, 1861, Davis referred to Lincoln's proclamation of April 15 calling for volunteers as a "declaration of war."[22] He reviewed negotiations with the Lincoln administration, "so wanting in courtesy, in candor, and directness," before official word arrived of the relief expedition.[23]

> Even then, under all the provocation incident to the contemptuous refusal to listen to our commissioners, and the tortuous course of the Government of the United States, I was sincerely anxious to avoid the effusion of blood, and directed a proposal to be made to the commander of Fort Sumter, who had avowed himself to be nearly out of provisions, that we would abstain from directing our fire on Fort Sumter if he would promise not to open fire on our forces unless first attacked. This proposal was refused and the conclusion was reached that the design of the United States was to place the besieging force at Charleston between the simultaneous fire of the fleet and the fort. There remained, therefore, no alternative but to direct that the fort should at once be reduced.[24]

Davis's explanation may have pleased Confederate loyalists but won few converts. In reality, Confederates had missed a second chance to avoid firing on Sumter. When Major Robert Anderson received and refused the demand for evacuation, he remarked that he "would be starved out anyway" if not bombarded.[25] Secretary of War Leroy P. Walker instructed General Beauregard: "Do not desire needlessly to bombard Fort Sumter. If Major Anderson will state the time at which, as indicated by him, he will evacuate and agree that in the mean time he will not use his guns against us unless ours should be employed against Fort Sumter, you are authorized thus to avoid the effusion of blood. If this or its equivalent be refused, reduce the fort as your judgment decides to be most practicable."[26] This second ultimatum received Anderson's reply that

> cordially uniting with you in the desire to avoid the useless effusion of blood, I will, if provided with the proper and necessary means of transportation, evacuate Fort Sumter by noon on the 15th instant, and that I will not in the mean time open my fires upon your forces unless compelled to do so by some hostile act against this fort or the flag of my Government by the forces under your command, or by some portion of them, or by the perpetration of some act showing a hostile intention on your part against this fort or the flag it bears, should I not receive prior to that time controlling instructions from my Government or additional supplies.[27]

Beauregard and his advisers at Charleston hastily concluded that the last condition invalidated the pledge of evacuation. Believing that Anderson was merely stalling while the relief fleet assembled outside the harbor, Beauregard decided to open the bombardment without further consultation with Montgomery.

In November 1863, speaking at City Hall in Charleston, Davis reminded the audience of a previous visit when he had escorted home the body of John C. Calhoun. He then imagined that Calhoun looked down upon Confederate Charleston like a guardian angel.[28] Without irony, Davis alluded to the Union blockading fleet and its recurrent bombardment of Fort Sumter. "Though crumbling in her ruins, she yet stands, and everyone looks with the anxious hope that the Yankee flag will never float over it. Nobly has the little heroic garrison that now holds it responded to every expectation. The commanding officer there is worthy to be the descendant of that heroic band that defended the pass at Thermopalye, and future records will record his name as glorious, for the defence of the approach to your harbor. Whatever may be in the future which is in the hands of the Supreme Being, we have written a proud page in our country's history."[29] Nobody recalls the "glorious" name of that Confederate commander; nobody forgets the Union garrison of 1861.

"No people ever warred for independence with more relative advantages than the Confederates," wrote Beauregard many years later.[30] "We needed for President either a military man of a high order, or a politician of the first class without military pretensions, such as Howell Cobb."[31] He remembered a nasty wartime quarrel with Davis, and he was not the only general "with whom Mr. Davis's relations were habitually unwholesome."[32]

Discounting Beauregard's prejudice and overstatement, is there any validity to his appraisal, especially as it related to Fort Sumter? Lincoln's strategy caught Davis at his weakest by refusing to recognize his government. Davis had political celebrity when Lincoln was unknown; Davis's apparent qualifications for the presidency far exceeded those of Lincoln. To follow a passive policy while Lincoln controlled events would prove impossible for Davis, even if toleration of the Sumter garrison might have brought strategic rewards. Surrounded by secessionist hotheads clamoring for action to vindicate Southern honor, Davis had no check on his own pride. To argue, then, that Lincoln provoked or tricked the South into firing the first shot is ridiculous; the decision to attack Sumter was the decision that Davis was born to make.

In his message to the special session of Congress of July 4, 1861, Lincoln devoted considerable attention to the events at Sumter, concluding that "the assault upon, and reduction of, Fort Sumter was, in no sense, a matter of self defence on the part of the assailants."[33] Instead, Lincoln asserted, Confederates attacked "to drive out the visible authority of the Federal Union, and thus force it to immediate dissolution. That this was their object, the Executive well understood; and having said to them in the inaugural address, 'You can have no conflict without being yourselves the aggressors,' he took pains, not only to keep this declaration good, but also to keep the case so free from the power of ingenious sophistry, as that the world should not be able to misunderstand it." Davis responded directly that Lincoln's message was based upon the "unfounded pretense that the Confederate States are the assailants," an argument he reiterated through the rest of his life.[34] During the past 130 years, a great deal of "ingenious sophistry" has been directed toward Fort Sumter, chiefly to palliate Confederate responsibility. In 1861, however, misunderstandings were fewer: by refusing to respect Lincoln's statements in his inaugural address, Davis had set his nation on the road to needless defeat.

Since eleven Confederate states nearly achieved independence, it is hardly outrageously speculative to argue that fifteen slaveholding states would have succeeded. Secession was based on an assumption that Lincoln's administration posed a threat to slavery throughout the South, an assumption plausible enough to create a new government at Montgomery. Had war ignited over any issue related to slavery, Southern unity, nationalism, and will to fight would have exceeded anything that Davis ever achieved. Instead, however, Davis assaulted the American flag, a symbol of national pride and patriotism. He could have rendered Lincoln no greater service.

4

"Freeing Some and Leaving Others Alone"

Lincoln's Emancipation Policy

Lincoln's Emancipation Proclamation of January 1, 1863, had "all the moral grandeur of a bill of lading," complained historian Richard Hofstadter.[1] Lincoln punished traitors by freeing their slaves. He based emancipation not on the evil of slavery but upon the necessity of suppressing rebellion. He did not free the slaves of disloyal persons except in states that had seceded, leaving slavery secure in Missouri, Kentucky, Maryland, West Virginia, and Delaware. Furthermore, he exempted from emancipation certain counties in Virginia, some parishes in Louisiana, and the entire state of Tennessee. The *London Times* sneered that "where he had no power Mr. Lincoln will set the negroes free; where he retains power he will consider them as slaves."[2] The final proclamation struck the British foreign minister as "very strange. . . . It professes to emancipate all slaves in places where the United States' authorities cannot, exercising jurisdiction, now make emancipation a reality, but it does not decree emancipation of slaves in any States or parts of states occupied by Federal troops and subject to Federal jurisdiction, and where, therefore, emancipation, if decreed, might have been carried into effect. . . . There seems to be no declaration of principle adverse to slavery in this proclamation."[3]

The draft of the Emancipation Proclamation that Lincoln read to his cabinet on September 22, 1862, opened with a statement that the war would continue for the same object as before: "restoring the constitutional relation between the United States, and each of the states, and the people thereof, in which states that relation is, or may be suspended, or disturbed." Lincoln reaffirmed his intention to urge Congress to pass measures facilitating compensated emancipation and added a promise, not included in an earlier draft, to support colonization of freedmen. Then he declared that slaves in rebel territory would be freed as of the first of next year.[4] By freeing slaves in insurrectionary areas, Lincoln duplicated, extended, and usurped congressional action.

In July 1862, the Thirty-seventh Congress had passed a confiscation bill to punish rebellion by seizing property of traitors to be sold for the benefit of the treasury, specifying, however, that slaves would be freed rather than resold. Congressional debate made abundantly clear that this was a Republican plan for emancipation. Profits realized from confiscation were expected to barely cover the cost of civil proceedings, if any, indeed, would be undertaken despite legal obstacles. Once set free, however, slaves could never be reenslaved, since this form of property was covered under the law of capture rather than that of legal seizure. Sixty days after the law went into effect, slaves of persons aiding the rebellion would be free whenever they came under control of the Union army. Confiscation would eventually free almost all slaves held within the United States and jeopardize the human property of remaining exempt slaveholders.

Early drafts of the Confiscation Bill conceded that war policy was an executive prerogative to be implemented with legislative warrant. As the sentiment of the Republican majority stiffened, while Lincoln's opposition to emancipation became better known, Congress revised confiscation bills to make them binding on the president. By providing for a presidential proclamation of confiscation sixty days after the bill became law, the final bill left nothing to executive discretion.

After Congress had adjourned, Lincoln presented to his cabinet a draft of an emancipation proclamation. As in the later version, this proclamation freed slaves only in those areas not under U.S. control. When Secretary of State William H. Seward protested that military setbacks made this an inauspicious time for such an edict, Lincoln put the proclamation aside for two months, until after the battle of Antietam in September.

Both Secretary of the Navy Gideon Welles and Secretary of the Treasury Salmon P. Chase recorded in their diaries that Lincoln said he had vowed to issue his proclamation if God gave victory in Maryland.[5] Lincoln did not account for the action of Providence in granting General Braxton Bragg temporary success in Kentucky at the same time

Robert E. Lee retreated from Maryland. Nor did Lincoln explain the divine aspects of a proclamation that freed only those slaves with no immediate prospects of benefiting while ignoring all those under the current jurisdiction of the Union.

Had Lee won at Antietam, did Lincoln intend to enforce the Second Confiscation Act? The sixty-day warning period of the Confiscation Act expired the day after the Proclamation appeared and this dubious legislation would automatically take effect. Although Lincoln might prevent the army from cooperating through his powers as commander in chief, civil officials in pacified regions were free to bring legal process. St. Louis authorities were already after the property of Senator Trusten Polk, expelled from Congress and last reported to be a private in the army of Confederate major general Sterling Price.[6] Under these circumstances, even if Confederates had been successful in Maryland, Lincoln probably would have issued the Proclamation nonetheless.

After John Pope's disaster at Second Bull Run at the end of August, Lincoln had recalled George B. McClellan to command. Radicals regarded his recall as a political affront. Combined with the president's quarrel with Congress, this had inspired Republican governors to plan a meeting at Altoona on September 24, a gathering labeled, with some justification, "a Roundhead Conspiracy."[7] In response to a charge that Lincoln had issued the Proclamation to forestall pressure from the Altoona meeting, Lincoln disclaimed his political sagacity by claiming that he "never thought of the meeting of the governors" and telling the standard story that Antietam had triggered a divine bargain.[8] The appearance of the preliminary Emancipation Proclamation just before the governors met, however, so neatly undercut their position that little was heard of their recommendations then or since.[9]

The entire North did not welcome the Emancipation Proclamation; a few days after its appearance, New York Republican Roscoe Conkling was forced to tell irate constituents that while serving "in Congress I never, by word or by act, have introduced the subject of the negro or of slavery, never save once."[10] Rather than winning public support, the Proclamation united two factions of the Republican Party behind the president. It pleased moderates by eliminating the dubious constitutionality of the Second Confiscation Act (even though it raised a new constitutional issue), and it pleased radicals by offering more in the way of ultimate emancipation that they had dared provide in the Confiscation Act and certainly far more than they had ever expected from

Lincoln. Radicals rejoiced in the uncompensated emancipation of the slaves of the lower South, while moderates welcomed the promise of border-state compensation; moderates liked the extension of the grace period, while radicals fancied that Lincoln had finally been converted to their cause.

For practical purposes, the Confiscation Act became a dead issue. Republican senator Ira Harris of New York, who represented the conservatives Lincoln hoped to impress, commented on the Proclamation. "I was *startled* when I first saw it. But it did not take me long to get reconciled to it. And now I find, every day, that men vastly more conservative than I have ever been are giving us their adhesion to the doctrine of the proclamation. It is producing a very happy effect here. . . . Those who have been *clamoring* for a *policy* have got it."[11] "Now, hurrah for Old Abe and the *proclamation*," wrote Ohio senator Benjamin Wade, ordinarily an implacable radical critic of Lincoln.[12]

In conventional interpretations, Lincoln as emancipator bides his time for the opportunity to strike the great blow against slavery that he wanted to deliver ever since, as a young man, he had witnessed a slave auction in New Orleans. Lincoln, however, intended to wage the war for the Union and not against slavery. He was eager to work out arrangements based on compensation and colonization that would pacify the border states and successfully terminate the war. Congress forced him to emancipate in order to preempt the vindictive Second Confiscation Act and to prevent further outcries from the radicals. Whatever Lincoln's satisfaction in implementing the antislavery views he had held all his life, he was pushed by radicals far beyond policy he had once thought appropriate. The preliminary Emancipation Proclamation of September 22 was neither the expression of pious gratitude for the stalemate at Antietam, nor the achievement of a cherished ambition, but a tactical move in a continuing struggle with Congress.

Lincoln had declared that he would free the slaves in states or parts of states still in rebellion on January 1. To establish a standard to judge loyalty, he provided that any state represented in Congress would be presumed loyal.[13] In this way Lincoln averted charges that he flouted Congress, since each branch judged the qualifications of its members and thus could determine which states or parts of states were actually loyal.

In the hard-fought delaying action against emancipation, Democrats overlooked no possible advantage, and this representation provision had aspects of a loophole. Those who opposed emancipation had one hundred days to find a way to stop the proclamation. Rumors flew that Democrats were planning to arrange dummy delegations from Confederate states to Congress solely to prevent emancipation.[14]

The substance of such rumors lay in the activities of Fernando Wood, publisher of the *New York Daily News* and recent mayor of New York. During the secession winter, he had alarmed the North by writing a letter of apology to Georgia secessionist Robert Toombs after arms destined for Georgia had been seized in New York, and he proposed that New York declare itself a free city, trading with both North and South. After Sumter, however, he offered Lincoln his services "in any military capacity consistent with my position as Mayor of New York."[15] Wood frequently wrote to Lincoln pledging his personal support and denying constantly published allegations of his disloyalty.[16] Since Wood continued to act with the most extreme wing of the Democrats, his letters to the White House were apparently designed to ward off the danger of arrest.

In early December 1862, Wood informed Lincoln that he had reliable evidence that Southerners were willing to return to Congress if granted a general amnesty. He asked permission to open correspondence with rebel friends.[17] In his reply, Lincoln asked upon what terms the Southerners would return and asserted that if amnesty "were necessary to such end, it would not be withheld." He asked Wood to keep the matter quiet and to tell him what information he had of Southern intentions, mentioning what must have been already obvious to Wood, that "such information might be more valuable before the first of January than afterwards."[18]

When Lincoln asked Wood for information, he did not give the authorization for negotiation that Wood requested. Wood's next letter expressed regret that his offer had been rejected and acceded to the request for secrecy.[19] Wood never revealed his source, and all that came of the exchange was a telegram from Wood two months later asking permission to publish the correspondence.[20] Aware that this was a political maneuver, Lincoln read the entire correspondence to his cabinet, preparing for publication which he expected to occur regardless of whether he assented.[21] Lincoln did not reply to the telegram, and Wood did not publish the correspondence; if Wood had embarrassed Lincoln, Lincoln might have arrested Wood. It is impossible to know if Wood had ever had any word from the South or any support from other Democrats, but it is fairly clear that he hoped to play on Lincoln's obvious reluctance to take the extreme step of emancipation while any hope of peaceful reunion remained.

In areas under Union military control, Lincoln, military governors, and local Unionists cooperated in a desperate effort to hold elections before January. In some districts where Congress had previously sanctioned irregular elections, new elections were held lest emancipating Republicans expel men who were formerly valuable as examples of Southern Unionism. Like most elections held before the Proclamation in seceded states, those held to prevent emancipation were often a grotesque mockery of correct procedure.

Limited coastal areas held by the North in North Carolina offered scant justification for elections, but one week after the appearance of the preliminary Emancipation Proclamation, Lincoln informed Governor Edward Stanly that he would be "much gratified . . . to have congressional elections held in that State before January."[22] North Carolina returned Jennings Piggott, private secretary to Stanly, who was not even a permanent resident. He had 595 of 864 votes; the majority of counties in the district were under rebel control.[23] The House quickly and easily rejected him.

In Virginia, one district represented in the last Congress elected Lewis McKenzie, mayor of Alexandria. McKenzie received a plurality of 12 of the 554 ballots cast amid serious irregularities: the governor neglected to set a definite date for the election and gave insufficient notice, while the polls were open in only two of nine counties in the district.[24] McKenzie was not seated.

In the Norfolk area, John B. McCloud was elected over W. W. Wing. McCloud, a former clerk in the navy yard, had lately worked as a day laborer, giving the *New York Tribune* opportunity to exult in the election of a "mudsill" from proud Virginia.[25] Once Lincoln ascertained that an election had taken place, he exempted the district from emancipation.[26] In one precinct where McCloud received a heavy vote, polling had been by printed ballot instead of voice vote, hence invalid under the laws of Virginia. This gave Wing an excuse to contest the election. The Committee on Elections, after examining an election that could not stand such scrutiny, rejected both contestants.[27]

In the eighth district, located in northern Virginia, Christopher L. Grafflin, a prominent Unionist, worked closely with the Francis Pierpont government.[28] As the fateful date for emancipation approached, he requested an election.[29] Federal troops usually controlled the district, but rebels mounted intermittent raids. Pierpont delegated a certain Downey to visit the district to determine if the time set for the election was suitable, and when rebels invaded just before the election day, Downey advanced the date. Because the laws of Virginia did not allow the governor to delegate the power to set the date of an election, Grafflin was rejected. As he had received only 342 votes, the House could have found other reasons.[30]

Much the same thing occurred in the ninth district of Tennessee. A group of loyal citizens met in convention and determined to hold an election on December 13 unless Governor Andrew Johnson issued a proclamation assigning some other day. At the last moment, the proclamation arrived, changing the day to the twenty-ninth, but arrived too late to prevent many from casting their votes on the thirteenth. Just before the twenty-ninth, Brigadier General Nathan Bedford Forrest launched a surprise raid into the district. In areas unaffected by the raid, voters again went to the polls. As Major General Stephen A. Hurlbut chased out the Confederates, he changed election day to January 5. Alvin Hawkins won all three elections, but in view of manifold irregularities was denied a seat.[31]

Another unusual case involved John B. Rodgers, who had served under Andrew Jackson in the Seminole War and won high favor that carried him to the attorney generalship of Tennessee and to the U.S. Senate. In 1845, he retired to private law practice and hotel keeping. One of the few Lincoln men of his state, Rodgers had attended the Chicago convention of 1860. He asked Lincoln for the Nashville post office, but Confederates made the appointment.[32]

In March 1862, Rodgers went north to help some Tennesseans captured at Fort Donelson who had been forced unwillingly into the Confederate army.[33] While in the North he purchased Sharps rifles with his own money and brought them back to equip three hundred cavalry.[34] In July, when Andrew Johnson heard that Lincoln planned to appoint Rodgers to a federal judgeship in Tennessee, he wrote strong letters of protest. Although he gave no reasons, perhaps he had in mind that for many years Rodgers had been more active in operating the Bon Air Health Resort than in the law.[35] He was then recommended for prison commissioner with the special duty of preventing the exchange of any loyal Tennesseans conscripted by the Confederacy.[36] This also fell through. Rodgers was once wealthy, but all his property was now behind rebel lines. He was so desperate for money that he offered to pledge his holdings at a tenth of their value as security on a loan.[37]

The election of four Unionist congressmen from east Tennessee in August 1861 had greatly embarrassed Confederate state officials. After redistricting, elections took place in November 1862. In a new district comprising parts of areas already represented by two Unionists, loyal Tennesseans elected Rodgers, one of the few Republicans in Tennessee. Rodgers did not press his claim for a full year, but then, under twin threats of personal bankruptcy and emancipation in Tennessee, presented himself for admission. Since he could not be seated without expelling two incumbents, Congress rejected his claim.[38]

Of eight claimants who appeared during the third session of Congress from the states of North Carolina, Virginia, and Tennessee, only one was admitted. Bridges of Tennessee, elected in August 1861, had been prevented by capture from appearing earlier. Elections in late 1862 had greatly reduced the number of Republicans, and now they were wary of new admissions which would obviously strengthen the opposition.

The most dramatic admissions controversies involved Benjamin F. Flanders and Michael Hahn, elected to Congress in December 1862 from the occupied areas of Louisiana. A new issue emerged of fundamental importance in the development of Reconstruction policy. Republican congressmen, who had no objection to the rule of a military government, resented Lincoln's assumption that such officials could be appointed by and solely responsible to the president as commander in chief. If the president maintained such control, he might eventually rule the entire South by independent authority. Already Lincoln had appointed five military governors: Stanly in North Carolina, Johnson in Tennessee, John S. Phelps in Arkansas, George Shepley in Louisiana, and Andrew J. Hamilton in Texas (who had no territory as yet). Stanly held an election won by his personal secretary; Andrew Johnson proclaimed an election thoroughly disrupted by Forrest's raid; Phelps had insufficient voters for any election; and Hamilton had none at all; only Stanly conducted elections legal enough to furnish a fair test of the right of a military governor to proclaim elections. Although Flanders and Hahn deserved admission more than a number of sitting members, to admit them would be a step toward conceding to the president the power of Reconstruction.

John E. Bouligny, U.S. representative from Louisiana in the Thirty-sixth Congress, had not resigned when his state seceded; instead he had returned to Louisiana to work against the Confederate government.[39] In the fall of 1862, he proposed elections in Louisiana, expecting an easy victory. Lincoln appointed Bouligny a special agent to organize elections, commending him to local authorities and reminding them: "All see how such action will connect with, and affect the proclamation of September 22nd."[40] When a citizen of Louisiana spoke to Lincoln of his apprehension that Northerners might be elected, Lincoln wrote to Shepley: "We do not particularly need members of congress from there to enable us to get along with legislation here. What we do want is the conclusive evidence that respectable citizens of Louisiana, are willing to be members of congress & and to swear support to the constitution; and that other respectable citizens there are willing to vote for them and send them."[41]

With voting limited to those who could take an oath of allegiance, about half the normal voters turned out.[42] In one district, Hahn received an overwhelming majority; in the other, Flanders received a plurality over four other candidates. Bouligny did not even come close to success. His reputation for heavy drinking told heavily against him, as did his indiscreet attempt in 1861 to run for local office under the Confederate government.[43]

Flanders, born in New Hampshire and educated at Dartmouth, had moved to Louisiana to practice law. He had also been superintendent of a school, editor of the *New Orleans Tropic*, and treasurer of the Opelousas Railroad. His outspoken Unionism so disgusted his Confederate neighbors that they exiled him to Tennessee, and he did not return until New Orleans was captured.[44] He was an abolitionist, "but not of the blood-thirsty kind," and an ally of Chase and Benjamin F. Butler.[45]

Michael Hahn was a young man of thirty-two, born in Bavaria, who had been brought to Louisiana when quite young and soon left an orphan by a yellow fever epidemic. He succeeded in obtaining a law degree, supported himself by selling real estate and writing for newspapers, and won election to local office. He had been a Douglas Democrat, and his loyalty was unquestioned.[46]

Nearly all of both districts were under Union control when the election was held. There were two matters of irregularity: some of the election laws of the secession regime were violated (including that requiring voters to swear allegiance to the Confederacy), and a military governor had ordered the election. In view of the general correctness of the procedure, the Committee on Elections recommended that the men be seated.[47]

Most complaints in the ensuing debate came from Democrats. Daniel Voorhees of Indiana attacked the concept that military governors could replace those elected by the people and asked "how many voters . . . desired to be represented in this Congress, and how many . . . [voted] to save their slaves under the proclamation of the President?"[48] The violence of the opposition's onslaught tended to weld Republicans together, but the debate did not close before some had registered their dislike for Lincoln's theory of Reconstruction.

In accordance with the second paragraph of the preliminary Emancipation Proclamation, Lincoln's December message to Congress offered a plan for compensated emancipation. Lincoln drafted three amendments to the Constitution. The first offered interest-bearing government bonds in payment to states abolishing slavery before 1900; the second freed all slaves entering Union lines during the war without prejudice to possible claims for compensation from loyal owners; the last authorized the appropriation of funds for voluntary colonization. Lincoln employed an elaborate argument, first demonstrating that the United States as a cohesive geographical unit could not be divided permanently. He believed that the present division could "be hushed forever" by the adoption of his amendments, which represented a compromise between the most extreme views of the slavery question.

Congressmen expected Lincoln's message to deal with the progress of the war. They were shocked to discover that he had omitted all mention of it. Few noted that he had presented the only plan of emancipation ever to come from the White House. In their wrath, they gave little attention to Lincoln's eloquent final plea: "Fellow-citizens, *we* cannot escape history. We of this Congress and this administration, will be remembered in spite of ourselves. No personal significance, or insignificance, can spare one or another of us. The fiery trial through which we pass, will light us down, in honor or dishonor, to the latest generation."[49]

Lincoln had never been further from the spirit of Congress. In Missouri, a strong group was working successfully to persuade the state to take advantage of compensation; Lincoln had spoken to a delegation of Kentucky Unionists of the advantages of compensation and had assured them of strong allies, but the situation looked dark there;[50] nowhere else in the slave states was there significant interest in Lincoln's plan. Orville H. Browning thought Lincoln suffered a "hallucination" if he thought there was any chance of success.[51] Representative Henry Dawes of Massachusetts claimed that Lincoln's message made his "heart bleed," for "whether the Republic shall live six months or not is the question thundering in our ears, and the Chief Magistrate answers, I've got a plan which is going to work well in the next century."[52]

Since Lincoln so prominently advocated a moderate solution to the problems of slavery, some Republicans feared that he would not issue the final decree of emancipation on January 1, 1863. He reportedly said that he "would rather die than take back a word of the Proclamation of Freedom,"[53] but nothing Lincoln could say would be interpreted as conclusive, for even if he intended to back down, he would lose credibility by revealing this beforehand.

On legal grounds, Browning violently opposed the Proclamation and used the last of his influence with Lincoln. On December 28, Senator Charles Sumner's anxiety vanished after Lincoln said that "he could not stop the proclamation if he would, and he would not if he could."[54]

On December 29, when Lincoln showed the proclamation to the cabinet, Chase, Seward, Welles, and Postmaster General Montgomery Blair argued against excluding fractions of states. Lincoln reminded them of his pledge in the first Proclamation that representation in Congress would be the test of loyalty. With reference to the exempted parishes of Louisiana, he had made a pledge to ex-Congressman Bouligny. Chase reminded him that Hahn and Flanders of Louisiana were yet to be seated. Lincoln angrily asserted that he would not be "bullied" by Congress.[55] When cabinet members made verbal changes on December 31, Lincoln stood firm on the issue of fractional exemption.[56]

Andrew Johnson believed that emancipation in Tennessee would harm the Union cause. Although only east Tennessee was represented in the House, Johnson argued for exempting the entire state because all Tennessee would have had representation in the Senate had he not resigned his seat to serve as military governor. On December 23, Lincoln received a petition requesting exemption signed by Johnson and other prominent Tennesseans.[57] Presumably on the strength of Johnson's protest, Lincoln exempted Tennessee, thus failing to carry out the threat of emancipation contained in the preliminary proclamation.[58]

The final document was simple and direct. Lincoln omitted mention of compensation or colonization, but referred to military use of former slaves.[59] The Washington correspondent of the *Chicago Tribune* called it "the greatest event since the crucifixion."[60] An abolitionist called for "three cheers for God!"[61] When Democratic brigadier general John A. McClernand hinted that rebels might return to their allegiance if Lincoln retracted the Proclamation, Lincoln would have none of it.[62] He refused to retreat after January 1, 1863.

Through a political masterstroke, Lincoln had become the leader of his party and his nation. He had struck against slavery so as to maintain maximum support from those who favored preserving both the Union and slavery. In August, he had responded to a demand from Horace Greeley for action against slavery by declaring: "If I could save the Union without freeing *any* slave I would do it, and if I could save it by freeing *all* the slaves I would do it; and if I could save it by freeing some and leaving others alone I would also do that."[63] As he penned these words, the proclamation enacting the third of these possibilities lay in his desk, awaiting the strategic moment. Lincoln's policy doomed slavery, untenable in exempted areas whenever Northern arms prevailed in the Confederate South. Some legal slavery survived until ratification of the Thirteenth Amendment in December 1865, but in Missouri and elsewhere state initiatives had previously achieved emancipation. Yet Lincoln's strategy bore a price. Historians have since focused on slaves unaffected by the Emancipation Proclamation, questioning Lincoln's determination to destroy slavery. They might better focus upon slaveholders in those exempted areas, frequently persons of tenuous allegiance at best to the Union cause. Failure to exempt would have created new allies for the Confederacy, hardly expedient at the midpoint of the Civil War. A few such recruits might have tipped the balance in a context not foreordaining a Union victory. To Lincoln, the Union was paramount, not least because Confederate triumph protected slavery indefinitely. Union victory was an indispensable prerequisite to destroying slavery. By framing emancipation strategically, Lincoln followed the sole policy, that of hardheaded military necessity, that could ultimately free any slaves. By freeing some slaves and "leaving others alone," Lincoln combined the goals of Union and emancipation.

5

Lincoln and
"Old Brains" Halleck

President Abraham Lincoln's appointment of Major General Henry W. Halleck as general in chief in July 1862 might rank as one of the most outstanding blunders of the Civil War. Within weeks of his arrival in Washington, Halleck had thoroughly demonstrated his inadequacy for the position. "Of all men whom I have encountered in high position, Halleck was the most hopelessly stupid," wrote Major General George B. McClellan. "I do not think he ever had a correct military idea from beginning to end."[1] Secretary of the Treasury Salmon P. Chase thought that Halleck "was good for nothing, and everybody knew it except the President."[2] Despite constant condemnation by generals in the field and the scorn of political leaders, Lincoln nonetheless kept Halleck in Washington for the remainder of the Civil War.

Halleck's performance exposed his obvious deficiencies. He evaded responsibility, provoked unnecessary quarrels, and truckled to political power. Why did Lincoln keep Halleck in Washington? Despite Halleck's superb background qualifications, Lincoln came to value Halleck less for his virtues than for his faults. This explanation requires looking beyond Halleck's military aptitudes toward Lincoln's style of leadership.

When Lincoln assumed office, General Winfield Scott served as general in chief, as he had for a generation. Seventy-five years old by this time, Scott was too heavy to mount a horse and too old to remain awake throughout important meetings. A hero of the War of 1812 and again a hero for his brilliant campaign in Mexico, Scott recognized his current limitations. Although a Virginian, Scott maintained a sturdy Unionism, attempted to retain Robert E. Lee in the Union army, and offered Lincoln seasoned advice on military matters. His intimate knowledge of the talent of the old army enabled him to provide sound suggestions about potential commanders. Scott early devised an overall wartime strategy, known as the "Anaconda Plan," to defeat the Confederacy by maintaining constant pressure on all points of the enemy perimeter, including a blockade, then bisecting the South by a campaign down the Mississippi River. Those who anticipated a quick and glorious victory over the rebellion ridiculed Scott's plan. In retrospect, however, Scott's plan closely resembles the blueprint ultimately resulting in Northern victory. Conscious of the burdens of age, and aware that Congress had pointedly provided the first military retirement plan in American history, Scott recommended Halleck as his replacement.[3]

Halleck seemed a perfect choice. At forty-six, he was neither immature nor overage for such weighty responsibilities. He had achieved his military reputation and standing through his own merits and hard work. Born to a poor farm family in upstate New York, he had run away from home to escape a life of rural drudgery. Aided by a sympathetic grandfather, he had acquired an academic education and eventually an appointment to West Point. There he flourished, graduating third in his class. He began to teach chemistry at the military academy even before graduation and remained to teach engineering. As a young officer, he received choice assignments in Washington, to the fortifications in New York Harbor, and finally to a tour of inspection in Europe.

Following his return from Europe, he published a book on coast defense that led to an invitation to lecture at the Lowell Institute of Boston. His lectures grew into the book *Elements of Military Art and Science*, first published in 1846, then reprinted, revised, and enlarged in 1861.[4]

In his book, Halleck advocated the merits of professional soldiers. He reminded readers of George Washington's complaints about the militia and his use of trained foreigners to win the Revolutionary War. War was not, Halleck argued, "a mere game of chance. Its principles constitute one of the most intricate of modern sciences; and the general who understands the art of rightly applying its rules . . . may be morally certain of success." For the troops, skill and discipline rather than numbers represented the formula for victory. Recognizing that Americans would fund only a small army, Halleck emphasized the education of engineer and artillery officers, those most difficult to prepare in wartime, and the training of all officers, no matter how few troops they commanded, to lead larger forces in wartime.[5] Halleck advocated a strategic offensive as the path to success. Little wonder, then, that this author appeared to be the ideal officer to take command of the U.S. Army.

Halleck was assigned to California at the outbreak of the Mexican War. While fellow officers played cards to kill time during the seven-month voyage around the tip of South America, Halleck translated four thick volumes of Jomini's life of Napoleon.[6] In California, Halleck was appointed secretary of state, translated complex Spanish land laws, initiated the movement for statehood, and wrote most of the new constitution. Before leaving the army, Halleck became the senior partner in Halleck, Peachy, and Billings, the foremost law firm in San Francisco. He resigned from the army in 1854 with the rank of captain, effective the day after the resignation of Captain Ulysses Grant. Younger officers blocked from promotion by a stagnant seniority system frequently resigned in frustration, some to pursue promising alternatives. Unlike Grant, who planned to start over again as a farmer, Halleck went straight to a lucrative legal career, enhanced by his mastery of Spanish land law. During seven civilian years, he refused a professorship at the Lawrence Scientific School of Harvard, was elected president of the largest mercury mine in the country, served as a railroad president, declined an appointment to the state supreme court, and rejected overtures for a U.S. Senate seat. In his spare time, he wrote a lengthy treatise on international law, published in 1861.[7]

Scott selected Halleck as his successor because of these dazzling accomplishments in military and civilian life. Besides, Scott was under heavy pressure from General McClellan, selected to command troops in the field when Scott could not. After Major General Irvin McDowell, first in that role, had suffered defeat at Bull Run, McClellan was summoned from western Virginia to train and organize the forces around Washington, now named the Army of the Potomac.

McClellan soon quarreled with Scott, whom he privately denounced as "a perfect imbecile. He understands nothing, appreciates nothing & is ever in my way."[8] McClellan—of all people—claimed that Scott was "for inaction & the defensive."[9] McClellan refused to forward reports through the "dotard," as he called Scott. For his part, Scott noted that the "remedy of arrest and trial before a court-martial would probably soon cure the evil," although such a trial would be "encouraging to the enemies and depressing to the friends of the Union." Consequently, wrote Scott, "I shall try to hold out" until Halleck reached Washington.[10]

When urged to advance, McClellan had offered a series of excuses for delay, some shifting blame to Scott. When Lincoln's close friend Edward D. Baker lost his life while blundering into unnecessary and humiliating defeat at Ball's Bluff on October 21, McClellan increased his complaints about Scott, who was soon hustled off to retirement at West Point even before his intended successor could complete the lengthy journey from California. In his message to Congress one month later, Lincoln announced McClellan's appointment, noting that "the retiring chief repeatedly expressed his judgment in favor of General McClellan," an incredible misrepresentation abetted by Scott's patriotic refusal to publicize his contempt for his successor.[11] Lincoln thus demonstrated a propensity to use his senior commander as a shield rather than a counselor.

Halleck had arrived in Washington to find McClellan holding the position of general in chief. McClellan immediately ordered Halleck to command the Western Department, recently mishandled for one hundred days by Major General John C. Frémont. Halleck arrived in St. Louis on November 19 determined to eliminate corruption, to institute sound military procedure, and to rid Missouri of armed rebels. Halleck had never commanded troops and had no inclination to leave his desk for the field. He defined his first task as concentrating troops in Missouri.

At the eastern edge of Halleck's department, at Cairo, Illinois, Brigadier General Ulysses Grant chafed at his inactivity. Already guilty of launching an attack at Belmont before Halleck could reorganize his department, Grant's initial request in January 1862 to attack Fort Henry was rebuffed by Halleck.[12] Wringing reluctant approval, Grant attacked successfully, then marched toward Fort Donelson while Halleck averted his eyes, ready to take credit for victory or to disclaim responsibility for defeat. Grant's victory encouraged a jubilant Halleck to request enlargement of his department and promotions for many officers besides Grant. Still distrusting his aggressive subordinate, Halleck dispatched a flurry of charges against Grant to McClellan, including one that Grant had "resumed his former habits," an accusation that meant only one thing to any officer familiar with gossip that Grant had drunk himself out of the service. Unaware of this last charge but outraged nonetheless, Grant asked to be relieved, yielding only when Halleck portrayed himself as Grant's defender and restored him to command the Tennessee River expedition. Surprised at Shiloh on April 6, Grant more than redeemed himself in a second day of battle, but Halleck decided to take personal command of the advance on Corinth, Mississippi, assigning Grant to a meaningless role as second in command.[13]

Having united three armies, Halleck eventually occupied Corinth after a six-week campaign notable for unnecessary caution, crowned with an opportunity for the foe to withdraw intact. Controlling an army of 120,000 at Corinth, Halleck could have advanced in any direction, but went nowhere. While fortifying Corinth on an elaborate scale, Halleck sent Don Carlos Buell eastward to pursue the enemy, with strict orders to repair the railroad as he advanced. This prevented Buell from reaching his opponents and did the railroad no good, since guerrillas destroyed track more quickly than Union troops could rebuild it.

In the meantime, McClellan had eventually moved against Richmond. As he left, Lincoln had relieved McClellan as general in chief and retained McDowell's corps for the defense of Washington. Though McClellan still commanded the Army of the Potomac, on which rested the nation's hopes, Lincoln had publicly demonstrated a lack of faith in him. Under such circumstances, the wonder is not that McClellan failed to take Richmond, but that he came so close. Following the climactic Seven Days battles, McClellan withdrew to Harrison's Landing and refused to advance unless massively reinforced. Consistent with earlier conduct, he blamed Lincoln and Secretary of War Edwin M. Stanton for the campaign's failure. Further, in his celebrated Harrison's Landing letter, much to Lincoln's dismay, he discussed war aims rather than strategy. Yet McClellan remained the idol of his troops. As Lincoln put it, McClellan "had so skillfully handled his troops in not getting to Richmond as to retain their confidence."[14] Lincoln brought Major General John Pope to Washington to take command of forces defending the capital. Pope urged Lincoln to appoint Halleck to overall command.

Late in June, Lincoln visited Scott at West Point. Scott reaffirmed his confidence in Halleck as general in chief, and Lincoln began a curious courtship that included sending Senator William Sprague of Rhode Island to Halleck's headquarters. Halleck telegraphed to Lincoln, "If I were to go to Washington I could advise but one thing—to place all the forces in North Carolina, Virginia, and Washington under one head, and hold that head responsible for the result."[15] Encouraged by this aggressive perspective, Lincoln appointed Halleck general in chief. Desperately frustrated by McClellan's passivity at Harrison's Landing, Lincoln sought an intermediary who would either force him to advance or would terminate his command.

Had Lincoln known more about Halleck's command in the West,

he might have hesitated before making this crucial appointment. Halleck had already displayed excessive caution, avoidance of responsibility, duplicity, petty tyranny, and military ineptitude. Excelling in managerial capacity, he lacked any skill in personal relations. He placed his own welfare above all other concerns. He had, however, so successfully concealed those faults that his reputed achievements, actually those of his subordinates, appealed to Lincoln, a man in search of victory rather than congeniality. Even Grant, Halleck's chief victim, had welcomed him to Shiloh, naming him "one of the greatest men of the age."[16] As Halleck left for Washington, Grant praised him as "a man of gigantic intellect and well studied in the profession of arms. He and I have had several little spats but I like and respect him nevertheless."[17]

From Lincoln's perspective, Halleck seemed the engineer of the successful Tennessee River campaign that had carried Union arms from Cairo to Corinth. After Shiloh, he successfully commanded the largest army ever assembled in North America. He had Scott's respect and endorsement, as well as Pope's enthusiastic backing. In matters of military procedure, Halleck had long been an acknowledged expert. Furthermore, Lincoln had no better candidate for general in chief, and to continue that vacancy meant direct and unprofitable contact with the hostile McClellan when what Lincoln needed was an intermediary.

Halleck's appointment made him McClellan's superior, exchanging their roles of three months earlier. Neither handled this reversal well. Halleck held the post of general in chief "contrary to my own wishes," he wrote to McClellan, who responded, "I would have advised your appointment," and offered "full and cordial support."[18] Privately, McClellan called Halleck's appointment a "slap in the face" and thought it "grating to have to serve under the orders of a man I know by experience to be my inferior."[19] Halleck thought McClellan a "selfish" general who "does not understand strategy and should never plan a campaign."[20] Lincoln gave Halleck authority to remove McClellan, anticipating that he would use it, yet Halleck rejected such a drastically unpopular procedure. Had Lincoln thought that he could remove McClellan without adverse political or military consequences, he might have done so himself without entangling Halleck.

Halleck came to Washington at a moment of unparalleled Northern opportunity. McClellan lay idle at Harrison's Landing with ample men to capture Richmond, while Pope had assembled troops south of Washington sufficient to defend the capital and to advance toward

Richmond. Had Halleck coordinated a renewal of McClellan's offensive with Pope's advance, Lee could have been crushed between two mighty armies. Instead, Halleck listened to McClellan's unrealistic demands for reinforcement, decided that they could not be met, yet declined to order McClellan forward with the enormous army he already possessed. Halleck eventually ordered McClellan's troops back to Washington, a move that McClellan resisted and delayed. When it became clear that McClellan was sullenly withdrawing from the peninsula and that not all of his troops had joined Pope, Lee skillfully and devastatingly struck at Second Bull Run.

Lee's defeat of Halleck's protégé Pope brought McClellan back to command all the forces defending Washington. His return to power was announced in orders attributed to Halleck. Lincoln, who had made this decision without informing Halleck in advance, took every step to evade responsibility.[21] Lincoln artfully convinced even his chief advisers that he had recalled McClellan to command on Halleck's advice. McClellan now freely expressed his contempt for Halleck while leading the Army of the Potomac to meet Lee's invasion of Maryland. Believing that he had won a substantial victory at Antietam, McClellan expected as his reward the removal of Halleck, "an incompetent fool" and "the most stupid idiot I ever heard of."[22] Halleck relayed to McClellan Lincoln's repeated orders to pursue the enemy. By ignoring them, McClellan achieved his own final removal from command. Halleck should then have been in firm control of the army.

However, he clearly did not want that power and responsibility. Three months of field command in the West had convinced Halleck that he belonged behind a desk reining in ambitious subordinates rather than urging them to attack. With McClellan's successor, Major General Ambrose E. Burnside, Halleck played a game of deadly errors. Burnside proposed to move his army to Falmouth, opposite Fredericksburg, and cross the Rappahannock on pontoons. Halleck insisted that the army cross above Fredericksburg where pontoons would be unnecessary. Burnside moved to Falmouth, found that Halleck had neglected to send the pontoons, and refused to cross the river, which was then easily fordable. Instead, he awaited the pontoons, giving Lee more than ample time to assemble his army and to fortify his position. Apprehensive of impending calamity, Lincoln asked Halleck to order Burnside to abandon plans to attack. Halleck refused, arguing that a general in the field was the best judge of operations. Halleck told Lincoln that if he wanted to control Burnside, he would have to do so himself.[23] When the battle of Fredericksburg turned into inevitable disaster, Burnside accepted responsibility. Critics, however, blamed Halleck. Burnside later advocated the removal of himself, Stanton, and Halleck, all of whom had lost the nation's confidence.[24] When Burnside proposed yet another move across the Rappahannock despite the doubts of corps commanders, Lincoln asked Halleck to visit the army, then submit an opinion. Halleck refused. "Your military skill is useless to me if you will not do this," wrote Lincoln.[25] In response, Halleck submitted his resignation. Lincoln endorsed his own letter: "Withdrawn, because considered harsh by Gen. Halleck." Harsh? Certainly. Justified? Absolutely. Halleck had managed to work himself into a position of essential uselessness to the country. Lincoln's annual message in 1862, unlike that of one year earlier that had so enthusiastically heralded the appointment of McClellan as general in chief, did not mention that Halleck had replaced McClellan.

Burnside's replacement, Major General Joseph Hooker, had bargained with Lincoln to receive no orders through Halleck, whom he detested. Lincoln had not consulted Halleck in advance about Hooker's appointment. Hooker's removal after his defeat at Chancellorsville in May was foreshadowed by the restitution of Halleck's authority. Originally on better terms with Hooker's successor, Major General George G. Meade, Halleck served as a conduit to convey Lincoln's disgust with the failure of the Army of the Potomac to pursue and crush Lee after the battle of Gettysburg. Like every previous commander of the Army of the Potomac, Meade came to detest Halleck.

In the West, Halleck proved more useful. His strong sense of professionalism assisted Grant during the Vicksburg campaign. Grant faced pressure from two directions. Lincoln believed that his own former congressman, Major General John A. McClernand, deserved an opportunity to command an expedition against Vicksburg. McClernand had negotiated with Lincoln to command troops recruited among Democrats in the Midwest. Halleck did everything possible to frustrate McClernand's dream of an independent command. Removed from command by Grant on a technicality shortly before Vicksburg capitulated, McClernand appealed in vain to Halleck.

Grant's brilliant Vicksburg campaign, which Halleck compared to one of Napoleon's finest triumphs, also eclipsed another uniformed politician. When Grant had finally disembarked his troops on dry ground south of Vicksburg, Lincoln had wanted Grant to move south and unite his command with that of Major General Nathaniel Banks, whose qualifications consisted chiefly of Massachusetts electoral triumphs as a Democrat, Know-Nothing, and then Republican. Halleck's belief that operations were best left to generals in the field worked in Grant's favor, as did his abhorrence of political generals like Banks. When Vicksburg fell, Lincoln wrote to Grant a celebrated letter acknowledging "you were right and I was wrong."[26] By implication, at least, Lincoln acknowledged that Halleck, also, had been right.

In March 1864, Grant replaced Halleck as general in chief when he assumed the rank of lieutenant general. In accordance with the Constitution, Congress had created this rank without specifying who should receive the appointment. Concerned about creating a rival candidate for the Republican nomination for president, Lincoln first required assurances that Grant held no political ambitions. Had he remained concerned, Lincoln could have promoted Halleck to the new rank—leaving command relationships unaltered. However, he had earlier concluded that Halleck was but little more than a "first-rate clerk" who had "shrunk from responsibility wherever it was possible."[27] When Grant was appointed, Halleck immediately resigned as general in chief, but Grant, who had professed "great confidence in and friendship for" Halleck, cooperated with Lincoln to have Halleck appointed chief of staff.[28] Since Grant intended to stay away from Washington, Halleck's appointment freed Grant from office chores, frequent communication with Lincoln and Stanton, and potential political pressure. Grant had Halleck's assistance in purging political generals including Banks, Franz Sigel, and Benjamin F. Butler.

Halleck's achievements as military manager were forgotten in July when Lee sent Jubal Early to threaten Washington. Halleck dithered while Early moved ever closer. Halleck was left behind when an anxious Lincoln conferred with Grant at Fort Monroe. As a result of that meeting, Grant sent General Philip H. Sheridan to take command of all forces near Washington to pursue Early "to the death."[29] Shortly afterward, Grant recommended that Halleck take command on the Pacific Coast.[30]

Grant and Lincoln drew closer while Halleck sat at his desk amid diminished expectations of his role. After Lee surrendered and Grant returned to Washington, Halleck's role disappeared. Immediately following Lincoln's assassination, Stanton sent Halleck to command at Richmond, as if to exile him from the capital. While there, Halleck quarreled with Sherman, his last and most loyal friend among senior commanders.

In less than three years, Halleck's reputation metamorphosed from potential savior of the Union to pariah. Shortly after arriving in Washington, Halleck demonstrated incapacity to direct McClellan or, indeed, any significant commander. Why did Halleck remain in Washington? Offered an opportunity by Grant to take command from Banks, Halleck avoided that assignment, perhaps aware that whatever his failings as a desk general, he performed even worse in the field.

Why, then, did Lincoln retain his services? Halleck remained a master of military technique, adept at moving troops and supplies. He knew how to translate Lincoln's wishes into proper orders and to offer suggestions about secondary matters. He provided Lincoln with a buffer against senior commanders; Halleck's name consistently appeared upon orders for removal. Halleck persistently opposed uniformed politicians, whereas Lincoln unified wartime support by appointing officers for both political and ethnic reasons. Halleck received blame when such appointees failed, again protecting Lincoln. As chief of staff, Halleck performed a similar task for Grant, offering counsel concerning the removal of political appointees, warning Grant against moving too quickly or with imprudent timing. Unlike Grant, the unpopular Halleck posed no threat of political rivalry to Lincoln. Critics who assailed Halleck's weakness and ineptitude rarely noticed that he shielded Lincoln, who once proclaimed himself "Halleck's friend because nobody else was."[31]

The otherwise friendless Halleck had not sought the post of general in chief. He admitted that he did not "understand and cannot manage affairs in the East," especially "the quarrels of Stanton and McClellan."[32] Lincoln summoned Halleck to Washington either to force McClellan to advance or to remove him from command; Halleck's hesitation to choose between these alternatives transferred the initiative to Lee for his great victory at Second Bull Run. Halleck then appealed to McClellan "to assist me in this crisis with your ability and experience. I am utterly tired out."[33] Lincoln later remarked that Halleck "broke down" after Pope's defeat "and has ever since evaded all possible responsibility."[34]

Many found Halleck's personal manner obnoxious; some thought that he might have some serious problem. Attorney General Edward Bates heard gossip in 1863 that Halleck "was a confirmed *opium-eater.*" Bates noted that Halleck was "something bloated, and with watery eyes. . . . But whether from brandy or opium I cannot tell."[35] Halleck's personal physician during the Corinth campaign, John H. Brinton, recalled him as "somewhat inert; he was fond of good living, and of good wine—notably of hock. After dining, he was often sleepy. From my own knowledge of him, I think that at first I overestimated him."[36] During Early's campaign against Washington, Charles A. Dana believed that "Halleck's mind has been seriously impaired by the excessive use of liquor and . . . is regularly muddled after dinner each day."[37] George Templeton Strong had accompanied a delegation to Washington that called on Halleck. "God help us!" exclaimed one member after leaving, something the entire group understood. Halleck was "weak, shallow, commonplace, vulgar," concluded Strong. "His silly talk was conclusive as to his incapacity, unless he was a little flustered with wine."[38] Halleck died in 1872, just short of his fifty-seventh birthday, "of softening of the Brain supervening upon chronic disease of the *heart* and of the *liver*."[39]

Halleck's curiously passive behavior in the decade following Pope's defeat supports a theory that he may have had alcohol problems. When Grant assumed the position of general in chief, Halleck submissively accepted his diminished role as chief of staff and uttered no protest when sent from Washington to Richmond or into postwar exile in California. When other commanders vehemently condemned his wartime role, Halleck made no response. The general who so carefully avoided combat even more assiduously shunned the battle for reputation. Ironically, Halleck's refusal to employ extensive military authority increased his value to Lincoln, who consistently dominated war policy even when he needed to conceal that mastery.

6

Lincoln's Despair

The Crisis during the Summer of 1864

On August 23, 1864, President Abraham Lincoln asked each member of his cabinet to sign a paper folded and sealed so that none could read it. "This morning, as for some days past, it seems exceedingly probable that this Administration will not be reelected. Then it will be my duty to so co-operate with the President elect, as to save the Union between the election and the inauguration; as he will have secured his election on such ground that he can not possibly save it afterwards."[1] Such a curious document demands attention. Written more than one year after the twin triumphs of Union arms at Gettysburg and Vicksburg and eight months before the effective end of the rebellion, its despondent tone raises questions as to its rationality. Did Lincoln have adequate cause to believe that he would lose the election? If so, why did he expect the president-elect to cooperate in a last desperate effort to save the Union?

Little over a year earlier the fall of Vicksburg and the repulse of Robert E. Lee's army at Gettysburg had appeared to represent a turning point in the Civil War. By capturing Vicksburg, Ulysses S. Grant's Western army had effectively bisected the Confederacy by rendering U.S. control of the entire Mississippi River all but inevitable. By prevailing at Gettysburg, George G. Meade's eastern army had effectively barred Confederate armies from Northern soil and deflected the rebel thrust for foreign recognition. In November, midway between Vicksburg and Gettysburg, Grant smashed Braxton Bragg's Army of Tennessee at Chattanooga. Of three sizable Confederate operational forces in early 1863, Grant had captured one and decimated another, while Meade had repelled the third and most fearsome.

The campaign of 1864 opened in May amid high hopes that the North could complete the destruction of the rebellion during one more season of battle. Promoted to lieutenant general and given command of all Union armies, Grant determined upon a unified advance with all forces moving simultaneously to forestall any Confederate use of interior lines to transfer troops from one theater to another. When Lee had sent James Longstreet's corps from Virginia to reinforce Bragg, Confederates had won their last major victory of the Civil War at Chickamauga. Grant accompanied the Army of the Potomac in an overland campaign against Lee, while Sherman led a mighty host from Chattanooga south toward Atlanta. Of the two, Grant's forces encountered the most savage fighting and suffered disheartening casualties. Battered in the Wilderness, Grant's army pushed forward to heavy losses at Spotsylvania and a devastating repulse at Cold Harbor. Grant's next move, a brilliant crossing of the James River, left Lee baffled and the vital rail center of Petersburg undefended. Some of the most dramatic bungling of the war by Grant's subordinates gave Lee time to save Petersburg and to establish a strong defensive line that compelled Grant to commence tedious siege operations. An ingenious scheme to breach the defenses with explosives, devised by Pennsylvania volunteers with mining experience, once again resulted in a brilliant success, when the explosives opened a huge crater, followed by devastating failure, when Union troops were trapped helplessly in the very crater they had created. This disaster made Grant physically ill.

One month earlier, Lee had sent a corps under Jubal A. Early to the Shenandoah Valley to force Grant to detach troops from Petersburg. Early's success had brought him to the gates of Washington and had, indeed, panicked the administration. Grant sent enough troops north to imperil Early but not enough to free Lee. By August, war on the eastern front had become an unsatisfactory stalemate.

In the West, Sherman had moved from Chattanooga to the outskirts of Atlanta in a campaign of maneuver with Confederate commander Joseph E. Johnston. Then Jefferson Davis replaced a Fabian with a fool as John B. Hood commenced his disastrous attacks. In late August, Sherman lay before besieged Atlanta, his long supply lines vulnerable and the ultimate outcome of the campaign seriously in doubt.

As of August 23, then, both major Union armies lay becalmed in siege without having administered crushing blows that would engender confidence in ultimate success. The human cost of bringing those armies to Richmond and Atlanta seemed too high for many in the North. Various forms of war weariness stimulated pressure for a negotiated settlement to the struggle. To complicate all else, 1864 was a presidential election year.

After a midsummer crisis in 1862, brought about by lack of military success and growing Republican dissatisfaction with Lincoln's policy of sustaining slavery in the loyal border states, Lincoln had gained control by restoring to command General George B. McClellan, who stopped Lee's invasion of Maryland. Lincoln then issued a preliminary Emancipation Proclamation that usurped and extended the antislavery legislation of Congress. The day after the fall congressional elections, Lincoln removed McClellan from command, sending him into idleness and political temptation.

The midsummer crisis of 1864 offered some uncomfortable parallels. Once again the Army of the Potomac lay immobilized below Richmond, and again Lee capitalized on the deadlock to detach forces to threaten Northern stability and determination to prosecute the war. Republican radicals, preempted on emancipation, now challenged Lincoln on reconstruction. The Wade-Davis bill paralleled the Second Confiscation Act by advancing beyond what Lincoln advocated as sound reconstruction policy to develop a scheme that would prolong military government in the South while guaranteeing the civil rights of freedmen. Lincoln refused to sign the bill on the premise that the proposed Thirteenth Amendment, rather than legislation, offered the constitutional means to end slavery and that the bill would destroy loyal governments already established.

Senator Benjamin F. Wade of Ohio and Representative Henry Winter Davis of Maryland lashed back at the president, denouncing "executive usurpation" as "a studied outrage on the legislative authority." If he wanted Republican support for reelection, Lincoln would have to "leave political reorganization to Congress."[2] The Wade-Davis manifesto, coming in the midst of a presidential election from two members of the president's own party, signaled a determination on the part of at least some radicals to dump a catastrophic candidate.

In this respect, the Wade-Davis blast represented only one of a series of Republican efforts to find an alternative candidate to Lincoln. In February, Senator Samuel C. Pomeroy of Kansas had issued a circular denouncing Lincoln as incapable of winning the war and touting Secretary of the Treasury Salmon P. Chase as just the man to bring victory. In response, Francis P. Blair Jr., brother of Postmaster General Montgomery Blair and the most outspoken member of a powerful political clan closely allied to Lincoln, denounced Chase as incompetent to administer the Treasury Department, much less the presidency. With this, Frank Blair punctured the Chase balloon. Chase soon disavowed all connection with the Pomeroy circular, and, equally disingenuously, Lincoln disclaimed his role in Frank Blair's counterattack.

At the end of May, a coalition of abolitionists and German-Americans, chiefly from Missouri, nominated John C. Frémont for president. Calling themselves the Radical Democratic Party, these dissenters hoped to push Republicans to drop Lincoln in favor of a radical candidate, possibly Chase. The general ineptitude of the party organizers, however, produced something of an opposite effect. Rather than mobilizing Republicans against Lincoln, the Frémont movement isolated the president's opponents.

As a result, Lincoln won overwhelming support for renomination at the June convention of the Union Party, a change of Republican name and tactics designed to unite Republicans with War Democrats to forge a majority dedicated to victory at the ballot box and on the battlefield. To cement this Union, Andrew Johnson, the unrepentant Jacksonian Democrat serving as governor of Tennessee, received the vice-presidential nomination. At the time, Lincoln so carefully concealed his political role that he could feign surprised gratification at Johnson's nomination. In later years, other Republicans rushed to join Lincoln in disclaiming responsibility for Johnson's selection. In the summer of 1864, however, few paid much attention to the vice-presidential nominee, largely seen as an enhancement of the Union ticket, destined for the same obscurity that shrouded Hannibal Hamlin.

Although the Union ticket claimed the nominal support of every influential Republican leader, Frémont's Radical Democrats still lurked in the background, ready to siphon the votes of the dissatisfied from Lincoln. Their inauspicious beginnings served as no clear indication of November ballots. Dissatisfaction with the conduct of the war and plans for reconstruction made these dissenters appear more prescient. Stalemate on the battlefield combined with the fury of the Wade-Davis manifesto made the Radical Democrats seem more dangerous.

Republican strategists pointed to an ominous precedent set by votes for the Liberty Party in 1844, when supporters of abolitionism apparently derailed enough Whig support to deprive Henry Clay of the

White House. Despite the misleading party name, only Republicans would vote for Frémont.

Democrats had wisely postponed their presidential nominating convention from July 4 to August 29. So much depended upon the conduct of the war that time would enhance their perspective on electoral strategy. Less than one week before the Democrats assembled, Lincoln wrote his despondent prediction of defeat.

Just as Lincoln had been the inevitable nominee of the Union Party, McClellan was the inescapable Democratic choice. Stephen A. Douglas, the 1860 nominee and then leader of the War Democrats, had died in June 1861 at the age of forty-eight. Had he lived, he might well have united Democrats as a loyal opposition and presented a formidable challenge to Lincoln in 1864. Instead, Democrats had broken into War and Peace factions, so serious a split that they sought a candidate who could somehow unite a fractured party. To do so, they necessarily looked to the battlefield for a general who shared their antipathy to Republican policy.

After his victory at Chattanooga in November 1863, Grant began to receive Democratic overtures. A prewar Democrat whose political views had been muffled during the war, Grant seemed an ideal candidate to reunite the Democrats. Born in Ohio and a resident of Illinois when the war came, he had footholds in two states essential to electoral victory. Immense popularity combined with apparent political naiveté made him irresistible to party strategists. Grant so quickly and decisively rebuffed political overtures as to discourage Democrats. Ironically, his attitude encouraged Republicans to think of him as an alternative to Lincoln. Before promoting Grant to lieutenant general and giving him overall command in March 1864, Lincoln required assurances that Grant would abstain from political activity. Even then, Lincoln kept up his guard. At the Union convention, all the first ballot votes went to Lincoln except twenty-two from Missouri cast for Grant.

The death of Douglas and the unavailability of Grant clarified Democratic thought. McClellan became the inevitable candidate. While in command in 1862, McClellan seemed to play a greater political role than after his removal from command. Not until the summer of 1863 did he endorse a Democrat—in this case the candidate for governor of Pennsylvania, who lost anyway—and he did little to take a prominent political role or to clarify his policy. Yet who else could carry the Democratic standard? When Democrats convened, they had two choices: McClellan or defeat at the polls.

Lincoln had relieved McClellan from command after Antietam, when he had halted Lee's invasion of Maryland. His skillful organization of the Army of the Potomac and his great concern for the welfare of its troops had not been forgotten. When critics charged that he had never won a victory, defenders responded that he had never lost a battle.

Preparing for the spring campaign of 1864 with such questionable commanders as Benjamin F. Butler, Nathaniel P. Banks, and Franz Sigel, no wonder Grant thought of restoring McClellan. Nor was he alone in that thought, and the clamor grew when Early threatened the capital while Chief of Staff Henry W. Halleck dithered. Since McClellan had twice saved the capital, why not turn to him once more? As Lincoln saw it, recalling McClellan could have the twin benefit of employing his military skill and popularity with the troops while depriving Democrats of their prime presidential candidate.

Two fateful meetings occurred in July. Francis P. Blair Sr., father both of the postmaster general and of Chase's assailant, met McClellan at the Astor House in New York City to advance the proposition that if McClellan renounced all interest in the Democratic nomination, Lincoln would restore him to a suitable command. Blair had just heard some advice for Lincoln from James Gordon Bennett, editor of the *New York Herald*. "Tell him to restore McClellan to the army, and he will carry the election by default."[3] Blair hardly needed to hear this. His mission to New York involved this very proposition, and he scarcely would have advanced the idea without expectation of White House support. McClellan took the matter home. While Blair and Lincoln anxiously awaited a written response, McClellan began to draft an answer that he apparently decided not to send. From the draft, however, McClellan's rejection of the offer emerges unmistakably. For somebody like McClellan to accept command under such circumstances required that he sell "his self respect honor & truth—as well as his country—for a price." Furthermore, added McClellan, "I do not approve of the policy and measures of the present President." The original purpose of the war, as McClellan defined it, "the preservation of the Union, its Constitution & its laws," had been abandoned for "secondary" goals, by which he clearly meant emancipation.[4] Had Lincoln received such a letter, he would have known better than to take his next step, but the dilatory commander apparently put his draft away and never sent Blair the promised reply.

On July 31, Lincoln conferred with Grant at Fort Monroe, a meeting

never discussed later by either man. Assuming that Grant omitted painful topics from his *Memoirs*—as he did in other cases—suggests that
the Fort Monroe meeting produced little that Grant cared to recall.
Following the meeting, at which Lincoln must have discussed the sorry
situation of Grant pinned down at Petersburg and Early rampant near
Washington, Grant sent Sheridan to consolidate and lead the pursuit of
Early. Also on the cryptic agenda that Lincoln jotted down on the back
of a telegram was the single word "McClellan."[5] Believing that McClellan was still considering Blair's offer, Lincoln discussed its implementation. Just what command would McClellan have received? During
the presidential campaign, Montgomery Blair stated that Lincoln "had
concerted with Gen. Grant to bring [McClellan] again into the field as
his adjunct, if he turned his back on the proposals of the peace junto at
Chicago."[6] This statement, a parenthetical remark in a political oration,
prompted Blair's father to a full and circumstantial account of his meeting with McClellan, yet one that concealed information on the command dangled before McClellan. At the end of August, Secretary of the
Navy Gideon Welles blamed Secretary of State William H. Seward for
some of Lincoln's most grievous errors. Welles believed that Blair had
arranged for McClellan to replace Halleck but that somehow Seward
had aborted the scheme.[7] Yet Welles referred to Blair's plan of the previous year, which did call for McClellan to replace Halleck, and did not
illuminate what Blair had offered in the summer of 1864. By then, the
issue was moot; McClellan had received the Democratic nomination
for president.

As of August 23, Lincoln had received numerous warnings of impending electoral defeat. He had been, declared the *New York Herald*,
"an egregious failure," and "under no circumstances can he hope to be
the next President of the United States."[8] Old political pro Thurlow
Weed told Lincoln the same thing,[9] and on August 22, Henry J. Raymond, editor of the *New York Times* and chairman of the Republican
Party, wrote to Lincoln that the "tide is setting strongly against us." Despairing reports had come to Raymond from such trusted Republicans
as Elihu B. Washburne in Illinois, Simon Cameron in Pennsylvania,
and Oliver P. Morton in Indiana that they expected to lose their states.
Raymond recommended that Lincoln send a proposition at once to Jefferson Davis asking him to end the war by "restoration of the Union,"
leaving all other issues to negotiation.[10] On this occasion Lincoln considered abandoning emancipation as a war issue, but only briefly; after

drafting the letter Raymond specified, he put it aside and later said that such an offer would represent surrender.[11]

If Raymond's proposition seemed excessive both to Lincoln and to posterity, it presented an alternative to what other Republican leaders had suggested: Lincoln's withdrawal as a candidate. Horace Greeley led a group of New Yorkers favoring this course, while Massachusetts contributed Senator Charles Sumner, Governor John A. Andrew, and Major General Benjamin F. Butler. The plotters expected support from Chase, recently evicted from the cabinet, and their trump card was the anticipated withdrawal of Frémont to match that of Lincoln. Who would replace Lincoln remained vague amid general agreement that anybody would be better.

In this dreary summer of defeatism, Lincoln prepared his curious secret memorandum for cabinet signatures. Not only did he tell his trusted advisers that he did not want them to read what they were signing, but he even folded and pasted the document to ensure against peeking. What cabinet officers thought of this, we know little. The two diarists, Welles and Attorney General Bates, omitted all mention of it, suggesting that the occasion lacked some of the drama later attributed to the event.

General Sherman furnished the drama by the occupation of Atlanta on September 2. Somehow this single piece of glorious war news relieved Northern despondency and paved the way to Lincoln's reelection. Although details of the bargain remain obscure, Montgomery Blair left the cabinet, and Frémont withdrew from the presidential election. When the votes were counted, Lincoln's victory was so overwhelming that the midsummer despair seemed like some dreadful dream. On November 11, amid rejoicing, Lincoln asked John Hay to unseal the secret memorandum.

> The President said, "You will remember that this was written at a time (6 days before the Chicago nominating Convention) when as yet we had no adversary, and seemed to have no friends. I then solemnly resolved on the course of action indicated above. I resolved, in case of the election of General McClellan, being certain that he would be the candidate, that I would see him and talk matters over with him. I would say, "General, the election has demonstrated that you are stronger, have more influence with the American people than I. Now let

us together, you with your influence and I with all the executive power of the Government, try to save the country. You raise as many troops as you possibly can for this final trial, and I will devote all my energies to assisting and finishing the war." Seward said, "And the General would answer you 'Yes, Yes;' and the next day when you saw him again and pressed these views upon him, he would say, 'Yes, Yes;' & so on forever, and would have done nothing at all." "At least," added Lincoln, "I should have done my duty and have stood clear before my own conscience."[12]

If cabinet members blanched when they learned what they had signed in August, they left no record. Less than a month before the president asked for their signatures, Chase had submitted his resignation one time too many and Lincoln had snapped it up, comfortable after receiving renomination. Although Lincoln feared defeat at the polls, he had mastered his own household so that cabinet members knew their place.

Although the secret memorandum reflected Lincoln's depression concerning the progress of the war and prospects at the polls, this depression had its basis in a realistic appraisal of the situation. Two days earlier radicals had written a letter advocating the joint withdrawal of both Frémont and Lincoln. Republican chieftains had predicted Lincoln's defeat. Lincoln may have hoped for good news from the battlefield but had no reason to presume it. Votes cast that day might have fulfilled his anguished prediction. Once again Lincoln fell into depression—as he had on previous occasions—in the face of depressing reality. Creating a hidden memorandum surely has bizarre aspects without meaning that Lincoln had abandoned rationality.

Had McClellan won, Lincoln reserved one last card to play. His July 18 call for five hundred thousand men, the largest of the war, had met a discouraging response. Even the most loyal governors quibbled about quotas, while recruiting lagged. McClellan's return to command might have stimulated enlistments and encouraged reenlistments among troops of the Army of the Potomac who still admired the Little Napoleon.

Finally, Lincoln knew that McClellan, for all his faults as a commander, was a patriotic soldier. The political and psychological pressure upon him when assuming command in July 1861 might have defeated an abler general. Seward's laughter about McClellan's response might not have been entirely warranted. McClellan's conduct since his removal from command had been less than consistent. Although he had opposed both conscription and emancipation, he had not opposed war for the Union. His removal had been a severe personal calamity that did not necessarily translate into obstruction of the war effort. More important than what McClellan thought is the matter of what Lincoln thought of him. By gaining the assent of his cabinet to McClellan's recall, Lincoln indicated his belief that the general might serve.

Was there yet time to save the Union? Although the months between November and March were customarily those in which warfare ebbed, they need not have been. As it happened, the month of December 1864 brought the Union two of its greatest triumphs: Sherman's capture of Savannah (the celebrated "Christmas gift") and George H. Thomas's decisive victory at Nashville. Although war weariness and despondency tormented the North in midsummer, victory was even then within reach, a proposition demonstrated when Atlanta fell some ten days after the Lincoln memorandum.

Was the memorandum, then, a reflection of Lincoln's depression or of his strategy? Surely it held elements of both, yet pessimism about reelection was sustained by the opinion of trustworthy political professionals. Did Lincoln have a rational plan in calling upon president-elect McClellan to retake the field? Perhaps this is best considered a last desperate chance to save the Union. After inauguration, McClellan might be expected to dismantle emancipation policy and to negotiate with the Confederacy. Would Lincoln's party have sustained a partnership with McClellan? Not without difficulty, thought Lincoln, as he gained cabinet endorsement without disclosing his intention.

When would Lincoln have disclosed this memorandum? Despite the reference to McClellan as president-elect, the proposition would have had most impact if made during the election campaign, challenging McClellan to recruit troops rather than voters. Only then would the stinging reference to the Democratic platform prove significant. Aware that the party intended to nominate a War Democrat on a Peace Democrat platform, Lincoln could effectively demonstrate the disharmony of his opponents. Whether McClellan accepted or declined Lincoln's challenge, he would alienate some potential voters. As it was, McClellan suffered through several drafts of an equivocal letter accepting the nomination before he retreated into the familiar silence of any presidential candidate—except an incumbent. Had Lincoln disclosed his memorandum, he could have further embarrassed his opponent.

Does anyone really know Lincoln? Can anyone follow his thought to the point of predicting his policy? This wondrously unique statesman continually frustrates such efforts. Confronted with the secret memorandum of August 23, we can only speculate about Lincoln's course had he continued to believe in his imminent defeat or even lost the election, but with some dim conviction that his inventiveness might yet have saved the Union.

7

The Personal Sentiments
of Mr. Lincoln

During the congressional elections of 1866, the first nationwide elections held since the death of Lincoln, heated debate centered on whether President Andrew Johnson had followed the Reconstruction policy of his predecessor. Although a staunch Democrat, Johnson had been elected vice president on the Union ticket with Lincoln, still retained most of the Lincoln cabinet, and honestly believed that his conciliatory policy toward the states of the former Confederacy was Lincoln's own. During the congressional campaign, letters were published in the newspapers in support of Andrew Johnson from two of Lincoln's oldest friends, Dennis Hanks and Ward Hill Lamon. The majority of Republicans in Congress, however, had broken with Johnson, passing the Civil Rights and New Freedmen's Bureau acts over his veto and submitting the Fourteenth Amendment to the states for ratification. The congressional Republicans were equally armed with personal reminiscences and apt quotations to prove that Lincoln was on their side. By winning a two-thirds majority in both houses of Congress, Republicans destroyed Johnson's dream of a National Union Party and seemingly gained permanent possession of the mantle of Lincoln. Not until the time of Woodrow Wilson did Democrats attempt again to associate themselves with the ideals of Lincoln.[1]

No major political organization of the past century has failed to find some justification for its policy somewhere in the life and words of the great emancipator. Cuckoos in the Lincoln nest are supremely confident that they alone are the rightful inhabitants. The interests of a historical Lincoln as opposed to one with a partisan usefulness have been submerged so long that the truth may now be buried forever. Nor did Lincoln himself make the recovery of his views easier. As a shrewd politician he sought to avoid committing himself until necessary—even then he might assert that his "policy is to have no policy." When it caused no harm he let people think as they pleased about his policy. To the end of his life General Grant believed that Lincoln had given him a free hand with the army in 1864. This was what General McClellan had thought in 1861, the only difference being that it became necessary for McClellan to learn the truth. Concerning a haughty Massachusetts senator, Lincoln was once heard to chuckle: "Sumner thinks he runs me."[2]

High on any list of those who did not run Lincoln would be Ward Hill Lamon and Dennis Hanks. Lamon, a beefy, good-humored Virginian, had practiced law in Danville, Illinois, from 1852 to 1859 and had been a local partner of Lincoln. After he accompanied president-elect Lincoln to Washington, he undertook a private mission for the president to Charleston, South Carolina, returning to take up duties as marshal of the District of Columbia. A loud anti-abolitionist, Lamon clashed with many prominent Republicans who demanded his removal, but Lincoln relied on Lamon's companionship.

Shortly after Lincoln's death, Lamon entered a law partnership in Washington with Jeremiah S. Black, formerly secretary of state under James Buchanan. Lamon planned to write a biography of Lincoln, purchasing William H. Herndon's notes on Lincoln's early life and enlisting Chauncey F. Black, as staunch a Democrat as his father, to do the writing. The biography blended Herndon's backwoods gossip and Black's Democratic partisanship into a monstrous affront to Lincoln idolators.

After Lincoln's death, Lamon had sought unsuccessfully an appointment as governor of either Idaho or Colorado territories.[3] Five months after writing the letter to Johnson printed below, Lamon wrote to Johnson again, telling him that "many of your warmest friends, from delicacy, have refrained from troubling you with their views relative to removals from and appointments to office." Never troubled long by delicacy, however, Lamon offered to come to the White House with advice, assuring Johnson of his friendship by asserting that "Mr. Lincoln's administration as well as his good name suffered much by the men who are now on the corners of the streets denouncing you as a traitor."[4]

Lamon's pleas were unsuccessful, and the February letter apparently went to the press through Lamon rather than Johnson. But, as late as 1868, the persistent Lamon wrote to Johnson from the Executive

Mansion waiting room, where he had spent several idle days, to say that he hoped to be appointed minister to Mexico. "You might find an *abler* man for the place," Lamon disarmingly admitted, "but a better friend never." That Johnson would be willing to give him the mission to Mexico after refusing him a few minutes in his office would have occurred only to Lamon. With equal innocence Lamon believed that because Lincoln had been his friend he had shared his political views. His first letter to Johnson, then, although colored by his Democratic politics and his hopes for office, was essentially sincere.

Washington, D.C.
Feb. 26th 1866

To his Excellency, Andrew Johnson
Mr. President

Among the numerous allegations made against you by the ultra abolitionists, I hear none repeated so often as this: That you have deserted the principles upon which you were elected and turned aside from the path in which your lamented predecessor would have walked if he had lived. It seems to be believed by some that Mr. Lincoln could have been used by the radicals for all their purposes including the destruction of the Government, the overthrow of the Constitution and the indefinite postponement of Union or harmony among the States.

I need not say to you or to any well informed man that the masses of that powerful party which supported Mr. Lincoln & you in the canvass of 1864 were sincerely attached to the Union and devoted believers in the Constitution.

They every where asserted that the object of the war was to reestablish the Union with the least possible delay and one of the resolutions of the Baltimore Convention pledged you both to restore the paramount authority of the Constitution in all the States. It is true that the party included some malignants who hated the Union and tried to destroy it before the war began and their pretended love of the Union during the war was more than suspected to be insincere and hypocritical. But they kept prudently silent. Mr. Thaddeus Stephens [*sic*] was to the best of my knowledge the only leading man in the party shameless and impudent enough to avow his hostility to the Union. He was not the exponent of our views and he represented not even a fractional part of the honest millions who cast their votes, spent their money and shed their blood to bring back the Government of their fathers.

All this you know. I write now to tell you what I know concerning the personal sentiments of Mr. Lincoln himself. I was his partner in the practice of the law for a number of years. I came here with him as his special friend, and was Marshal of this District during his whole Administration. Down to the day of his death I was in the most confidential and intimate relations with him. I knew him as well as one man can be known to another; I had many and free conversations with him on this very subject of restoration. I was made entirely certain by his own repeated declarations to me that he would exert all his authority, power and influence to bring about an immediate and perfect reconciliation between the two sections of the Country. As far as depended upon him he would have had the Southern States represented in both houses of Congress within the shortest possible time.

All the energies of his nature were given to a "Vigorous prosecution of the war" while the rebellion lasted, but he was equally determined upon a "Vigorous prosecution of peace" as soon as armed hostility should be ended.

He knew the base designs of the radicals to keep up the strife for their own advantage and he was determined to thwart them as he himself told me very often. If any corrob[o]ration of this statement is needed it may be found in the fact that the Ultra abolitionists had actually begun the outcry against him before his death, and the moderate men every where North & South sincerely mourned his fall as a calamity which deprived them of their best friend. If that inscrutable Providence whose ways are past finding out had permitted his life to continue until this time, there can be no doubt that the Northern Disunionists would now be as loud in their denunciation of his policy as they are of yours—Mr. Stephen's demand for the head of "that man at the other end of the avenue," would not have been a whit less ferocious. Of course he could not and did not anticipate the precise shape of the measures which the radicals might adopt to prevent reconstruction.—

The "Freedmen's Bureau Bill" which recently met its death at your hands was not born in his life time. But I pronounce it a foul slander upon his memory to assert that he would have signed a bill so palpably in conflict with the Constitution and so plainly intended to promote the one bad purpose of perpetual disunion.

I did love Mr Lincoln with a sincere and faithful affection; and my reverence for memory is intensified by the horrible circumstances in which his high career was closed—Now that death has disarmed him of the power to defend himself, his true friends should stand forth to vindicate his good name.

If there be any insult upon his reputation which they should resent more indignantly than another it is the assertion that he would have been a tool and an instrument in the hands of such men as those who now lead the heartless and unprincipled contest against you.

I have the honor to be your friend & obedient Servant

Ward H. Lamon[5]

Ten years older than his cousin Abe, Dennis Hanks remembered the day when he heard, "Nancy's got a boy baby." Hanks had indeed been close to Lincoln for the first twenty-one years of his life and claimed: "I taught Abe his first lesson in spelling—reading & writing."[6] Thus Hanks's view of Lincoln's political ideals delighted Democrats. "Coming from one who was the preceptor of the lamented dead—from his relative—from one who was recognized as his personal, particular friend, this testimony is invaluable. We commend every word of it to the calm, sober thoughtful attention of intelligent republicans."[7] In the letter which follows. the effrontery seems to be Dennis's own, though the style and composition must be the work of an unknown Democrat.

DECATUR, ILL, October 2, 1866.

EDITOR STATE REGISTER:—For the past five years there has been no warmer supporter of the administration of Abraham Lincoln than myself. My support of him was to some extent controlled by my knowledge of him. I have known him from his infancy, and was intimately associated with him during his whole career, up to the day of his death. In his school boy days, I was his teacher; and, when President, he recognized me as his friend, and as his relation. Knowing him thus intimately, it is but natural that I should know something of his intentions in regard to the settlement of the grave questions that were submitted to his control. His whole Presidential career was a continual struggle against the rapacity, the cruelty, and the recklessness of the Radical faction of the great Union party—that faction led by [Benjamin F.] Wade, [Benjamin F.] Butler, [Wendell] Phillips, [Horace] Greeley, Fred Douglass, and their confederates;

and, whenever any movement was inaugurated that promised a speedy overthrow of the rebellion, the Radical class imposed upon him conditions before they would pledge their support, or the support of their representatives in Congress, that compelled him either to sacrifice the country or to yield to their demands. I have private evidence that he was in this way compelled to inaugurate policies that were repugnant to the dictates both of his judgment and his heart. Unfortunately for the country, at the hour when he did not require their aid to accomplish the restoration of peace, the hand of an assassin removed him, and prevented him from accomplishing that good he intended.

Mr. Lincoln was well beloved by the people. Had he lived, the Southern States would by this time have been represented in Congress. The Radical curs would have barked at his heels, but the people would have had confidence in his purity and judgment.

President Johnson's policy, as now enunciated by him, would, ere this, have been carried into practical effect by Mr. Lincoln, not because Mr. Lincoln was a purer or greater man than President Johnson, but because the people had, through the gloomy years of the dreadful struggle through which we had been passing, reposed confidence in his judgment and his honesty, and the factious partisan lash could not have destroyed his power with the people. I hope that every honest supporter of President Lincoln—every man who fought in the field or who battled at home in behalf of the glorious Union of ours—will not only cast their ballots, but will as well exert all their influence against the miserable combination of fanatics, charlatans and plunderers, who, under the name of Union Radical party, are now attempting to rob Mr. Lincoln of his good name, and our country of liberty.

Yours truly,
DENNIS F. HANKS[8]

Dennis Hanks's position as a Lincoln oracle was far below that of Lamon. Hanks had seen little of Lincoln for thirty-four years when he went to Washington in 1864 to beg lenient treatment for his neighbors in Charleston, Illinois, involved in antiwar rioting. Although Lincoln received him cordially, Secretary of War Stanton declared that "every one of them should be hung." Stanton, a "frisk, little Yankee with a short coat-tail," so angered Hanks that he later asked his cousin "why he didn't kick him out. I told him he was too fresh altogether." Lincoln sent Dennis home with a new silver watch, though deciding to keep his secretary of war.[9]

It was after the assassination that Dennis set himself up as a Lincoln expert, wearing a stovepipe hat in hopes that strangers would note a family resemblance. He was well known to Lincoln biographers for his full (if contradictory) accounts of Abe's early life, and to Herndon he declared, "Now William be Shore and have My Name very Conspikus."[10] After his one foray in divination he tended to his reminiscences to old times in Kentucky and Indiana. But he was rewarded for his apostasy when Nicolay and Hay mentioned his name only once in their compendious ten-volume biography of Lincoln. The two Republicans grudgingly conceded Dennis's presence in the 1830 Lincoln trek from Indiana to Illinois in a paragraph which began with a pointed reference to John Hanks as "the steadiest and most trustworthy of his family . . . though an illiterate and rather dull man."[11]

Part 2

Ulysses S. Grant

8

Ulysses S. Grant
One Hundred Years Later

The death of Ulysses S. Grant one hundred years ago plunged an entire nation into mourning. In every American city ceremonies took place with massive displays of civic grief. The Chicago City Council declared that "the death of Gen. Grant is a calamity affecting the entire Nation," a sentiment echoed in Columbia, South Carolina, where a newspaper editorial stated that Grant's death "will be honestly felt as a national affliction all over the wide Union, without reference to section or party."[1] The *Vicksburg Post* predicted: "When prejudices pass away and time brings calmness, justice and reason to pass upon General Grant's life, character and achievements, he will hold a very high place in the esteem of the citizens of this country, . . . and all of them will have great admiration for his character, a just pride in his patriotic services, and a profound respect for his memory."[2] The *Advertiser* of Montgomery, Alabama, proclaimed that "no man since Washington has better illustrated the genius of American institutions or the temper of Americans as a people."[3]

Two detachments of veterans volunteered to guard the isolated cottage where Grant had died, believing their presence necessary to protect the privacy of the family and to deter souvenir hunters. Perhaps they remembered that twenty years earlier virtually every item that furnished Wilmer McLean's parlor at Appomattox Court House had been carried away. Across the country citizens draped their homes in mourning, purchased memorial trinkets, and sought ways to honor Grant.

On August 8, the Grant funeral in New York City brought together ranking surviving Confederate generals and their Union counterparts riding together in carriages in a ceremony of reconciliation. General Winfield Scott Hancock led the funeral procession; once one of Grant's commanders, he had been the Democratic nominee for president in 1880, and Grant had campaigned against him. Southerners and Democrats now vied with Northerners and Republicans to honor Grant. The estimated one and one-half million spectators who lined the streets to watch five hours of procession by some forty thousand marchers long remembered the impressive pageantry.[4]

To understand such public mourning, older Americans might recall the emotional impact of Franklin D. Roosevelt's death, and all should recall John F. Kennedy's assassination. Few people, I suspect, can even remember exactly when it was that Dwight D. Eisenhower died, and Douglas MacArthur did, indeed, "fade away." A president who dies in office or a general who is killed in battle touches chords that inspire public grief. Grant, however, had survived the Civil War, served two terms as president, and completed his *Memoirs* before dying. Looking back on that national mourning, after one hundred years during which Grant's reputation has not always been high, we must ask how he had so captured the hearts of the American people.

Even in appearance he represented the average citizen. For much of his life, he passed unnoticed in a crowd; he looked like a man who might deliver wood in St. Louis or might clerk in Galena. Grant's indifference to dress became most evident in military service, where he avoided regalia and weapons even when facing photographers. In this he followed General Zachary Taylor, his commander in the Mexican War, who "never made any great show or parade, either of uniform or retinue."[5] Once Taylor had donned full uniform to receive a naval flag officer, Grant recalled, but the officer, knowing Taylor's tastes, wore civilian clothes, and the meeting embarrassed both.[6] Grant, taking the lesson to heart, never overdressed for any military occasion. In 1863, when Secretary of War Edwin M. Stanton came to meet him, Stanton stepped directly up to the medical director, whom he mistook for Grant, largely because the medical director was wearing a military hat. Not only did Grant not look like a general, he hardly looked like a person of any importance. Arriving in Washington to take command of all the armies of the United States, he was accompanied only by his son and went unrecognized by the desk clerk at Willard's Hotel, who assigned him an undesirable top-floor room before reading the register. Both at Willard's and later at a White House reception, people who saw him whispered reassurances to each other that this unprepossessing man was really General Grant. Cartoonists later called upon to portray Grant in either heroic or villainous light always had trouble with his ordinary features.

Similarly, biographers had trouble with Grant's ordinary boyhood. Born in Ohio, the son of Jesse Grant, who had known poverty as a boy but was beginning to prosper when his son was born, Ulysses grew up in the middle class of the day. Little about his early life, education, or character appears remarkable. Tales of his boyhood that prefigure his later career are the most unreliable.

At age seventeen when he learned that his father had arranged an appointment to West Point, Ulysses said, "I won't go."[7] Traveling to West Point at his father's insistence, Grant hoped that a steamboat or railroad accident might cause some temporary injury to prevent his enrollment. The reluctant cadet enjoyed reading novels, rarely read an assignment twice, and graduated in the middle of his class, with a recognized aptitude for mathematics and horsemanship.

Reminiscing after leaving the White House, Grant clearly established himself as an unmilitary soldier.

> I did not want to go to West Point. . . . My father had to use his authority to make me go. I hear army men say their happiest days were at West Point. . . . The most trying days in my life were those I spent there, and I never recall them with pleasure. . . . I never liked service in the army—not as a young officer. . . . I do not think there was ever a more wicked war than that waged by the United States on Mexico. I thought so at the time, when I was a youngster, only I had not moral courage enough to resign. . . . When I resigned from the army and went to a farm I was happy. When the rebellion came I returned to the service because it was a duty. . . . I never went into a battle willingly or with enthusiasm. It was only after Donelson that I began to see how important was the work that Providence devolved upon me. . . . When the bill creating the grade of Lieutenant-General was proposed I did not want it. . . . I never held a council of war in my life. . . . I never want to command another army. . . . The one thing I never wanted to see again was a military parade.[8]

Grant's easily perceived distaste for pageantry, proclamations, and martial display contributed to his success as a commander and also to his reputation among the American people, ever suspicious of military formality.

The U.S. Army entered the Civil War torn between the merits of military professionalism and the need to call upon citizen volunteers. President Abraham Lincoln responded by appointing to command both leading professional soldiers and prominent political leaders of both parties, but the mixture did not work. Perhaps again inspired by Zachary Taylor, Grant combined the essential elements of military professionalism with an informality of manner and a businesslike approach to war that served effectively to make him a superb commander of volunteers. For example, while pondering the problems of the Vicksburg campaign, Grant took time to write to an anxious mother of two privates: "I cannot see your sons immediately . . . but I will take the very first opportunity of doing so and do all in my power to cheer them up."[9] Grant's troops, somehow inspired by his confidence and determination, fought for him with great courage and persistence. The boy who said "I won't go" to West Point became the general who captured three Confederate armies. Under his command, raw volunteers became superb soldiers.

No student of historic battles, Grant thoughtfully pondered the lessons of the Mexican War but approached the Civil War in terms of improved weapons, new conditions, and the vast scale of the conflict. As Grant put it, "The laws of successful war in one generation would insure defeat in another."[10] His strategic genius found fullest expression in the May 1863 campaign against Vicksburg, ending with the encirclement of the Confederate citadel. Major General Henry W. Halleck declared, "In boldness of plan, rapidity of execution, and brilliancy of results, these operations will compare most favorably with those of Napoleon about Ulm."[11] Grant, who "always had an aversion to Napoleon," never responded to the compliment.[12] Lincoln wrote a remarkable letter to Grant, praising him for "the almost inestimable service you have done the country" and admitting his doubts about Grant's strategy during the Vicksburg campaign. Lincoln concluded: "I now wish to make the personal acknowledgment that you were right, and I was wrong."[13] Grant did not answer that letter until Lincoln asked about its receipt, then did so by writing that "your letter of the 13th of July was also duly received."[14] Described by Confederate vice president Alexander H. Stephens as "not aware of his own power," Grant found more difficulty in accepting praise than in capturing Vicksburg.[15] Innate modesty made written responses to compliments painful and public speaking impossible.

Both North and South had entered the Civil War following command patterns established in the regular army, one by inheritance, the other by adoption. Victory required innovation. When Grant went to Washington to accept his commission as lieutenant general and to assume the duties of general in chief, common military expectation held that he would direct operations from Washington and place a successful western general, probably William T. Sherman, in command of the Army of the Potomac. Grant surprised the army by leaving his predecessor, Halleck, an excellent desk general, behind a desk in Washington as chief of staff, an innovative step toward a modern command system, and establishing his own headquarters with the Army of the Potomac without displacing its able commander, Major General George G. Meade. Grant based his decision to leave Washington in part on an understanding that the telegraph, a modern tool of warfare, enabled him to direct the war from wherever the campaign carried him; indeed that his absence from Washington would free him from details of administration and provide a closer view of actual military operations.

Supervision rather than direct command of the Army of the Potomac provided further freedom from detail and time to concentrate on broad strategy. Grant's presence with the army raised fears of wholesale command changes, which he soon allayed with remarkable tact. Retention of Meade and current corps commanders heightened morale throughout the army, and Meade eventually appraised Grant as "the best man the war has yet produced."[16] Acceptance of Grant's leadership spread to the troops when he turned south after the bloody encounter in the Wilderness; as Grant rode by, a spontaneous nighttime demonstration erupted among war-weary troops who suddenly realized that they had begun the final campaign of the conflict under a commander who refused to turn back.

Only superficially could Grant's victories be credited to luck and larger armies. Qualities exhibited in his correspondence—clarity, decisiveness, equanimity, and versatility—were demonstrated as well in his campaigns. Paramount to his success was the resiliency with which he recovered from the bloody surprise of the first day at Shiloh and the misbegotten assaults on Vicksburg on May 22, 1863, and on Cold Harbor on June 3, 1864. The failure of the Army of the James to capture Petersburg and the ghastly debacle at the Crater would have disheartened another commander, but Grant could be defeated, never beaten. When successful, he proved relentless in pursuit, but pressed toward victory rather than glory. The fall of Petersburg and the capture of Richmond in April 1865 he treated as mere incidents in a lightning campaign designed to force Lee to surrender. Only at Appomattox could he display the magnanimity appropriate to a true cessation of hostilities.

Grant at Appomattox reached the apex of his career. With power to negotiate severely constricted by Lincoln, Grant found latitude for generosity that converted the simple surrender meeting into a ceremony of peace. His letter to Lee, written without forethought in a crowded parlor, exhibited the same clarity and directness of his field orders; the provision that officers could retain their horses and sidearms forestalled any ceremonial tender by Lee of his sword. Grant later decided to permit privates to retain their horses for farmwork, attended to feeding the captured Confederates, and stopped the loud celebration by his own army. He created a tableau of gracious reconciliation as important as any victory in the field.

The officer who had taken command of a regiment at Camp Yates in Springfield, Illinois, in 1861 was not the Grant of Appomattox. Fifteen years in the old army had taught him the mechanics of army bureaucracy and the procedure of supply and discipline. He had never commanded more than a handful of men in battle before 1861, and then only with the limited responsibility of a young lieutenant. Not quite thirty-nine years old when the Civil War began, a civilian for seven years, he was better prepared to learn, in a sense, than fifty-four-year-old Colonel Robert E. Lee, one of the most respected officers in the army. Grant's first battle, fought at Belmont in November 1861, showed the faults of a neophyte commander: lack of clarity about objectives, failure to coordinate army and navy, and loss of control over his troops. He made many other mistakes through the remainder of the war, but not the same ones. A relatively minor command early in the war gave Grant a chance to learn, and perhaps he recognized that when commenting many years later that if George B. McClellan "had fought his way along and up," he might "have won as high a distinction as any of us."[17]

Both McClellan and Grant had understood from the onset of war that the conflict had political dimensions. Both were military professionals and prewar Democrats. One allowed himself to become entangled in the political issues of the day, especially those involving slavery; the other developed a sure touch in civil-military relations. Soon after Lincoln issued the preliminary Emancipation Proclamation, he removed McClellan from command. In 1864, Grant's effort to reassign

McClellan failed because McClellan was then headed toward the Democratic nomination for president. Grant had achieved top command only after Lincoln had received assurances that Grant would not seek a presidential nomination.

Grant quickly adjusted to political reality as war became revolution. The organization of black troops in the spring of 1863 had provoked many officers to resign, others to try to use the new soldiers for menial labor only. In July 1864, planning to create a corps composed almost entirely of black troops, Grant offered command to Major General Andrew A. Humphreys, who responded that he would "prefer not to command such troops."[18] Frederick Douglass, who observed that "neither West Point nor the Democratic party have been good schools in which to learn justice and fair play to the Negro," credited Grant, a prewar slaveholder, with "superiority to popular prejudice" in his quiet persistence in organizing the new troops.[19] Firmly accepting policy as duty, Grant used black troops as an increasingly decisive component of his armies.

Grant avoided politics during the war because of both his concept of military propriety and his genuine dislike for politics. In Washington after the war, he settled comfortably into the role of commanding a diminished army, enjoyed a stable family life, and anticipated lifetime employment. President Andrew Johnson, eager to associate Grant's personal popularity with a conciliatory Reconstruction policy, put such improper pressure on him that Grant eventually came to believe that his duty lay in accepting the Republican presidential nomination. "I have been forced into it in spite of myself," he wrote to Sherman, a man to whom Grant thought he owed an explanation.[20] "I did not want the presidency," Grant recalled, "and have never quite forgiven myself for resigning the command of the army to accept it."[21] As president, he served two terms without ever becoming a politician and did not deliver his first campaign speech until 1880, three years after leaving the White House.

If Grant believed that success as an unmilitary general presaged success as an unpolitical president, he was doomed to disappointment. He had become a general after fifteen years in the army; he entered the White House without adequately understanding the mechanics of its power, relying upon his own reforming instincts and the support of the American people. The American people, however, showed more enthusiasm for electing than for sustaining a determined nonpolitician.

Grant's reform efforts met frustration in his first term when Southern white intransigence blocked full civil rights for blacks, congressional opposition crippled civil service reform, and religious bickering hindered implementation of a "peace policy" in Indian affairs. Still, Grant deserved credit for trying.

If Grant had served only one term as president, he might now be remembered for the successes of his administration: his support of Reconstruction laws upholding civil rights, his assistance in securing passage of the Fifteenth Amendment guaranteeing the right to vote, his generosity in granting amnesty to former Confederates, his reform initiatives in civil service and Indian affairs, and his peaceful settlement of grievances with England through the Treaty of Washington. Only his persistence in attempting to annex Santo Domingo and his brother-in-law's involvement in the Black Friday scheme to corner the gold market clouded an otherwise creditable record.

When impatient reformers, denouncing what they labeled "Grantism" and calling themselves Liberal Republicans, joined with Democrats in 1872 to oppose Grant's election to a second term, they made the president the central target of their campaign, but drew no response from the White House. Embarrassed by acclaim, passive in response to criticism, Grant seemingly valued his privacy more highly than his reputation. In that, he maintained a lifelong practice. As a young officer he had been distressed when a letter he wrote to his parents from the Mexican War appeared in a newspaper. When falsely charged in 1852 with neglect of duty when his regiment crossed the Isthmus of Panama, he wrote nothing in his own defense. In response to severe criticism after the battle of Shiloh in 1862, he wrote home that "I have been so shockingly abused that I sometimes think it almost time to defend myself."[22] For Grant, that time never came. Grant had assured a friend that the "S" in his name stood for "*nothing*," but remained silent when others gave him the middle name of Simpson.[23] A man who declined to correct error about his name was unlikely to answer political accusations.

Grant's apparent indifference to what was said about him masked reality. When he had been forced to accompany President Andrew Johnson on a tour of the Northern states in 1866—ostensibly to dedicate the tomb of Stephen A. Douglas but actually to rally public support for presidential programs—Grant observed firsthand the disastrous effects of Johnson's vituperative attacks on his opponents followed by his intemperate responses to hecklers in the crowd. Grant avoided Johnson's thin-skinned reaction to criticism, but under Grant's thicker skin resentment festered. Republican leaders learned how to exploit that resentment to influence policy and, by the close of the second Grant administration, had reshaped the Republican Party. Grateful for his defense by others when cruelly castigated, Grant defended private secretary Orville E. Babcock and Secretary of War William W. Belknap during their exposure as wrongdoers who had disgraced the Grant administration. Such stubborn loyalty raised suspicions, however unjust, of Grant's acquiescence, or even complicity, in scandalous misconduct of government.

The depression of 1873 forced Grant to confront new problems with which he had less experience and less certainty about solutions. Congressman James A. Garfield wrote to a friend in late 1874: "The President's Message is in the main a very good document. We had somewhat of a struggle to keep him from drifting into that foolish notion that it was necessary to make large appropriations on public works to give employment to laborers. But the Secretary of the Treasury [Benjamin H. Bristow] and I united our forces in dissuading him from the scheme, insisting that the true remedy for the finances at present was economy and retrenchment, until business restored itself."[24] Often Grant's instincts proved superior to the conventional wisdom of the day. Within his own party, Grant drew criticism for his ignorance of economics, as well as his persistence in maintaining Reconstruction legislation, charges especially ironic a century later. In his final message to Congress, Grant admitted to "errors of judgment, not of intent," attributing them to lack of "previous political training."[25] That candid statement, though sometimes misread as an apology because other presidents so rarely admit any mistakes, has stood for more than a century as an accurate and fair self-appraisal.

During a post-presidential trip around the world, a leisurely journey consuming more than two years, the Grants received state welcomes and generous hospitality from rulers everywhere. Experiencing some of the restlessness of other former presidents uncertain as to their proper role, Grant continued to travel after returning to the United States. He had decisively rebuffed overtures for a third-term nomination in 1876, but appeared more receptive as Stalwarts launched a similar but unsuccessful movement in 1880. After the 1880 Republican convention, he began to dabble in business and eventually moved to New York City to become a silent partner in Grant and Ward, in which the Grant was his son, Ulysses S. Grant Jr., and the Ward (Ferdinand) was belatedly exposed as a clever swindler. The firm's collapse in 1884 brought financial ruin to the Grant family and some public disapproval of the former president for allowing himself to be so easily tricked.

Driven by the necessity of earning money to support his family, Grant began to write magazine articles about his battles and found the work so satisfying that he decided to prepare his *Memoirs*. Almost at the same time, he began to feel the pain in his throat that was soon diagnosed as inoperable cancer. He wrote his *Memoirs* amid excruciating pain, in a desperate race with death, to provide for his wife and children.

This last battle roused again the Grant of Shiloh and the Wilderness. His declining days, lavishly reported in the press, dramatized close family bonds as well as indomitable will. Details of his wasting illness drew the sympathies of families with similar experiences. Two periods of adversity in his adult life, one at St. Louis and Galena, the other as he neared death, also repeated familiar American patterns.

The unmilitary general and unpolitical president survived long enough to complete a manuscript immediately hailed as an American literary classic. He opened with the motto "Man proposes and God disposes," surely the best summary of his astonishing career.[26] During his lifetime, then, his countrymen knew just enough about Grant to form bonds of close identification. His posthumously published *Memoirs* revealed more about him; their candor, scrupulous fairness, and grace of expression completed the process of creating an American hero.

In his career and character, Grant had combined the ordinary and extraordinary to become a quintessential and archetypical American. He exhibited, as Walt Whitman concluded, "the capacities of that American individuality common to us all."[27] His remarkable self-confidence, stubborn determination, and basic integrity reflected the strengths of the American people. As president, his flaws became more evident as he sometimes misplaced his trust or misdirected his stubbornness. As an aspiring financier, he had been both naive and inattentive. Yet even his faults stemmed from a simplicity and innocence that made him all the more typically American.

He accepted success with modesty, failure with equanimity, and an amazing career without self-consciousness. He had brilliantly fulfilled the Military Academy motto—"Duty, Honor, Country"—without entirely understanding those qualities he possessed that gave him the power. Sherman, who had known him ever since West Point, concluded that he was a mystery to himself as well as to others.[28] Henry Adams observed, "One seemed to know him so well, and really knew so little."[29] Adams was correct: the Grant honored by millions of his countrymen in 1885 was a man dimly understood.

In the century since Grant's death, has the mystery deepened or dissipated? Those who regard him as a symbol of the age and render judgment on him for reasons extraneous to the man and his career do not even perceive the mystery, much less solve it. Some have attempted to understand Grant by diminishing him to manageable proportions, since mediocrity is more readily explained than greatness.

In 1935, the year marking the fiftieth anniversary of Grant's death, William B. Hesseltine, professor of history at the University of Wisconsin, published *Ulysses S. Grant: Politician,* a study that conveniently marks the low point of Grant's reputation. Written with verve and contempt, the book opens with a chapter titled "Forty Years of Failure," an account of "a plastic person" incapable of creating his own success, instead destined to be shaped by the events of the day.[30] Hesseltine sardonically portrayed Grant as "peculiarly ignorant of the Constitution and inept in handling men," adding "dogs did not like him."[31]

Even when Hesseltine wrote, military historians analyzed a far different Grant than did political historians, and the two portraits hardly seemed to show the same person. Reviewing a new edition of the *Personal Memoirs* in 1953, Edmund Wilson wrote of Grant as author of "nothing less than one of the great American books," thereby opening yet another area of interpretation.[32]

A century of scholarship has created long bookshelves of Grant source materials and interpretations without inspiring confidence that the man himself has been understood. Continuing scholarly controversies as well as dim public perceptions, however discouraging to those demanding certainties, pay tribute to the continuing fascination of the man. Like Lincoln, he remains on the historical horizon, always in view but never clearly visible.

9

The Paradox of
Ulysses S. Grant

Among American leaders of a century ago, Ulysses S. Grant is perhaps the most easily remembered. Time has eroded much of the complexity of his character and career, leaving behind a popular image of a slightly bewildered man in rumpled clothes with a cigar in his mouth, smelling of liquor and horses, oblivious both to needless death in war and to corruption in peace. For the past quarter century, however, historians and biographers taking a fresh look at Grant have usually discovered a man vastly more interesting, who deserves better from his countrymen. None of this would surprise Americans who had watched Grant win his last victory.

Early in 1885 newspapers spread word that Grant was writing his personal memoirs in a desperate race for time against an incurable cancer. Only one year earlier the former general and president had been the center of the news when the Wall Street firm of Grant and Ward—in which he was a silent partner and his son a full partner—collapsed under the massive swindling of Ferdinand Ward. Although Grant himself was clearly the chief victim of the swindle, not all newspapers could refrain from criticism of the ex-president's involvement with Wall Street finance or his naïveté and ignorance in allowing the swindle.

Newspaper comment on Grant's last days, however, was uniformly favorable. Most Americans were aware of the general's strong love for his family, which drove him on amid excruciating pain to complete a manuscript which could repair the family's shattered finances. Reporters camped outside the Grant New York City brownstone awaiting medical bulletins which chronicled the contest between death and Grant's indomitable will. The doctors expected Grant to die in April. They were wrong: the memoirs were still incomplete. Grant lived on into the summer and died on July 23, three days after completing his work.

Grant's funeral brought Americans North and South together in a mass outpouring of public grief. In New York City, Grant's lieutenants, William Tecumseh Sherman and Philip Henry Sheridan, were joined in the funeral by former Confederate generals Joseph E. Johnston and Simon Bolivar Buckner. The *Memoirs* sold wondrously, bringing some $450,000 to the Grant family, with sets standing in the parlor of many an unbookish family as a symbol of respect and patriotism.

Mark Twain, hardly unprejudiced since he was the publisher of the book as well as a friend of the author, compared the *Memoirs* to Caesar's *Commentaries* and defended them against all critics.

> People may hunt out what microscopic motes they please, but, after all, the fact remains and can not be dislodged that General Grant's book is a great, (and in its peculiar department) unique and unapproachable literary masterpiece. . . . There is that about the sun which makes us forget his spots: and when we think of General Grant our pulses quicken and his grammar vanishes: we only remember that this is the simple soldier who, all untaught of the silken phrase-makers, linked words together with an art surpassing the art of the schools, and put into them a something which will still bring to American ears, as long as America shall last, the roll of his vanished drums and the tread of his marching hosts.

Despite the popularity of the *Memoirs,* biographies of Grant continued to appear: by the end of the nineteenth century the 91 biographies of Grant almost matched the 110 biographies of Lincoln. The inspiring Grant story seemed to deserve constant retelling.

Walt Whitman was typical of many Americans in appraising Grant as "the typical Western Man: the plainest, the most efficient: was the least imposed upon by appearances, was most impressive in the severe simplicity of his flannel shirt and his utter disregard for formal military etiquette." Grant, said Whitman, illustrated "the capacities of that American individuality common to us all." And yet, "in all Homer and Shakespeare there is no fortune or personality really more picturesque or rapidly changing, more full of heroism, pathos, contrast."

The decline of Grant's reputation after 1900 suggested that Lincoln belonged to the ages, but Grant belonged to the nineteenth century. In the twentieth century, the Twain and Whitman view of Grant was destined to be less influential than that of Henry Adams, one of the unhappiest men in Washington during the Grant presidency. His great-grandfather and grandfather had been presidents of the United States; his father, who had been Lincoln's minister to England, was prominently mentioned for the Liberal Republican nomination in 1872; but Henry Adams never came close to political eminence. He wondered why, concluding that there must be something wrong with the country. In his book *The Education of Henry Adams,* he made Grant a symbol for post–Civil War America. "The progress of evolution from President Washington to President Grant," he concluded, "was alone evidence enough to upset Darwin." Adams found in Grant pure energy without evidence of intellect. After attempting to follow his reasoning without success, Adams reported, his staff officers had given up. "They were not sure that he did think."

An elaborated version of the Grant of Henry Adams can be found in *Meet General Grant,* a 1928 biography by William E. Woodward, whose novel entitled *Bunk* had added a word to the English language. As Woodward traced Grant's rise from "the bottom of his pit, a forlorn figure" in Galena, to "a complacent bourgeois" in New York, he lost no opportunity to express contempt for the period and to emphasize the sordid aspects of the Grant administration. As late as 1981, William S. McFeely's biography of Grant, far superior in style and scholarship, emphasized the same themes, presenting Grant as a completely ordinary man of an extraordinarily bad period of American history.

The generation between two world wars undertook a thorough reappraisal of the years of Civil War and Reconstruction. Unhappiness with the results of the war to end all wars influenced a revisionist concept of the Civil War as a needless war or repressible conflict brought on by a blundering generation. Disillusionment with the noble experiment of prohibition influenced a skeptical attitude toward efforts to transform race relations in the South during Reconstruction. Finally, the collapse of the American economy in the Great Depression influenced hostility toward the age of the "robber barons" in which America had hurried into industrialization. While a rash of biographies idealized Andrew Johnson as a heroic agrarian and conscientious constitutionalist, Grant became the popular symbol of a misguided and materialistic age.

Because historians often are slow in communicating new ideas to the public, and teachers often continue to teach long after they learn, a Grant image designed to meet the needs of fifty years ago is still all too lively. Surely a theory of inevitable Northern victory in the Civil War due to more men and industrial capacity is untenable after Vietnam; a portrait of a shockingly corrupt Grant administration inappropriate after Watergate. In polls taken among professional historians in 1948 and 1962, judging U.S. presidents on their presidential records, Grant was twice one of the two men ranked flat failures, and perhaps the only consolation was that Warren G. Harding won last place in both polls—and has since strengthened his claim to that position, challenged only by Richard Nixon.

Surveying the changes in the Grant image across a century, one is drawn to the conclusion that his image tells us far more about the needs of the American people than about the reality of Grant's character and career. Nor is this an uncommon fate for great American public figures, for a type of secular theology has grown up about them. The phrase "Lincoln Shrine" comes too easily to the lips. Americans believe that, with a word, President Monroe surrounded a hemisphere with a defensive wall; with a stroke of the pen President Lincoln struck the shackles from all slaves; with a nod of inattention President Hoover made the grass grow in the streets. It is all godlike, untrue, and virtually ineradicable. Only a few years ago a Washington, D.C., department store held a special sale on Washington's Birthday, attracting customers with a relic furnished by a historical society: a piece of wood from the actual cherry tree alleged to have been cut down by George Washington.

Grant's life lent itself, in part, to symbolic use because of its varied nature and paradoxes. Sherman, one of Grant's oldest and closest friends, concluded that Grant had "a strange character. Nothing like it is portrayed by Plutarch or the many who have striven to portray the great men of ancient or modern times. I knew him as a cadet at West Point, as a lieutenant of the Fourth Infantry, as a citizen of St. Louis, and as a growing general all through the bloody Civil War. Yet to me he is a mystery, and I believe he is a mystery to himself." Grant must have agreed, at least in part, when he opened his *Memoirs* with the motto: "Man proposes and God disposes." Through the *Memoirs* runs an untheological yet profound belief in the guiding force of some higher power. In discussing the Mexican War, of which he disapproved both as a young officer and as an old man, he wrote: "The Southern rebellion was largely the outgrowth of the Mexican War. Nations, like individuals, are punished for their transgressions. We got our punishment in the most sanguinary and expensive war of modern times."

It was characteristic of Grant to be vague about who arranged the punishment. Through his adult life Grant almost never attended church, perhaps because of his great dislike for music; but as a boy he had lived in a strict Methodist household, for the Methodist Church was the cornerstone of his mother's life. As a West Point cadet, Grant complained to a cousin that "we are not only obliged to go to church but must *march* there by companys. This is not exactly republican. It is an Episcopal Church." Although not religious in a formal sense, he was conscious of following pathways he never chose.

Grant's whole life was filled with strange twists and turns. Despite his military achievements, Grant never sought nor enjoyed the life of a soldier. "I never entered the army without regret or left it without pleasure," he recalled. He went to West Point because his father insisted upon it, and he never studied more than necessary. Had it not been for his sense of obligation to remain in the army through the Mexican War, he would have resigned as soon as possible. He never took pleasure in privileges of rank or military display; to him war was always a dirty job to be finished quickly. After the Civil War some Bostonians decided to give General Grant a military library and asked a staff officer what books Grant already had; they were told he had no military books. Of course, this was exaggeration, for when Grant went off to war in 1861 he wrote home for his copy of George B. McClellan's report of the Crimean War, and he studied Hardee's tactics until he realized that his regiment was camped on too small a field to carry out the recommended maneuvers. Grant eventually raised ignoring the military past to the level of principle during the Vicksburg campaign.

> When I determined on that campaign I knew, as well as I knew anything, that it would not meet with the approval of the authorities in Washington. I knew this because I knew Halleck, and that he was too learned a soldier to consent to a campaign in violation of all the principles of the art of war. But I felt that every war I knew anything about had made laws for itself, and early in our contest I was impressed with the idea that success with us would depend upon our taking advantage of new conditions. No two wars are alike, because they are generally found at different periods, under different phases of civilization.

Instead of a military career Grant had first hoped to return to West Point as an assistant professor of mathematics. As a young officer at Jefferson Barracks near St. Louis, he studied for the day when he might abandon garrison duty. But he lost touch with mathematics during the Mexican War and decided to stay in the army. As late as the 1850s he still considered an academic career.

During the war Grant began to buy land near the site of his Hardscrabble farm near St. Louis, planning an eventual retirement to the life of gentleman farmer. After the war and through the early years of his presidency, he continued to expand his acreage and directed tenants to begin the improvement of his property. At his direction a large horse barn was built, larger and sturdier than anything Confederates built at Vicksburg. But after the Whiskey Ring scandal involved too many of his St. Louis friends, Grant lost interest in the property, never lived there, and showed no remorse when it went to Vanderbilt in his final financial collapse.

After his presidency and a triumphal tour around the world, Grant settled in New York City and began to move into the business world. He was first involved in the Mexican Southern Railroad Company with Jay Gould and then became a silent partner in Grant and Ward. The railroad was never built, and the investment firm turned into a disaster.

Grant had a well-deserved reputation for resoluteness of purpose and determination. Yet of the three careers he planned for himself—professor of mathematics, gentleman farmer, businessman—not one was successfully fulfilled. Three others into which he drifted or was forced—soldier, politician, man of letters—were brilliantly successful. Little wonder then that Sherman concluded that Grant was a mystery to himself as well as to others.

Adding to the paradoxical quality of his career was the fact that the conqueror of the South had many sympathetic connections with it. He was born in Ohio within sight of the Ohio River and had relatives who lived on the slaveholding side. Several fought for the Confederacy, including at least one young cousin who surrendered at Appomattox. At West Point he formed lifelong friendships with cadets from the South, like James Longstreet. While stationed at Jefferson Barracks, south of St. Louis, Grant fell in love with Julia Dent, daughter of a slaveholding family—distant relatives of Longstreet—and at least two future Confederate generals attended the small wedding four years later. When Grant resigned from the army in 1854, his father-in-law, Colonel Frederick

Dent, gave him a place to live and land to farm, while his own father, a far wealthier man, offered only an unappealing clerkship in Galena. While farming in Missouri, Grant owned at least one slave—whom he freed in 1859, during a time of considerable financial hardship. Slaves given to his wife, however, remained her property when Grant accepted the surrender of Lee, who had freed all his slaves years earlier. Grant's sympathy for the South remained late in life when a reporter introduced himself as a former Confederate soldier who fought at Fort Donelson and Champion's Hill. "I honor all, Confederate soldiers," Grant replied, "as I do all brave conscientious men. You were not at fault; your leaders were. They knew that a Southern confederacy was impossible and ought not to be. I was fighting not *against* the South, but *for* it. In every battle I felt a sympathy for you, and I felt that I was fighting for North and South—for the whole nation."

When the Civil War began, Grant expressed concern that the slaves might rise in revolt; of course, he thought, the North would fight to suppress such an uprising. As a commander, his thinking underwent dramatic changes. He welcomed the fugitive slaves who brought him information of enemy movements and gladly undertook the menial tasks necessary to his army. By the end of the war, black troops constituted a crucial segment of his army and were not forgotten when the battles ended. The last slaveholder to serve as president enthusiastically supported the Fifteenth Amendment (which gave all American citizens the right to vote); enforced civil rights legislation; and attacked terrorist organizations such as the Ku Klux Klan, designed to rob Negroes of their legal rights. In his opinion, the goal of reuniting North and South could not be achieved at the expense of wartime black allies.

Contemporaries were dazzled by Grant's meteoric rise within three years from leather-goods clerk to general in chief. The youngest man ever elected president to that time, he had voted in only one presidential election before his own (and then for a Democrat) and made his first political speech three years after leaving the White House. Grant's own modesty encouraged cynics to believe that some wily manipulator had furnished the brains for his career. Speculation has centered on Elihu B. Washburne, the congressman from Galena who gave Grant his first star and defended his military career in Washington, and on John A. Rawlins, Grant's chief of staff and self-appointed guardian.

Washburne, of course, had done Grant a valuable service. Grant was promoted to brigadier general before he ever engaged the enemy because he was the likeliest candidate for general who happened to live in Washburne's congressional district. "I think I see your hand in it," wrote Grant to Washburne and promised, "you shall never have cause to regret the part you have taken." Washburne also accepted his responsibility to Grant to such an extent that his friends claimed he had "Grant on the brain." Washburne defended Grant in Washington against charges of intemperance, explained away his unpreparedness at Shiloh, and even helped Mrs. Grant find a cook.

During the Vicksburg campaign, so little went right for so long a time that faith in Grant was severely tested. Lincoln's mail included a letter from the influential editor of the *Chicago Tribune,* who moaned: "I hardly look for much success under copperhead Grant & crazy Sherman." Another editor called Grant "a jackass in the original package." Washburne heard from his brother, then a major general serving in the West, that "Grant has no plans for taking Vicksburg, and he is frittering away time and strength to no purpose. . . . You cannot make a silk purse out of a sow's ear." In this test of faith it was Lincoln who did best; in one account he put his hand on Washburne's shoulder and said, "Elihu, it is a bad business, but we must try the man a little longer. He seems a pushing fellow, with all his faults." Once Vicksburg had fallen, Washburne's faith in Grant was restored, but it was no longer necessary; the entire North had faith in Grant. In time, Washburne, a typical Western congressman, became a liability, but President Grant repaid Washburne many times over for his appointment as brigadier general.

Grant was still alive when newspaper reporter Sylvanus Cadwallader published an article in which he stated: "It has long been known to all the intimates of both that Rawlins was the power behind Grant, greater even than Grant himself." In this case, Grant's habitual reticence was undoubtedly strengthened by reluctance to attack his late and valued friend Rawlins, for Cadwallader was repeating a myth created by Rawlins himself. Rawlins, a Galena lawyer, had first joined Grant's staff in the summer of 1861. His father, a drunkard who kept his family in poverty, gave his son a lifelong fear of liquor. With no military training, Rawlins was tutored in his duties as adjutant by Grant himself, who often drafted orders for Rawlins to sign because of Rawlins's clumsy writing style. Indeed, the most valuable service Rawlins could perform for Grant was to be his friend. After Grant's seven years in St. Louis and Galena following his resignation from the army in 1854, years filled with financial distress and disappointment, he had great need of reassuring friendship and loyalty, and his staff, a military family, was a substitute for his true family. Rawlins remained with Grant throughout the war and was appointed to his cabinet as secretary of war.

In December 1861, when Washburne heard rumors that Grant was drinking, he wrote to Rawlins for the truth. Rawlins replied that Grant did not drink; if he ever did, Rawlins would inform Washburne and then resign his commission. It was unfortunate that Rawlins fell into the position of watchdog over Grant, because the lawyer had an irrational attitude toward liquor, an excitable temperament, and an impatient attitude toward his subordinate position. Since Rawlins had promised to resign if Grant took to drink, his continued presence on the staff is ample evidence of Grant's sobriety. Yet Rawlins made the most of his watchdog position by discussing the drinking question frequently with other officers and newspapermen; by issuing stern, probably unnecessary, warnings to Grant; and by intimating much too often that only his presence at headquarters kept the general from lunging at the bottle. Rawlins's position depended on his good relationship with Grant, a man he genuinely admired and liked; his self-esteem depended on a portrayal of Grant as a man of bad habits and weak character. Acting as oracle to a worshipful crowd of staff officers and reporters, he often took credit for Grant's plans and suggested that he could influence Grant's thought. In the summer of 1861, lawyer Rawlins had hitched his wagon to a star, and within a few years he was hitched to four stars and even wore one himself. The ambitious Rawlins found it hard to admit to himself—much less to his wife and friends—that he had played a subordinate role in the ascent.

Old army gossip ran that Grant had been drinking heavily on the Pacific Coast in 1852–1854, and that this had something to do with his resignation from the army. Separated from his wife and children with no prospect of acquiring the money to reunite the family, recently promoted but not likely to rise again for many years, in poor health, assigned to a small and isolated post with a commanding officer he had previously disliked, Grant had plenty of reasons to resign, and documentary evidence demonstrates that the resignation was his own choice. If, on the Pacific Coast, he drank more than was necessary to maintain his standing as an officer, or if the financial hardships of the following years drove him to drink, the evidence is too meager and contradictory for any sound conclusion. But once in the Civil War, he quickly rose to an important position, then was watched closely by many who had heard the gossip. Aware of constant scrutiny and speculation, Grant wrote home a few weeks after Shiloh: "We are all well and me as sober as a deacon no matter what is said to the contrary." Belief in Grant's drinking is a legacy from Rawlins and his friends, gratefully accepted not because of its truth but because of its convenience in shaping an image.

As a young boy, Grant was anxious enough to escape the stench and filth of his father's tannery to go to West Point. There he found the first well-stocked library he had ever known, and his reading of Bulwer-Lytton, Cooper, Scott, and Irving set a lasting pattern. Later he read fiction extensively during lulls in garrison duty and served as reader to his weak-eyed wife. His oldest son remembered that his father read aloud to the family frequently and was especially fond of Dickens. West Point had, at least once, produced an officer and a gentleman.

Through his correspondence runs a thread of gentlemanly restraint. He was affectionate toward his wife and children, yet his family letters were not intensely personal. Unfailingly deferential to women, he abhorred unclean conversation. Lincoln won fame for skill in telling dirty jokes, Grant for not even listening. Grant's unusual gentleness even influenced his eating habits. He would eat no meat not thoroughly cooked—his cook said the closer he came to burning the meat the better the general liked it—and he rejected all fowl, saying he would eat nothing that walked on two feet. Vegetables and fruits were much preferred, with cucumbers a notable favorite.

As a gentleman, Grant did not boast or seek public acclaim, but he went far beyond this to value his privacy so highly that he retreated into silence when under attack. Bitterly criticized after Shiloh, he wrote ambivalently to his wife: "I have been so shockingly abused that I sometimes think it almost time to defend myself." When urged by his father to do so, however, Grant commented: "Dont he know the best contradiction in the world is to pay no attention to them?" Once he had weathered this storm, silence became habitual.

Until he found himself penniless, with no way of providing for his family except by writing memoirs, Grant had no intention of telling his own story to the American people. If he resented journalistic distortions of his career, he valued his privacy too highly to engage in efforts to correct the record. Originally named Hiram Ulysses Grant, but commonly called Ulysses, he had decided to reverse his first and middle names when he entered West Point, in order to avoid teasing about his initials. In the meantime, his appointment had been erroneously made in the name of Ulysses S. Grant, because the congressman who appointed him either remembered his mother's maiden name of Simpson or confused Ulysses with a younger brother actually named Simpson. The army being what it was—and still is—Grant's efforts to correct his name in the records failed, and after graduation he bowed to necessity and began to sign himself "U. S. Grant."

The army, then, had imposed a middle initial upon him, but no middle name. While Grant was serving on the Pacific Coast his wife gave birth to a second son whom she named Ulysses S. Grant Jr. "What does the S stand for in Ulysses' name?" asked the father; "in mine you know it does not stand for anything!" In an 1864 letter to Washburne, Grant wrote vehemently: "In answer to your letter of a few days ago asking what 'S' stands for in my name, I can only state *nothing*."

Yet as Grant rose to prominence, he made no effort to correct the general confusion about his middle name. A biography published in 1864 provided 316 pages of information about Ulysses Sydney Grant. Those familiar with his family background repeated an old mistake by misnaming him Ulysses Simpson Grant—an error now virtually canonized by its repetition on Library of Congress catalog cards and in standard reference books. Of course, the man most responsible for the error is Grant himself; one public word from him would have demolished acres of Simpsons.

In his lifetime, Grant became justly famous for his reticence. Many an office seeker who visited the White House was reduced to stammering incoherence after several minutes of flinging hot pleas against icy silence. Several politicians who wanted to solicit Grant's promises before the Republican convention in 1868 commented that Grant had turned the conversation to horses. Some thought it reflected the banality of his mind; others realized that he had avoided political commitments. Yet when Grant was with close friends, he did most of the talking and was remembered as a skilled conversationalist.

Evidence in his letters supports Grant as a master of words. Grant's letters are revealing because the man speaks directly. Few were written with advance thought, preliminary drafts, or secretarial assistance. Most express his thoughts just as they came to mind, and their remarkable clarity illustrates the clarity of Grant's own thought. Even the most important letters have crossed-out words or sentences indicating a shift of thought or emphasis. During the Civil War he wrote his own orders, as many as thirty-five a day, sometimes writing while conferring with his commanders. These orders were never misunderstood. Sentences were clear, even when circumstances were complex, and officers who received orders from Grant knew exactly what was expected.

Together with the *Memoirs*, the letters reveal that Grant had a quiet sense of humor. For example, on taking command at Ironton, Missouri, in August 1861, he reported to headquarters that he did not expect the enemy to attack. "It is fortunate too if this is the case for many of the officers seem to have so little command over their men, and military duty seems to be done so loosely, that I feel at present our resistance would be in the inverse ratio of the number of troops to resist with." Somewhat later, Grant complained that he could not find enough loyal men in southeast Missouri "to save Sodom." Someone mentioned that the pompous and arrogant Senator Charles Sumner did not believe in the Bible. "Of course not," said President Grant. "He didn't write it." But Sumner brought out the worst in Grant, and his joke at Sumner's expense was uncharacteristic. Usually, Grant's wit was of a sort which might pass unnoticed.

The latest edition of Bartlett's *Familiar Quotations* has eleven Grant selections, three for Robert E. Lee. In fact, a count ranked Grant ninth among the presidents in regard to memorable lines. Grant did have a gift for ringing words: "unconditional and immediate surrender," or "I propose to fight it out on this line if it takes all Summer," and, especially, "Let us have peace."

Forty years ago historians complained that Grant "wrote as little as possible" and that almost no manuscripts existed. Research based on collections overlooked then, supplemented by material only recently made available by the Grant family, completely reverses this verdict. The edition in progress of *The Papers of Ulysses S. Grant* has published ten large volumes, with at least another fifteen projected. Inspiration for such mammoth scholarship came from Grant biographers like Lloyd Lewis and Bruce Catton, who uncovered the complexity of Grant's character, and from military analysts like Kenneth P. Williams and T. Harry Williams, who attributed Grant's victories to more than luck and larger armies. Much remains to be done, and the White House years, once casually dismissed as a carnival of ineptitude, now loom as a scholarly frontier.

For many years ahead a Grant image will undoubtedly stand where the real man should be. But, for the first time, the material for a true likeness is emerging. And those who see it will find a man far more remarkable than myth makers have ever created.

10

A Marriage Tested by War

Ulysses and Julia Grant

Of the leading figures in the Civil War, Ulysses S. Grant had the happiest marriage. Julia Dent Grant wrote a sunny account of their life together.[1] Varina Davis, perhaps a more talented writer—although a less congenial wife—published a defensive memoir of her husband, Jefferson Davis. Although Mary Lincoln wrote nothing for publication, her side of the tortured Lincoln marriage has frequently engaged sympathetic biographers. The reclusive Mary Custis Lee remains an enigma to most Robert E. Lee scholars. Although a solid and affectionate marriage was not a prerequisite to Civil War achievement, notable benefits followed in Grant's case.[2]

Julia Dent, an eighteen-year-old schoolgirl, first met twenty-two-year-old Brevet Second Lieutenant Ulysses S. Grant in 1844 at the Dent family estate of White Haven in south St. Louis County. Born in St. Louis on January 26, 1826, Julia was raised at White Haven. She was the fifth child in a family that already had four boys. Three more girls followed, one of whom died in infancy.

Julia's father, Frederick Dent, was called "colonel" through wealth and social standing rather than military service. Born in Maryland in 1786, he had prospered as a St. Louis merchant and real estate speculator. He had acquired a country estate of nearly one thousand acres, which originally supplemented his downtown residence. He gradually withdrew from business to enjoy country life and domestic pleasures, at some cost to his once considerable wealth. A Southerner by birth and inclination, he farmed White Haven with slaves and never doubted the propriety of the institution nor his opinions on any subject. Neighbors considered him indolent, irascible, and litigious.

Julia's mother, Ellen Bray Wrenshall Dent, born in England and raised in Pittsburgh, was educated in Philadelphia. Her father, an importer and Methodist preacher, established a strong religious and genteel tradition. She was remembered as cultured and quiet, perhaps uncomfortable in frontier society. From her father, Julia acquired assertiveness and from her mother, a persistent use of feminine wiles.

Julia remembered her girlhood as idyllic. Her father's pet, she had young slave girls as attendants. Her schooling began nearby at a log schoolhouse, which she recalled fondly. Required to learn "those dreadful roman numerals" or face punishment with a rod, she faltered in class but was given a reprieve by a kindly schoolmaster, John F. Long, who later became a close friend to both Grants.[3] At age ten, Julia was sent to a St. Louis boarding school, where she remained about seven years. She remembered her years there as filled with reading romantic novels while neglecting English grammar and multiplication tables. Noticeably cross-eyed and rarely considered beautiful, she was nonetheless a belle. Willful and charming, she captivated Lieutenant Grant.

Ulysses was born at Point Pleasant, Ohio, on April 27, 1822. His father, Jesse, was the son of a Revolutionary War veteran too fond of drink, whose many children scattered on the frontier after the death of his second wife, Jesse's mother. Jesse received assistance from his prosperous half-brother Peter and from kindly families that took him in as a bound boy, including the family of Owen Brown, father of abolitionist John Brown. Jesse eventually learned the tanner's trade and established himself in Point Pleasant, where he married the daughter of a nearby farmer. Hannah Simpson was an educated young woman from Philadelphia noted for her Methodist piety.

Young Ulysses, the oldest of six children, apparently had an ordinary boyhood in Georgetown, Ohio, where he grew up and attended school. The Grant home was across the street from the tannery, which Ulysses came to detest. He preferred farmwork and anything involving horses, for which he seemed to possess a special aptitude. After Ulysses spent two terms at nearby academies, Jesse arranged his appointment to the U.S. Military Academy. Ulysses immediately said, "I won't go." Jesse responded that "he thought I would, *and I thought so too, if he did.*"[4] The unwilling cadet, who did not study "with avidity," enjoyed reading novels.[5] A natural talent for mathematics carried him to graduation in the middle of his class. This brought him a commission as brevet second lieutenant and assignment to Jefferson Barracks, then the largest military post in the United States. His West Point roommate, Frederick Dent, encouraged Ulysses to visit his parents at nearby White Haven. Ulysses enjoyed the company of two of Fred's brothers still living at home and two young sisters—Nellie, age fifteen, and Emma, eight or nine—as well as the hospitality of the Dent parents.

In February 1844, when Julia returned from a social season with the family of Colonel John O'Fallon in St. Louis, Ulysses and Julia met and soon found themselves in love without fully realizing the depth of their attraction. Orders in May sending Grant's regiment to Louisiana forced both to recognize the truth. Ulysses left with at least an informal engagement, not yet blessed with parental approval, something that Ulysses eventually wrung from Colonel Dent one year later, despite Dent's concern about whether his daughter would be happy as an officer's wife.

Neither of the young people shared Colonel Dent's apprehensions, and Ulysses hoped to leave active service soon for teaching. He had already corresponded with his mathematics teacher at West Point about returning there and eyed academic opportunities elsewhere. Military movements carried the regiment from Louisiana into Texas and then interfered with Ulysses's teaching plans. As Grant's regiment became entangled in the preliminaries of the Mexican War, then the war itself, the young couple's separation was bridged solely through ardent correspondence.

Julia carefully saved Ulysses's letters. Although he treasured her letters, they have not survived. His letters attest to the strong bond between them, intensified by separation. After the war, twenty-six-year-old Ulysses hurried to St. Louis to marry twenty-two-year-old Julia. Their quiet wedding on August 22, 1848, at the Dent house in St. Louis was conducted in accordance with Methodist practice. All three groomsmen later fought for the Confederacy, including James Longstreet, Julia's cousin as well as Ulysses's friend. None of the Grant family attended, a portent of trouble to come.

Although Ulysses and Julia had many common bonds and were deeply in love, the similarities in their backgrounds came from their quiet Methodist mothers. Their fathers differed enough to presage trouble. Jesse Grant held strong antislavery views and was a Whig; Colonel Dent was an opinionated slaveholder and Democrat. Julia was too fond of her father to challenge him; Ulysses had experienced his father's authoritarian personality when forced to attend the military academy but respected his financial success. By the 1850s, a partner in two tanneries and several leather stores, Jesse Grant had a net worth of some one hundred thousand dollars, although his grandson remembered him as "at no time a liberal man."⁶ Jesse Grant was probably wealthier than Frederick Dent, but the Dents lived as if they were rich, the Grants as if they were poor.

For four years, the young couple experienced the normal life of a young officer's family. Expecting an assignment at Detroit, the Grants found instead an unwelcome posting to Sackets Harbor, New York, a cold, dreary, lonely place to spend a winter. Nonetheless, they found enough society for comfort, enough privacy for bonding. Julia remembered that her husband once invited other officers home for dinner after church without informing her. She begged him to rescind the invitation until she could determine that her cook was sufficiently skilled. This he did, telling her later that his friends went without dinner that day. Later, they joined him in teasing Julia, pretending that they were afraid to enter the Grant home without her special permission.⁷

In spring 1849, the Grants went to Detroit, where they spent a pleasant year in a larger city with more society. Julia returned to St. Louis to give birth to Frederick Dent Grant on May 30, 1850. While she was gone, regimental headquarters moved to Sackets Harbor, where her husband found them a comfortable home.

The greatest trial of their marriage came with Ulysses's assignment to the Pacific Coast in 1852. Again pregnant, Julia, with two-year-old Fred, might not have survived the journey across the Isthmus of Panama, a nightmarish trek across fever-ridden swamps that cost the lives of many women and children who had accompanied the troops. Left behind for her safety, Julia gave birth to her second son, Ulysses S. Grant Jr., on July 22, 1852, while staying with the Grant family in Ohio, so he was nicknamed "Buckeye," later shortened to Buck. Assigned to Fort Vancouver, Ulysses tried to supplement his pay through various investment and farming ventures to enable him to bring Julia and the two boys to Oregon Territory. Everything he tried turned out badly. As the months dragged by, Julia went to St. Louis to await fruitlessly a summons to the Pacific Coast. Reassigned to the dreary and isolated post of Fort Humboldt, California, commanded by a martinet with whom he had quarreled years earlier, troubled by malaria and other ailments, and despairing of promotion beyond captain, Ulysses resigned in 1854 after two years of family separation, planning a new career as farmer on land given to Julia by her father.

In his *Memoirs,* Ulysses wrote little about the seven years between his resignation from the army and the start of the Civil War, and that chapter dealt chiefly with the politics of the period. His financially troubled adjustment to life outside the army threatened his capacity to support his family. Whatever the economic stresses of the time, the marriage thrived. Shortly after Ulysses's return from the Pacific Coast and the happy reunion at White Haven, the family traveled to Bethel, Illinois, where Jesse proposed to set his son up in the leather business in Galena, in the northwestern corner of Illinois, an attractive prospect before Jesse revealed his thrifty intention to have Julia and the children stay with the Grants or with her father while Ulysses learned the trade.[8] Indignantly declining the offer, Ulysses returned to Missouri, where he began to farm just in time to be overwhelmed by the Panic of 1857. At least once during her farm life Julia succumbed to despair about her future, and she hated the log house, Hardscrabble, that her husband had built himself. After Julia's mother died in early 1857, the Grants moved from Hardscrabble to the family mansion of White Haven, but eventually Ulysses had to move to St. Louis in search of employment.

In the spring of 1860, the Grants finally moved to Galena, where Ulysses worked with and for his two younger brothers. The Grants had a seven-room rented home. Fred and Ulysses Jr. had been joined by Ellen (Nellie), born on July 4, 1855, and Jesse Jr., born at Hardscrabble on February 6, 1858. Although Ulysses received only a small salary, Julia had a servant who did all the cooking. Ulysses disliked his employment, and Julia missed St. Louis, but family life provided compensations.

The outbreak of war impelled Ulysses, conscious of his obligations as a trained soldier, to volunteer immediately. He presided over a Galena war meeting, accompanied a local company to Springfield, and found employment in the governor's office. Acquiring a commission proved more difficult, but after two months Grant became colonel of a regiment of Illinois Volunteers. Julia sent eleven-year-old Fred to join his father in Springfield, and Fred accompanied the march to the Illinois River and the railroad trip to Quincy, where his father put him on a steamboat headed toward home. Julia protested because Fred had been sent alone, although both Grants later recalled that Julia protested that Fred should have stayed with his father.[9]

During the summer of 1861, Grant received promotion to brigadier general, and both Grants realized that the war would not end soon. Where should Julia and the children live? Galena did not seem like home to Julia without her husband, and Simpson, her favorite of Ulysses's brothers, slipped deeper into illness, dying in September. Ulysses considered sending Julia to live with his parents in Covington, Kentucky, but, remembering previous disagreeable talk about money, only as a paying guest. The Confederate sympathies of too many family members and friends made St. Louis uncomfortable. Although Julia's eldest brother, Fred, fought for the Union, her father and brother John sympathized with the South. Julia's love for her Dent family was overshadowed by her devotion to Ulysses, whose political views became hers as well. In part because the Grants truly had no other home, the family reunited at Cairo, Illinois, in November 1861. Grant had recently fought his first battle at Belmont, Missouri, an inconclusive engagement; the family remained in Cairo until Grant left for Fort Henry, Tennessee, in early February. Julia remembered the superior quality of the mess and the companionship of Mrs. William S. Hillyer of St. Louis, whose husband served on Grant's staff.

Other women, including Mary Logan, wife of John A. Logan, by then an Illinois colonel, joined their husbands at Cairo. Located farther south than Richmond, Virginia, Cairo was nonetheless a city in a Northern state. Grant's advance into the rebellious South presented new problems for officers' wives, especially those with young children. Few officers were as frequently accompanied by their families as Grant. Julia, who brought a welcome domesticity to her husband's army headquarters, also nursed Ulysses through devastating migraines.

Julia wept piteously as she left her husband at Cairo; being together meant much to both. Grant, however, now advancing southward, had wrung grudging approval from his commanding officer, General Henry W. Halleck, for a campaign to open the Tennessee River. They were separated during Grant's campaign against forts Henry and Donelson. When Confederate general Simon B. Buckner accepted Grant's terms of "unconditional and immediate" surrender" at Fort Donelson on February 16, 1862, Grant suddenly became famous. He had achieved the first major Union victory of the war, had captured some fifteen thousand prisoners, and had won promotion to major general. Grant's aggressive and successful campaigning increased the jealousy of Halleck, whose efforts to displace Grant after his success at Fort Donelson failed largely because of an injury to General Charles F. Smith, Halleck's preference for commander of the Tennessee River expedition.

Restored to command, Grant was surprised by an attack on his troops at Shiloh. A few miles away, waiting to meet the army of General Don Carlos Buell, joining him for an attack on Corinth, Mississippi, Grant had not anticipated that the enemy might strike first. Hurrying to the field, Grant rallied his forces and created a line on the banks of the Tennessee River to protect his army. The next day, reinforced by a dilatory division of his own army and forces under Buell, Grant more than redeemed the losses of the first day and drove Confederates from the field. The bloodiest fighting of the Civil War to date brought Halleck to the field, reacting to Grant's victory as if it had been defeat, and Northern newspapers attacked Grant's unpreparedness and alleged inebriation.

Not until Halleck left the Western armies for Washington, D.C., in July 1862 did Grant emerge from a cloud of suspicion and neglect so debilitating that he considered resignation. Once free of Halleck, he sent for Julia, who joined him at Memphis in July and then accompanied him to Corinth. During the summer, all their children stayed with them. In the fall, after they were placed in school, Julia returned to army headquarters with Jesse Jr., who was still too young for school.

Julia's frequent visits to her husband in the field fueled speculation that her presence kept Ulysses from drinking. Old army gossip that Ulysses had drunk himself out of the army in 1854 pursued him through the war, leading observers at headquarters to comment frequently on his sobriety. He did not drink when Julia was around but also abstained when she was not with him. Soon after the battle of Shiloh, Ulysses reassured Julia that he was "as sober as a deacon no matter what is said to the contrary."[10] Charging him with drunkenness at Cairo in late 1861, an anonymous writer demanded "pure men in habits and men without secesh wives with their own little slaves to wait upon them."[11] As Julia joined her husband whenever possible during the campaign that ended at Vicksburg, at least one slave given to her by her father was much in evidence through the early years of the war. When the Grants had moved from St. Louis to Galena in spring 1860, they left behind four young slaves. When Julia left St. Louis in 1861 to follow her husband, Jule, or "Black Julia," accompanied the Grants, especially to care for young Jesse. Julia gave little indication of consciousness of any incongruity, however much the scene startled others. In early 1864, concerned that an impending trip to Missouri might return her to slavery, Jule ran away. Residence in Mississippi should have freed her under the Emancipation Proclamation; in Missouri she could have become another Dred Scott.

Julia Grant, raised on a farm worked by slaves, owner of slaves in her own right, a Southern belle by disposition and training, tolerant of the Confederate leanings of members of the Dent family, was nonetheless devoted to her husband. In Holly Springs, sharing a house with rebel sympathizers, her position was quite easily misunderstood. The young women of the family invited Julia to join them in the parlor to listen to rebel songs, and those who saw Julia out shopping with Jule made similar assumptions. Julia set the record straight: "I am the most loyal of the loyal," she explained, and to arguments about the constitutionality of secession she responded that she "did not know a thing about this dreadful Constitution."[12] Her belief in her husband and his cause was strong and unwavering.

Grant's overland campaign in Mississippi failed when Confederate general Earl Van Dorn raided the Union supply base at Holly Springs on December 20, 1862. Narrowly avoiding capture, Julia had left Holly Springs shortly before the raid. During the early months of 1863, as Grant attempted to reach Vicksburg from a base across the river in Louisiana, Julia remained in St. Louis, but she had joined him when Union gunboats and transports ran the Vicksburg batteries in April. She always remembered the exciting nighttime spectacle. When Grant crossed the river in late April to campaign on dry land, she returned home to St. Louis, but thirteen-year-old Fred, who had gone ashore by subterfuge, accompanied his father through the campaign that ended on July 4 with the capitulation of the Confederate citadel.[13] Although Fred recalled the campaign as an adventurous lark, he returned to St. Louis seriously ill.

Julia rejoined her husband in occupied Vicksburg. The Grants lived on the first floor of the Lum mansion; the family lived above. Julia did favors for the Lums (including interceding with her husband to revoke the banishment of a family friend) that eventually changed their attitudes toward the Union; she also made friends elsewhere in Vicksburg by intervening in cases that touched her tender heart. She had established a circle of friends before she left at the end of the summer of 1863 to make arrangements for her children's schooling. She later returned to Vicksburg to nurse her husband, seriously injured when his horse fell in New Orleans, and accompanied him as far as Louisville when he was called to take command at Chattanooga. After Grant's great victories in the battles at Chattanooga in late November, she joined Ulysses at headquarters in Nashville.

Julia soon hurried to St. Louis upon receiving word that Fred was gravely ill with dysentery and typhoid. In late January 1864, Ulysses was called to his son's bedside, uncertain whether he would arrive in time.[14] As it turned out, Fred had already begun to recover before Ulysses reached St. Louis. In the meantime, Julia's persistent problems with her eyes had reached a crisis, and she thought that a long-deferred operation to cure her strabismus might improve her appearance as the wife of the great soldier. When a surgeon told her that it was too late, Ulysses reassuringly reminded her that he had fallen in love with those same eyes.

Grant's growing prominence in the Civil War gave Julia greater responsibilities and prominence. Willingly or not, she began to represent her husband. St. Louis neighbors scrutinized her actions and conduct for clues to her husband's beliefs. Those who knew the Southern sympathies of some of her Dent kinsmen expected some reflection of them. Although St. Louis held a substantial Unionist majority, Julia's prewar social circle represented the minority. Some of her St. Louis neighbors went so far as to assume the disloyalty of this Southern slaveholder. Julia eventually found living in St. Louis uncomfortable.

Grant's own distaste for burgeoning public recognition of his military achievements encouraged shifting the spotlight of publicity and attention to his wife. Because of her troublesome eye problems in early 1864, Julia did not accompany her husband to Washington in March for the ceremony marking his promotion to lieutenant general and assignment as general in chief, commanding all the armies of the United States. Instead, Fred accompanied his father. At a crowded White House reception where Grant first met President Abraham Lincoln, Grant had to stand on a sofa to allow all to see him. At a quieter ceremony attended by cabinet officers the following day, Lincoln made a brief speech investing Grant with authority; Grant responded with an even briefer speech, written out in advance, delivered awkwardly, and omitting points that Lincoln had specifically requested for inclusion. After a visit to General George G. Meade's headquarters in Virginia, Lincoln invited Grant to a state dinner. Grant declined, complaining privately that he had had enough of "this show business."[15]

Julia arrived in Washington later, after Grant had decided to accompany the Army of the Potomac on its Overland campaign in Virginia. As Major General William T. Sherman traveled with the Grants from Nashville to Cincinnati, Julia asked Sherman's advice on Washington etiquette, an apt subject since Sherman had been raised by a politically prominent family and had a brother serving in the U.S. Senate. Sherman advised Julia to return all calls, something that she eventually found impossible. One day in Philadelphia gave Julia an opportunity to improve her wardrobe. After Ulysses left Washington for the army, Julia attended her first White House reception, escorted by Admiral David G. Farragut and two of her husband's staff officers. Both the president and Mary Lincoln graciously welcomed Julia, who displayed impressive self-assurance and eluded flattering efforts by strangers to place her under obligation. Standing by Farragut's side, receiving the welcome of the most prominent leaders in wartime Washington, Julia gave every indication of relishing the attention that her husband abhorred. Asked if she thought her husband would capture Richmond, Julia answered that he would: "*Mr. Grant always was a very obstinate man.*"[16]

Before rejoining her children in St. Louis, Julia went to New York City as the guest of the Hillyers. Again she enjoyed meeting "many distinguished people."[17] Daily telegrams of war news received from Secretary of War Edwin M. Stanton reflected her new prominence. She also attended the great Sanitary Fair, an event organized to raise money for charitable work in military hospitals. For each dollar donation, fairgoers received one vote for a handsome jeweled sword for presentation to the most popular general. The two leading contenders were Grant and General George B. McClellan, the first commander of the Army of the Potomac, removed in November 1862, and the inevitable Democratic opponent of Lincoln in the presidential election of 1864. Julia cast her vote for McClellan on grounds of "good taste" and "etiquette."[18]

Newspaper attention given to Julia's gallant gesture distressed her husband, less because the vote went to McClellan than because the story was widely reported.[19] Like it or not, Julia had acquired some of the celebrity of her husband and enjoyed the spotlight. Grant won the sword but still regretted that Julia's name had been involved. Julia contentedly dawdled in New York, later claiming that she awaited a suitable escort to St. Louis. Nonetheless, she had previously traveled without one and was aware that her children were in the capable hands of her relative, Louisa Boggs.

As the spring campaign of 1864 opened, Ulysses wrote Julia that he did not "know exactly the day when I will start or whether Lee will come here before I am ready to move. Would not tell you if I did know."[20] Through much of the grim fighting that took such a terrifying toll on the Union army and on Grant himself, the lighthearted relationship between Grant and his family provided some measure of relief. Ulysses planned to bring Julia to his army, first intending that she stay at nearby Fort Monroe with Sarah Butler, wife of General Benjamin F. Butler. During the summer, the entire family joined Grant at City Point. Staff officer Horace Porter once came upon Ulysses flushed by exertion after wrestling with his boys.[21] Determined that his children receive an education, Ulysses looked that fall toward finding a home in Philadelphia before discovering that nearby Quaker-dominated Burlington, New Jersey, offered even better prospects. Julia put the three older children in school, then, with Jesse, rejoined her husband at City Point. Ulysses lived in a small cabin built by engineers in the shadow of Hopewell Manor, an elegant mansion that he declined to commandeer. Although the cabin contained few comforts, neither Grant complained. They were together. "I am snugly nestled away in my husbands Log cabin Head quarters," wrote Julia. "I enjoy being here, have such long talks with my husband, when all have retired."[22]

As a professional soldier, Grant shared the conservatism of the old army. Fifteen years in the army dating from admission to West Point had provided him with close friends among rebel commanders. Marriage into a family of border-state slaveholders strengthened his Southern ties, notably those to Longstreet. A prewar St. Louis slaveholder, Grant had voted in only one presidential election, casting a ballot for Democrat James Buchanan. Although famed for demanding "unconditional surrender," he had not yet been tested by Confederate offers to negotiate.

At the end of January 1865, Confederate emissaries arrived at City Point requesting permission to visit Washington to confer with Lincoln about terminating the "existing War."[23] Lincoln sent a War Department official to insist that no conference could take place unless the commissioners discussed a "common country." By welcoming and dining with the commissioners, Grant had already exceeded what Lincoln thought proper. To underscore that point, Lincoln ordered Grant to allow "nothing which is transpiring [to] change, hinder, or delay your Military movements, or plans."[24]

In a telegram to Stanton, Grant forced Lincoln's hand by asserting that the commissioners had shown him "that their intentions are good and their desire sincere to restore peace and Union."[25] "Induced by a dispatch of Gen. Grant," Lincoln wired Secretary of State William H.

Seward, "I Join you at Fort-Monroe so soon as I can come."[26] Grant was not invited to the unproductive Hampton Roads conference where Lincoln insisted upon reunion and emancipation. Jefferson Davis had empowered his emissaries to concede neither but only to promote an unrealistic alternative, first suggested by Lincoln's adviser Francis P. Blair Sr., to unite North and South in an expedition to drive the French from Mexico. Lincoln, who gained nothing by conferring, reported to Congress that he would not have gone without Grant's urging.

Grant was soon drawn into one of the most bizarre episodes of the war. Confederate commissioners at City Point had been favorably impressed by Grant's friendliness and especially that of Julia, who hoped that Confederates might be induced to release her brother John Dent, held prisoner in the South despite his ardent rebel sympathies. Grant refused to exchange any soldier for his civilian brother-in-law, especially since Dent had foolishly thought that his outspoken support of the Confederacy gave him license to travel freely in the South. Remembering Mrs. Grant's cordiality, though perhaps forgetting its cause, Julia's cousin Longstreet proposed to Union general Edward O. C. Ord that Louise Longstreet and Julia Grant, old friends from St. Louis, exchange social visits as a first step toward conversations between officers of both sides that might end with Grant and Lee suspending hostilities to negotiate. "How enchanting, how thrilling!" exclaimed Julia. "Do say I may go." Grant dismissed that proposal as "simply absurd."[27]

Conversations between Ord and Longstreet ostensibly concerning political prisoners wandered toward peace negotiations. Ord reported that Longstreet had asserted that Lee believed the Southern cause to be hopeless although Davis insisted on continuing the war. Ord suggested that Lee threaten to resign to force Davis to negotiate.[28] Lee requested a meeting with Grant, who forwarded the message to Washington and received an unequivocal reply from Stanton that was actually penned by Lincoln himself. "The President directs me to say to you that he wishes you to have no conference with Gen Lee unless it be for the capitulation of Lees army, or on solely minor and purely military matters[.] He instructs me to say that you are not to decide, discuss, or confer upon any political question: such questions the President holds in his own hands; and will submit them to no military conferences or conventions— mean time you are to press to the utmost, your military advantages."[29] Even more vigorously than Grant, Lincoln pushed toward what Confederates considered to be unconditional surrender. Julia's presence at headquarters may have strengthened Lincoln's determination to limit Grant's peacemaking authority.

As the war neared its end, Grant appointed Lincoln's son Robert to serve on his staff. Robert had previously attended Harvard College and remained in its law school. Well aware of the precarious nature of Mary Lincoln's mental health after the death of Willie in 1862, the president acquiesced in protecting Robert from danger. Finally, he requested Grant to appoint Robert to a staff position, something Grant agreed to do, not without a bit of grumbling, but did accede to Robert's request to attend his father's second inauguration.[30] Once at Grant's headquarters, Robert had little to do more essential than escorting his parents. At Julia's suggestion, Ulysses invited the Lincolns to visit City Point.

Mary Lincoln's behavior during this visit tested Julia. "How dare you be seated until I invite you," Mary said.[31] Worse followed when the two women, escorted by Grant's staff officer Adam Badeau, rode together in an ambulance to witness a review of the Army of the Potomac. Mary learned from Badeau that while other women were sent away from the army when campaigning loomed, the wife of General Charles Griffin had received special permission from Lincoln to remain. Mary exploded. "Do you mean to say that she saw the President alone? Do you know that I never allow the President to see any woman alone?" Julia later agreed with Badeau that neither would ever mention the dreadful episode again.[32] The next day, the same party started off for a review of the Army of the James, joined by Horace Porter, another staff officer brought along by Badeau for support. Mary soon discovered that Mary Ord, wife of General Ord, commanding that army, was on horseback by the side of President Lincoln. Mary Lincoln behaved even more irrationally and hatefully than the day before, finally turning on Julia, who had tried to mollify her. "I suppose you think you'll get to the White House yourself, don't you?" Meeting Mrs. Ord at the review, Mary brought her to tears through insults and refused to cease her abuse. Even at dinner she kept after the poor woman, demanding that Lincoln remove General Ord from command.[33] Julia learned to avoid Mary Lincoln.

On March 29, 1865, Grant left City Point for what he planned as the final campaign against Lee. Ulysses advised Julia to move to the dispatch boat anchored in front of their City Point cabin. She did so, along with the wife of General John A. Rawlins, Grant's principal staff officer. Mary Emma Hurlbut, a Connecticut governess stranded in Mississippi by the war, had married the widower Rawlins after the fall of Vicksburg, and Julia had been a delighted witness to their courtship. When Julia invited Mrs. Rawlins to come with her to City Point in November 1864, Rawlins raised a flurry of objections, but Julia eventually got her way.[34] Rejoicing in the success of Union arms, the two women now anxiously awaited the return of their husbands. One general sent Julia a bouquet picked in the gardens of Petersburg immediately after its occupation on April 2.

On April 7, the day Grant first asked Lee to surrender, the two women received a telegram from Ulysses telling them to return home. Grant expected to be absent ten or twelve days longer, to go to Danville, and to unite with Sherman, who was then in North Carolina, in crushing the remnants of the rebel forces. Julia proudly noted on the telegram that she "did not obey" but remained at City Point and eventually returned to Washington escorted by victorious generals.[35]

While Grant cornered Lee, Julia visited the Lincolns on the *River Queen*. She understood that Mary Lincoln did not welcome her company. Somewhat miffed that Lincoln had visited Richmond without her, Julia made her own visit to the Confederate capital, weeping when she reflected on the human cost of war. When she returned, she learned that the Lincolns, about to return to Washington, had not invited her to a final reception on board their boat. Julia decided to embark upon a James River cruise with her friends, took along a band, and had it play "Now You'll Remember Me" as her boat passed the *River Queen*. Julia had acquired a sense of social standing that eclipsed that of her husband.

Soon afterward, a telegraph operator delivered to Julia the news of Lee's surrender on April 9 before sending the telegram to Washington. When Ulysses returned, he rejected the idea of visiting Richmond, although Julia joined the chorus of those urging a triumphal entry. Grant had decided to return to Washington promptly to end the war. As always, Grant focused firmly on the business of war, leaving ceremony to others.

Back in Washington, however, even Grant could not evade the rejoicing over Lee's surrender. On April 13, all Washington was ablaze with lights to celebrate the triumph. Mary Lincoln had invited Grant to escort her to view the spectacle. Intending to accompany Secretary Stanton and his wife to view the illuminated public buildings, Julia insisted that her husband escort her. This he did, joining Mary Lincoln later, and remembering her bitterness when crowds cheered Grant instead of her husband.

Under the circumstances, Julia was determined to reject the theater invitation from the Lincolns for the following evening. An overdue visit to the children in Burlington served as an effective excuse as well as a legitimate reason for absence. Julia believed that the conspirators followed her to lunch that day and that John Wilkes Booth himself trailed the Grants to the railroad station. The Grants reached Philadelphia before learning of events at Ford's Theatre; Ulysses then returned to Washington, leaving Julia in the comparative safety of Burlington. In the aftermath of the assassination, none could predict the extent of the conspiracy. Julia believed that a locked railroad car door had foiled a plan to kill Grant on the train traveling to Philadelphia.[36] For his part, Grant regretted his absence from the theater, where he might have stopped Booth.

With Lincoln's tragic death, Grant became the North's single greatest living Civil War hero. Wherever he traveled crowds gathered to honor the victor. Ulysses's innate modesty and Julia's sense of propriety allowed the Grants to move unscathed through a tempest of adulation.

The Grants had come a long way from Galena. Then a couple in modest financial circumstances, still dependent upon Ulysses's father and younger brothers for employment, exiled by circumstance from the Missouri farm life that both preferred, their rise to prominence had been meteoric. Observers then and now have been quicker to marvel at this ascent than the Grants themselves. Julia had always believed that her husband possessed extraordinary qualities that eventually others would discern. Two years of prewar separation had prepared her to live independently during the Civil War. Her own social skills had been acquired in sophisticated St. Louis rather than some backwoods village. She was better prepared than her husband for the world of celebrity and leadership into which both were now thrust.

During the war, Ulysses wrote scores of lengthy letters to Julia, almost all closing with "kisses" for her and the children. Once after Julia visited military hospitals in Nashville and returned with petitions for discharges, her husband reminded her that he dealt with such matters daily. "I want and need a little rest and sunshine."[37] She needed no further reminder. Through victories and defeats in battle, vicissitudes of command, burdens of administration, and crushing responsibilities, Ulysses's love for Julia provided his core of strength and stability.

Grant continued to command the armies during the administration of Andrew Johnson. Detesting the political intrigue of Washington,

Ulysses first attempted to commute from Philadelphia. Finding this impractical, the Grants moved to Washington, living comfortably in a house purchased for them by wealthy admirers.

Grant became entangled in the turmoil he had sought to avoid. He found himself trapped when Johnson pushed a policy of rapid Reconstruction without fundamental Southern changes and congressional Republicans insisted on protection of the civil rights of freedmen. Johnson tried to harness to his cause Grant's immense popularity through having him replace Secretary of War Stanton during a congressional recess. When Congress reconvened and insisted upon Stanton's return, Grant resigned, touching off an acrimonious quarrel with Johnson that led to the impeachment trial, and Grant in turn became the inevitable Republican candidate for president in 1868.

When the Grants moved into the White House in 1869, Julia initially relied on Julia Fish, wife of Secretary of State Hamilton Fish, for guidance in the duties of first lady. Neither Mary Lincoln nor Eliza Johnson, a reclusive invalid, had provided effective role models. Julia plunged into refurbishing the White House; she replaced carpets and reupholstered furniture, hired an excellent chef, and served elegant state dinners.

As in wartime, Julia played little role in executive matters. Her sphere was, instead, personal and domestic. Unlike wartime, the Grants were rarely separated, and both treasured summertimes away from steamy Washington at their cottage in Long Branch, New Jersey, amid their closest friends. When the Civil War ended, the Grants had four school-age children. Fred left for West Point in 1866, Buck for Harvard in 1870, and Nellie for Miss Porter's School in Farmington, Connecticut. Both boys graduated, but Nellie returned almost immediately, preferring Washington society to education. When not quite nineteen, Nellie married Algernon Sartoris in 1874, a much-publicized wedding at which her father was tearful. Sartoris was a dashing Englishman and nephew to abolitionist and actress Fannie Kemble, but the marriage proved a mistake and eventually ended in divorce. The same year as Nellie's wedding, Jesse entered Cornell University, but Buck soon returned home to serve as his father's secretary.

The Grants also brought Colonel Dent to live at the White House. Before his death in 1873, he enjoyed sharing outspoken and outrageous political opinions with Republican visitors, to the delight of both Grants. When Jesse Grant visited Washington, he stayed in hotels, and Hannah never visited. President Grant appointed so many relatives to office that nepotism charges arose. The preponderance were, however, Dents rather than Grants.

Ulysses never wanted to be president and served two terms through a sense of duty and responsibility. On the other hand, Julia loved her years in the White House and made it a pleasant home for her family. Even more delightful were the two and one half years following, when the Grants traveled leisurely around the world. After they returned, supporters failed in an 1880 attempt to nominate Grant for a third term. The Grants settled in New York City, where Ulysses became a silent partner in Buck's investment firm of Grant and Ward, which collapsed in 1884 through the swindles of Ferdinand Ward. Impoverished and suffering from cancer, Ulysses began to write memoirs to support his family, completing that heroic task shortly before his death in 1885. The grieving widow was unable to attend the funeral.

A few years after Ulysses's death, Julia began to write her own memoirs, perhaps initially intending only to provide her children and descendants with a tribute to her beloved Ulysses. Accepting conventions of the day, she emphasized her husband's strength and wisdom and her own frailty and inadequacy. Although she repaid some scores with her husband's enemies, her memoirs generally present an affectionate and cheerful portrait of the life of both Grants. Civil War chapters provide delightful accounts of her naïveté in strategy and politics.

She gave herself less credit than she deserved. For four years she had balanced the needs of four young children with those of her husband. A resident of Galena for only one year before war began, she had no local network of family and friends to assist her with the children or other household responsibilities. Rebel sympathies of too many St. Louis friends and neighbors hindered her from using her old home as a base. Tensions in the Grant family pervaded Covington. Julia had no true home except with her husband. Otherwise she moved from place to place, sometimes boarding with distant relatives or strangers. With her husband's guidance, she assumed responsibility for the children's health and education and the management of the family finances. Simultaneously, she provided Ulysses with relief from the overwhelming cares and responsibilities of command. Her children and her husband needed the affectionate health care that only she could provide. The Grants together prevailed during the Civil War in ways creditable to both. A love story that began at White Haven endured until 1902, when they lay together in Grant's Tomb.

11

From Galena to Appomattox

Grant and Washburne

On April 1, 1840, a Mississippi River steamboat brought to Galena, Illinois, a classic specimen of Yankee. One of eleven children born to an impecunious storekeeper in Livermore, Maine, Elihu B. Washburne had spent his youth toiling on rocky farms. At sixteen he became a printer's apprentice to escape the hated farm labor, but was soon to give this up because of poor health. Still determined to escape farming, he studied for a time at Maine Wesleyan Seminary and later at Harvard Law School while a law clerk in Boston. After admission to the bar in Massachusetts, he hurried west. His original destination was Iowa, but his brother Cadwallader advised him that the booming lead-mining town of Galena offered the best legal possibilities.[1]

Soon Washburne was in virtual partnership with Charles S. Hempstead, a prominent Galena lawyer whose partial paralysis opened his office to the young lawyer. Washburne then struck out on his own, doing quite well as an odd Whig among the local lawyers, and returned to Hempstead in 1845 in a formal partnership sealed by Washburne's marriage to Hempstead's niece. At the age of twenty-seven, already successful in land speculation, Washburne was a delegate to the Whig convention in Baltimore.

Success apparently ran in the family. In the Congress which met on the eve of the Civil War, three Washburns represented as many states: Elihu, Illinois; Cadwallader, Wisconsin; and Israel, Maine. Five Washburn brothers eventually included one secretary of state, two governors, one senator, four representatives, two ambassadors, and one major general—a combination transcending arithmetic.

Washburns traveled all over the world, but spiritually never left

Maine. Elihu's restlessness, industry, brusqueness, independence, and shrewdness forever marked him a transplanted Yankee. He never drank, smoked, or approved of the theater; his antislavery sentiments were sincere. First elected to Congress as a Whig in 1852, Washburne joined the Republican Party as soon as there was a party to join and still kept his seat. This effortless conversion brought him a rich reward: by 1861 he had the longest continuous service of any Republican on the floor of the House.[2]

Washburne's New England antecedents never deflected his devotion to the economic growth of the Midwest; particular attention to matters of local concern separated him from those who attempted a national view. During the Civil War he became a dogged foe of corruption in army contracts and land grants. His persistent attacks on speculators brought him afoul of Radicals who were able to overlook the derelictions of their friends in their concern for a united front against Democrats and secessionists. He led the cry against corruption in Frémont's department in the early days of the war when Radicals sought to use the Republican Frémont in the West as a counterweight to the Democratic McClellan in the East. Washburne's relentless pursuit of Frémont's misdeeds infuriated Thaddeus Stevens, the virtual dictator of the House.[3] As the war progressed, however, Stevens's hard-driving tactics alienated many congressmen who had previously been acquiescent. Washburne's persistent quarrel with Stevens, a liability in the early days of the war, later became an asset.

Washburne's course as self-proclaimed watchdog of the treasury did not make him popular in Washington; one cabinet member called him "the meanest man in the House."[4] Always alert to the extravagant schemes of others, the watchdog slept when his own friends were on the prowl. But he had seniority, the chairmanship of the Committee on Commerce, a friend in the White House, and a long memory. Here was power that deserved respect.

The firing on Fort Sumter ignited a counterblast of oratory in every Northern community. The first war meeting in Galena was addressed by the Democratic mayor, whose hopes for conciliation were badly received; by Washburne, who gave the townspeople what they expected; and, finally, by the local lawyer and prominent Democrat, John A. Rawlins, who electrified the audience with a stirring war speech. Another Democrat, Ulysses S. Grant, a clerk in his father's leather store for the past year, walking home with his brother, told him that he would volunteer for service; brother Orvil then volunteered to keep the store.[5]

Two days later, Galena held another war rally, this time in response to Lincoln's call for troops. Ex-captain Grant was chosen to preside, and, unknown to Grant, Washburne had a hand in his selection.[6] After the meeting, Grant told Washburne that he planned to ask Governor William Dennison of Ohio for a commission. Washburne persuaded him to ask Governor Yates of Illinois instead, promising to introduce and recommend him.[7] Grant's skill in recruiting, outfitting, and training the volunteers, who drilled on the front lawn of the Washburne mansion, confirmed Washburne's favorable first impression.[8] So, as the Galena volunteers marched gaily to the Springfield train, they were followed by a seedy civilian with a carpetbag—a future lieutenant general, currently unemployed.

Despite Washburne's endorsement of his townsman, the commission did not come easily; Yates and Washburne were not friendly.[9] First Yates found Grant a clerk's position in the adjutant general's office and, when Grant had enough of drawing red lines on blank paper, gave him a temporary appointment as mustering officer. But after the regiments were mustered, there was nothing. Grant saw with disgust the political wire-pulling which gave important commands to men without qualifications.[10] Through Washburne he could have played the same game had his standards permitted, but he considered himself a competent soldier and remembered the ethics of his profession. Grant requested a commission from Washington in a letter never honored with a reply, then went to Cincinnati, where he tried in vain for two days to see Major General George B. McClellan.[11] Wherever Grant turned, a dark cloud of old army gossip preceded him. When he returned to Illinois, he learned that Yates had commissioned him as colonel of an unruly regiment that had already used up one colonel. It was not much, it came late; but without Washburne there might have been nothing.

Washburne's first effort in Grant's behalf had been a partial success; his next, which shaped the whole of Grant's Civil War career, developed from his influence with the president. Lincoln had first met Washburne when they had both been in attendance on the Illinois Supreme Court in the winter of 1843–1844. The court met in Lincoln's hometown of Springfield, and he enjoyed spending evenings in the Supreme Court library with out-of-town lawyers, entertaining them with his famous stories or enjoying the flow of legal gossip.[12] The Supreme Court reunion was an annual affair, and Lincoln also met Washburne at the River and Harbor Convention in Chicago in July 1847.[13] When Lincoln went to Washington in December of that year to take his seat in Congress, again he found Washburne, this time practicing before the U.S. Supreme Court and lonely enough for the company of an Illinois Whig to spend much time in Lincoln's room at Mrs. Sprigg's boardinghouse. A little more than a year later, they attended the inaugural ball together, ardent supporters of President Zachary Taylor, with enthusiasm undimmed by the loss of Lincoln's hat in the crowded cloakroom.[14]

Through the next decade they maintained their friendship. After 1852, it was Washburne who was in Congress, and, unlike Lincoln, he remained there. Twice Washburne did his best to further Lincoln's election as U.S. senator, both times strengthening his hold on Lincoln's affections.[15] With Lincoln nominated for the presidency, their positions were again reversed, but not their friendship. In the secession winter, Lincoln picked Washburne as a recipient of a statement of his no-compromise policy, asked him to tell General Winfield Scott confidentially to be ready to hold or retake the federal forts after inauguration day, and even had him make hotel arrangements in Washington.[16] When rumors of plots against his life forced Lincoln to enter Washington off schedule, only Washburne greeted him at the railroad platform.[17]

Washburne and the other Illinois Republican congressmen knew they had the inside track with Lincoln for federal patronage. At the same time they knew that competition among them could cancel this advantage. So they caucused and decided on a single slate of district attorneys, marshals, and territorial officers. They even decided that Senator Trumbull was entitled to two foreign service appointments and Congressmen Washburne and William Kellogg one each.[18] During the emergency session of Congress held that summer, Lincoln was authorized to appoint brigadier generals of volunteers. Again the Illinois congressmen huddled; this time they included the Democrats because it was everybody's war; besides, the Republicans had more votes. So successful was the caucus that six Illinois brigadiers were appointed, two more than the total for any other state.[19] After Washburne had been caught in the mob fleeing to Washington from Bull Run, he had denounced the "clamors of presumptuous ignorance" which had forced the army battle against the judgment of General Scott.[20] All qualms were forgotten, however, when it was possible to make brigadiers of his constituents.

At the time of his promotion to brigadier general, Colonel Grant had taken his regiment to Missouri, but had yet to engage the enemy. He was promoted because he was the likeliest candidate for general from Galena. In a Missouri army camp, a chaplain told his colonel about the list of newly nominated generals he had found in the newspaper. "Well, sir," said Grant, "I had no suspicion of it. . . . That's some of Washburne's work."[21] A month later, Grant wrote Washburne a letter of thanks, saying: "I think I see your hand in it," and promising, "you shall never have any cause to regret the part you have taken."[22]

Grant, with a commission dated back to May 17, stood eighteenth on the list of brigadier generals and thirty-fifth in the chain of command which began with Winfield Scott.[23] Whatever estimate Frémont might put on Grant's abilities, he could not be denied district command. When Brigadier General Benjamin M. Prentiss claimed to outrank Grant, it was Grant who was in the right.[24] When Grant was made commander of the southeast Missouri district, which brought him the opportunity to be the first Union commander to enter Kentucky, his career was fairly launched.

By his action, Washburne had earned Grant's gratitude and had also accepted him as a responsibility. Grant's military career and Washburne's military judgment were now wedded. Washburne's friends complained that he had "Grant on the brain," for the blunt congressman lost no chance to praise his discovery.[25] He helped arrange the appointment of reliable Galena friends to Grant's staff, chief among them the fiery War Democrat Rawlins. In December, Washburne asked Rawlins to give him the truth about Grant and liquor. Rawlins, son of a drunkard, was a temperance fanatic who could be trusted for a harsh judgment on any drinker. He answered that Grant drank rarely and moderately:

> Have no fears; General Grant by bad habits or conduct will never disgrace himself or you, whom he knows and feels to be his best and warmest friend (whose unexpected kindness toward him he will never forget and hopes some time to be able to repay). But I say to you frankly, and I pledge you my word for it, that should General Grant at any time become an intemperate man or an habitual drunkard, I will notify you immediately, will ask to be removed from duty on his staff (kind as he has been to me), or resign my commission.[26]

Had Rawlins failed to report any drinking or other misconduct, word would have come anyway from other Galenians indebted to the congressman for appointments to Grant's staff. The voluminous Washburne manuscripts in the Library of Congress are crammed with reports on Grant from many pens.

There were strong political cross-currents in the Western theater of war. Radicals were infuriated by Lincoln's removal of Frémont from overall command because of his premature proclamation of emancipation, failure to move against the enemy, and inability to control corruption. After Washburne had investigated contract frauds in St. Louis, he became a leading spokesman for the anti-Frémont position.[27] If Henry W. Halleck, the ultimate replacement, was only a professional trying to obey the laws of war and of the United States, he appeared positively proslavery in contrast to Frémont. Wherever a general moved he touched slaves, cotton, contracts, political appointees, and vague legislation; whatever he did could acquire a political connotation. While Grant fought the rebels, Washburne would fight the battle in the rear.

Not least among the dangers to Grant was the presence in his command of three Illinois Democratic congressmen. One of them, Philip B. Fouke, later returned to the House; John A. Logan and John A. McClernand continued with the army. All served under Grant at Belmont, his first engagement; McClernand and Logan remained to share the credit for forts Henry and Donelson. These first major victories of the war were greeted with such enthusiasm that Vice President Hamlin, presiding over the Senate, announced: "It is in order to hurrah."[28] But the House motion of thanks "to Generals Halleck and Grant" was buried by the Military Affairs Committee after Washburne agreed that McClernand and Logan deserved consideration.[29] It was small consolation when far-off Maine sent congratulations to the Illinois troops; the resolution was signed, of course, by Governor Israel Washburn.[30] Elihu would not be unprepared next time; his brother Cadwallader, a colonel, was assigned to Grant's department.[31]

Then came the low point in Grant's Civil War career, and Washburne was able to help him. First removed from command by Halleck over a misunderstanding concerning reports, then restored to command and caught off guard at Pittsburg Landing, Grant needed all the support he could get. The question of the Union preparations at Pittsburg Landing became the subject of newspaper controversy, with several midwest editors demanding the removal of Grant as incompetent and intemperate. Washburne even received complaints from Grant's subordinates.[32]

Answering newspaper charges from his seat in the House, Washburne affirmed: "There is no more temperate man in the Army than General Grant. He never indulges in the use of intoxicating liquors at all."[33] Perhaps the congressman was carried away, for most of his Galena informants on Grant's staff had said only that Grant drank rarely and moderately. Handling the military matter adroitly, Washburne concluded: "No matter whether there was a surprise or not, the manner in which all those gallant troops fought on that day has conferred upon them and upon the country imperishable renown."[34] One thousand copies of the speech were sent to Grant's headquarters for distribution.[35]

John Sherman of Ohio attempted to defend Grant in the Senate.[36] His interest in the matter was equal to Washburne's, for any lack of preparation would have reflected unfavorably on his brother, William Tecumseh. Senator James Harlan of Iowa was willing to have Sherman defend his brother and the Ohio troops, but drew the line at Grant. "I do not think General Grant is fit to command a great army in the field"; those who defended him "carry on their skirts the blood of thousands of their slaughtered countrymen.[37] Sherman reported that his efforts to defend Grant had "little success."[38]

Joseph Medill, editor of the *Chicago Tribune,* would tell Washburne, "I admire your pertinacity and steadfastness in behalf of your friend, but I fear he is played out. The soldiers are down on him."[39] On the same date, William R. Rowley, former clerk of the circuit court in Galena, placed by Washburne on Grant's staff, wrote that Grant would like to have a command in the East.[40] Now second in command under Halleck in the exasperatingly slow advance on Corinth, Grant was disheartened. In a letter to Washburne, he struck, for the first and last time, a plaintive note: "To say that I have not been distressed at these attacks upon me would be false, for I have a father, mother, wife & children who read them and are distressed by them and I necessarily share with them in it. Then too all subject to my orders read these charges and it is calculated to weaken their confidence in me and weaken my ability to render efficient service in our present cause."[41]

The midsummer crisis which took Halleck to Washington put Grant back in command. Halleck, Grant told Washburne, was "a man of gigantic intellect and well studied in the profession of arms. He and I have had several little spats but I like and respect him nevertheless."[42]

"Grant *is* the only regular Army Genl worth a cuss," wrote Cadwallader Washburn to his brother.[43] Elihu agreed; Grant would have his chance.

Trouble struck again late in the year when Grant, massing forces for the Vicksburg campaign, issued his controversial General Orders No. 11, expelling Jews from his department.[44] In both Houses of Congress resolutions of condemnation were offered even after Lincoln revoked the order.[45] Washburne had told Lincoln that Grant's blunder was "the wisest order yet made by a military command. . . . I want to be heard before the final order of revocation goes out. . . . There are two sides to this question."[46] In the House, Washburne moved that the matter be tabled since "this resolution censures one of our best generals without a hearing," an argument which would have been more convincing had Washburne requested a hearing. Washburne carried the motion, but by a close vote of 56–53.[47]

It was perhaps at this time, the start of the Vicksburg campaign, that Washburne ceased to be an asset to Grant. Lincoln's course in promptly revoking and forgetting General Orders No. 11 was wise; Washburne's "pertinacity and steadfastness" could have forced an investigation that might have been fatal to Grant's career.

Washburne, who wanted quick and glorious victories, was dismayed by Grant's campaign against Vicksburg. Brother Cadwallader criticized the Yazoo Pass expedition, for which he believed Grant sent too few men, and Elihu referred the letter to Lincoln.[48] Cadwallader later wrote, "Grant has no plans for taking Vicksburg, and he is frittering away time and strength to no purpose. . . . You cannot make a silk purse out of a sow's ear."[49] J. Russell Jones, Washburne's fellow Galenian and partner in advancing Grant, was equally concerned: "If Grant fails, I shall feel inclined to take to the brush for the next few months. You and I will be speared to death."[50]

Lincoln told Admiral Dahlgren that the canal at Vicksburg "was of no account." Dahlgren noted that Lincoln "looks thin and badly, and is very nervous."[51] Lincoln told his old friend Ward Lamon that "even Washburne, who has always claimed Grant as his by right of discovery, has deserted him and demands his removal; and I really believe I am the only friend Grant has left."[52] In one account, Lincoln put his arm on Washburne's shoulder and said: "Elihu, it is a bad business, but we must try the man a little longer. He seems a pushing fellow, with all his faults."[53]

The evidence that Washburne deserted Grant is far from conclusive, but it is clear that Lincoln had determined to stick by him even under enormous pressure. Medill, always a Grant doubter, said, "I hardly look for much success under copperhead Grant & crazy Sherman."[54] In another letter, which also found its way to Lincoln, Murat Halstead, the Cincinnati editor, called Grant "a jackass in the original package. He is a poor drunken imbecile. . . . Grant will fail miserably, hopelessly, eternally."[55] More serious, perhaps, was the judgment of a Springfield friend: "I have as much confidence in Grant's bravery as any man in the service; but in his capacity to take Vicksburg I have but little." Grant, he wrote, was "there without a plan wa[i]ting to see the Salvation of the lord. . . . Grant . . . would make a good Col. But can't keep House for so large a family."[56]

Grant apparently realized he had a new friend in Washington after Lincoln allowed Halleck to block McClernand's bid for command of the Vicksburg expedition. In an unusually frank letter from Grant to Lincoln about the proposed promotion of Napoleon Bonaparte Buford to major general, Grant asserted: "He would scarcely make a respectable Hospital nurse if put in petticoats. . . . He has always been a dead weight to carry becoming more burthensome with his increased rank."[57] Old friends were still useful, however, and while Grant wrote Lincoln, Rawlins wrote Washburne: "General Buford is a kind hearted and affectionate old gentleman, entertaining views at variance with our republican institutions, and believing the Government of England, because of its titled nobility, much preferable, and further, that the final result of this war will be the overthrow of our present system and give us dukes and lords and titled castes, and that his family will be among the nobility."[58] Both letters urged a promotion for Logan. They were hardly coincidental; they were planned, and their importance lies in the delegation— Grant wrote to Lincoln, Rawlins to Washburne.

After the adjournment of Congress, Washburne visited the army before Vicksburg, arriving in time for the successful crossing of the Mississippi. His letters to Lincoln were as enthusiastic as they were superfluous.[59] By now, Lincoln had read Stanton's reports from Charles A. Dana and General Lorenzo Thomas.[60]

No sooner had Vicksburg fallen than Benjamin Butler heard that Washburne was grooming Grant for the presidency.[61] But Washburne, addressing a triumphal gathering in Washington, praised the administration: "They had ever yielded to the torrent of obloquy that had at one time been heaped upon the pure and noble man, who, under a modest and unpretending exterior, wore the golden heart of a true soldier."[62] And Washburne was among the first to speak to Lincoln of prospects for a second term. An indication of Lincoln's trust in Washburne was embodied in the reply: "A second term would be a great honor and a great labor, which together, perhaps I would not decline, if tendered."[63]

In the next session of Congress, which began in December 1863, not long after Grant's success at Chattanooga, Washburne had no difficulty in passing a resolution of thanks and authorization for a medal, and he was given the responsibility of "getting up" the medal and accompanying scroll.[64] The lieutenant general bill presented more difficulty. Introduced in the House by Washburne, it was commonly understood that this revived rank was intended for Grant; indeed, so strong was the feeling of representatives that they attached an amendment recommending Grant for the rank, an act which raised the issue of intrusion on the president's power of appointment and the Senate's power of confirmation. Through the debates in early January ran a clear political theme: president making.[65]

In his full-length speech on the lieutenant general bill, Washburne spoke only of Grant. "How much, I would ask is now to be required of a general before he can have the confidence of this House?" In addition to his achievements, Washburne emphasized Grant's character: here was a man who had never sought advancement, a modest man who wanted to finish his task, an unpretentious soldier who, in the Vicksburg campaign, for six days carried only one item of baggage—a toothbrush.[66] This last might have given pause to those who remembered another simple soldier who had ridden a jug of hard cider into the White House.

In the end, the bill passed the House, 96–41, and went to the Senate, where it was shorn of mention of Grant. Washburne, on the conference committee, was unable to have it restored. Even so, senators were dubious about Grant. Fessenden of Maine claimed that he voted for the bill under strong pressure, and "most of us were cowards."[67] After Lincoln approved it, he had to fill the position.

Lincoln had already indicated his interest in renomination. If he could have the able Grant in the field, he would want him; if a lieutenant generalcy would move Grant closer to the White House, he might try someone else. He could, after all, elevate Halleck without altering existing field arrangements.

S. S. "Sunset" Cox, the Democratic congressman from Columbus, Ohio, had already given a shrewd analysis of Grant's political position.

"Grant belongs to the Republicans," he told John Hay. "We can't take him after his letter to Washburne. But for that we might have taken him. The Republicans won't take him either."[68] Lincoln, of course, received assurances from Washburne that Grant was no candidate; indeed, Washburne's own loyal support of Lincoln was evidence against Grant's presidential ambitions. He had been firmly advised by Cadwallader to keep Grant out of politics.[69] To be doubly sure, Lincoln spoke to another Galenian, J. Russell Jones, who was able to produce a letter in which Grant disavowed presidential ambitions. Lincoln was pleased, "for when this Presidential grub once gets to gnawing at a man, nobody can tell how far in it has got."[70]

Indeed, Washburne was already planning to put Grant in the White House; "after old Abe is through with his next four years, we will put him in."[71] Following Grant's nomination and confirmation as lieutenant general, he stood to Lincoln and received attention from all official Washington. Washburne could now only shine in reflected glory. As Cadwallader said, "You have crowded him about as hard as he will bear and anything more looks fulsome."[72] Through the spring, Washburne commuted between Grant's headquarters and Washington, busying himself with the promotion of John A. Rawlins and other matters of interest to Grant.[73] Washburne's interest in Grant extended to his middle name, and Grant replied: "In answer to your letter of a few days ago asking what 'S' stands for in my name I can only state *nothing*."[74] It would not be far off the mark to label him Grant's legislative agent. At the same time, a letter from Rawlins indicated that Washburne was regarded at army headquarters with increasing annoyance.[75]

Washburne not only acted as though he had invented Grant; he sought to improve his invention. His French-speaking wife had given him an interest in French customs and history.[76] Washburne, as familiar with the campaigns of Napoleon as any West Pointer, sought in Grant the Napoleonic flair. On the evening before the start of the Wilderness campaign, Grant told his staff at about 11 P.M. that he was going to sleep. "It is said," intoned Washburne, "that Napoleon often indulged in only four hours of sleep, and still preserved all the vigor of his mental faculties." "Well, I, for one, never believed those stories," Grant replied. "If the truth were known, I have no doubt it would be found that he made up for his short sleep at night by taking naps during the day."[77] Lloyd Lewis wrote of Washburne: "He'd bred a Napoleon and got a Coolidge."[78]

As the Army of the Potomac advanced into the Wilderness, Washburne, with permission from Grant to witness the fighting, rode with the headquarters staff and slept in Grant's tent. His black civilian clothes prompted one foot soldier to inquire if Grant had brought along his private undertaker.[79] After a few days of bloody battle, Washburne was ready to return to Washington. On May 11, he breakfasted with Grant, then prepared to leave with a cavalry escort. Reminding Grant that Washington would be anxious for news, he asked to carry some message to Lincoln and Stanton. Grant thought it better military etiquette to address a letter to Halleck. Neither Washburne nor Grant apparently realized the enduring significance of the phrase "fight it out on this line if it takes all summer."[80]

As the summer of 1864 wore on, Washburne became increasingly pessimistic about Lincoln's reelection. He thought the resignation of Salmon P. Chase disastrous and was active in the campaign to force Lincoln to remove Blair from his cabinet.[81] Washburne wrote in August to the chairman of the Republican National Committee: "Were an election to be held now in Illinois we should be beaten."[82] Lincoln wrote one word on the envelope of one of Washburne's despairing letters: "stampeded."[83] Despite his despair, Washburne was a tireless campaigner. He gave a private letter from Grant wide circulation in the press and later asked Grant to refute charges made by Democrats that Lincoln had interfered with Grant's plans.[84] Grant replied: "I have no objection to the President using any thing I have ever written to him as he sees fit. I think however for him to attempt to answer all the charges the opposition will bring against him will be like setting a maiden to work to prove her chastity."[85]

Shortly before election day, Washburne learned that Stanton had refused to divulge the location of some New York regiments to agents sent to distribute ballots. Washburne took the matter to Lincoln after explaining to the disappointed New Yorkers: "While he is a great statesman, he is also the keenest of politicians alive. If it could be done no other way, the president would take a carpet-bag and go around and collect those votes himself."[86] Washburne probably arranged the letter from Grant to Stanton defending voting in the field.[87] Lincoln and Washburne understood each other; after the election a flurry of requests for political favors descended from Galena.

A Washburne request was usually stated in a unique style. Recommending a move up the political ladder for a friend, Washburne would tell Lincoln, "You can stick some other gentleman in his present position." Another friend wanted to see the president, so Nicolay was told: "I will consider it a favor if you & Maj. Hay will run him in at the earliest practicable moment." When a constituent named Coltrin regretted the enlistment of his young son, Washburne scrawled, "Will Captain Ruggles try and *snake* this boy out of the service. Mr. Coltrin is one of the most respectable men in Jo Daviess County."[88]

Lincoln's reelection meant that Grant would be able to bring the war to a successful conclusion. Again Washburne busied himself with Grant's congressional business: Meade's overdue promotion, the exposure of fraud in Ben Butler's department, and staff matters; he even helped to locate a good cook for Mrs. Grant.[89] Washburne continued to use his influence to help his brother Cadwallader.[90] Rawlins now occupied a newly created post: chief of staff, with the rank of brigadier general.[91]

Although Washburne visited Grant in mid-March 1865, the fall of Richmond came with unexpected suddenness while the congressman rested from his labors in Galena. Leaving Galena at 5 P.M. on April 3, he reached Washington on the morning of April 6. Accompanied by James G. Blaine, he hurried to City Point in time to spend an evening with Lincoln on the *River Queen*. The next morning, bearing a letter from the president to his son Robert, now on Grant's staff, he left in search of Grant.[92]

Ironically, Washburne found Grant the day after Lee's surrender. He was warmly welcomed by Grant and his staff, nearly all indebted to him for promotions or favors.[93] Deprived of the privilege of bearing the news of the surrender to Washington, at least he was able to telegraph Lee's farewell order.[94] Washburne remained at City Point, waiting to accompany Grant on a triumphal tour of Richmond, but Grant was busy in Washington making peace; again Grant fell short of the Napoleonic.[95]

There is, of course, a great deal more to be said about Grant and Washburne: of their connection in politics after the war; of Grant's appointment of Washburne as secretary of state for less than two weeks, just long enough to gather prestige for eight years as minister to France; of the tension which developed in 1880 as two old friends both had support for the Republican presidential nomination; and of the final break, with no forgiveness on either side. But perhaps the wartime association can be considered alone.

From his study of democracy in the United States of the 1830s, Alexis de Tocqueville had concluded that a democracy goes to war with an army rusted by disuse and commanded by generals lacking vigor. But, says Tocqueville:

> As the war attracts more and more of public attention and is seen to create high reputations and great fortunes in a short space of time, the choicest spirits of the nation enter the military profession; all the enterprising, proud, and martial minds, no longer solely of the aristocracy, but of the whole country, are drawn in this direction. As the number of competitors for military honors is immense, and war drives every man to his proper level, great generals are always sure to spring up. A long war produces upon a democratic army the same effects that a revolution produces upon a people; it breaks through regulations and allows extraordinary men to rise above the common level.[96]

True enough; yet the selection of Union generals was never free of political considerations. Party loyalties, sectional bonds, and personal entanglements were never forgotten in an age of superheated politics. Politicians intrigued for important commands, while military professionals competed against them. In this struggle for command, an obscure ex-captain, dogged by old army gossip concerning his fondness for drink, would stand little chance. He needed influential friends—and he didn't have any.

Grant had once been badly hurt by political maneuvering when he failed to get the post of county engineer of St. Louis.[97] A sensitive man, unable to bear rebuffs and failures, he detested politics. When he wrote to Washington for a commission in May 1861, both Governor Yates and Senator Trumbull offered to endorse his letter, but Grant politely declined.[98] Although aware of the political implications of the conduct of the Civil War, he chose to ignore them. His avoidance of politics helped to make him a great general; at the same time, he was continually vulnerable to those who chose to make political capital of his military career. He needed a political manager; Washburne assumed the job.

Nearly every member of Congress who was not a diehard opponent of the war had his pet officers to protect and advance, just as Washburne had Grant. Sponsorship of Grant was part of Washburne's political program of picking successful generals or furthering the military careers of useful men. In addition to Grant, he helped McClernand, Logan, Stephen A. Hurlbut, and others, to say nothing of his brother Cadwallader.

As Grant had moved up the ladder of command, he had brought with him a host of Galenians, largely to please Washburne. Among the generals from a town of some ten thousand were Grant, Rawlins, Augustus L. Chetlain, Jasper Maltby, William R. Rowley, and two named John Smith.[99] All in all, Congressman Washburne made a good thing of the war, and services rendered to Grant were amply repaid. In 1869, President Grant would appoint two Galenians, Washburne and Rawlins, to his original cabinet; neither was a wise appointment.

Even a conscientious reader of Grant's *Memoirs* may forget a man named Washburne who is mentioned only four times, twice fleetingly. The memory of the nomination quarrel in 1880 was still fresh in Grant's mind as he wrote, less than five years later. In a sense, Washburne reciprocated, for, although he lived in Chicago for the last ten years of his life, occupying himself industriously with the activities of the Chicago Historical Society, he wrote almost nothing about his association with Grant.

Neither assisted, then, in analyzing the Grant-Washburne relationship, but perhaps this much can be concluded: Grant was fortunate in living in Galena when the Civil War began. He had slight chance for a regiment, even less for a general command, without the intervention of an effective politician. Later, endangered by unpleasant relations with his superior, Halleck, and a public outcry after Shiloh, Grant might have succumbed without Washburne. But Washburne had his limitations: he spoke for a narrow Western economic interest, lacked finesse in debate, and antagonized unnecessarily by injecting politics into military matters. In time he would be a liability to Grant.

But whatever his faults, whatever harm he did Grant, it is easy to understand Grant's extended loyalty. In the early days of the war, when political considerations took precedence over professional qualifications in assigning command, Washburne had done big things for an unprepossessing townsman. Perhaps Tocqueville had been correct in sanguine prediction that a democratic nation could discover its natural leaders during a long war; but for Grant, and for Washburne, there was no assurance.

12

That Obnoxious Order

"That obnoxious order," Julia Dent Grant called it. She disliked General Orders No. 11, issued by her husband, Major General Ulysses S. Grant, on December 17, 1862. The order read:

> I. The Jews, as a class, violating every regulation of trade established by the Treasury Department, and also Department orders, are hereby expelled from the Department. II. Within twenty-four hours from the receipt of this order by Post Commanders, they will see that all of this class of people are furnished with passes and required to leave, and any one returning after such notification, will be arrested and held in confinement until an opportunity occurs of sending them out as prisoners unless furnished with permits from these Head Quarters. III. No permits will be given these people to visit Head Quarters for the purpose of making personal application for trade permits.

Why did Grant issue such an order? This remains a puzzle with only a partial solution.

On the day of the order's issue, Grant advanced into Mississippi along the line of the Mississippi Central Railroad and reached Oxford. From there he instructed Major General William T. Sherman to lead an expedition down the Mississippi River to Vicksburg, the ultimate objective of Grant's campaign.

Though he planned a pincer's movement on the Confederate citadel, Grant knew relatively little about the strength of the army before him or of the Vicksburg defenses. Already two Confederate cavalry commanders, Major General Earl Van Dorn and Brigadier General Nathan B. Forrest, were preparing to cut Grant's supply line. They struck three days later: Van Dorn at Holly Springs, Mississippi; Forrest farther north, in Tennessee.

On December 17, Grant knew that his army had advanced deep into Mississippi with a tenuous supply line, that enemy forces remained intact and mobile, and that his divided army ran the risk of fighting the same Confederate forces on separate fields. Given his military anxieties, he could hardly be expected to devote enough thought to matters of trade. But such concerns constantly intruded.

Grant's victory at Fort Donelson, Tennessee, in February 1862 had cracked the Confederate defense line in Tennessee, opening part of the cotton kingdom to Federal occupation, and through the year, as U.S. armies advanced, more of the plantation South came within Federal lines. The outbreak of war had so increased the value of cotton in the North and in Europe that planters continued to grow it, despite the Confederate embargo. By the end of the year, Grant's advance carried him toward the richest plantations, some storing both 1861 and 1862 crops.

A confused and ambivalent U.S. government policy on trade provided generous loopholes for the enterprising and unscrupulous. When war began, Secretary of the Treasury Salmon P. Chase moved immediately to halt the shipping of "munitions of war" to the Confederacy, but not until August 1861 did President Abraham Lincoln give the treasury authority to regulate trade with insurrectionary regions. Chase believed that trade should follow the flag, and as armies moved southward, treasury agents gave permits to loyal citizens to resume normal commerce. Such a policy, Chase believed, would reconcile citizens to the federal government and benefit the Northern economy through the flow of needed Southern products.

What looked sound and sensible from Washington looked disgraceful from army headquarters in Mississippi, where everyone knew how often goods traded by "loyal" persons behind the lines seeped southward to the Confederacy in exchange for cotton. The war had cut off the supply of cotton to New England mills and the world market, multiplying traditional prices. The government expected the army to seize captured and abandoned cotton for sale to benefit the treasury, thus defraying the staggering cost of war and ending the cotton famine. But as the army advanced, patriotic Confederates burned their cotton, rather than lose their hoards without payment and help the North win the war. Rebels aware of the imminent arrival of the enemy and reluctant to torch their only capital asset did have an alternative. Traders or their agents who slipped through the lines offered gold, weapons, or medicine in return for these doomed bales. Such illegal and unpatriotic practices were lucrative enough to warrant the risk, and speculators who bought the cotton stood to make sufficient profit to enable them to bribe officers and officials to look away or even to assist as they smuggled cotton through the lines. Once through the lines, cotton might pass through different hands on the way to market, and smuggled bales, looking the same as those from occupied regions, defied efforts to trace their origin.

Wartime cotton trade in the Mississippi Valley outraged patriotic Northerners, soldiers and civilians alike. Unscrupulous traders enabled Confederates to fight more effectively by supplying gold and scarce goods, deprived the U.S. Treasury of revenue, and corrupted the military. Officers and journalists frequently blamed this trade on Jews.

When the war began, some 150,000 Jews lived in the United States, about two-thirds of whom, born abroad, had crossed the Atlantic for much the same reasons motivating other recent immigrants from Europe. Like other immigrants, they more often settled in the North than the South and disproportionately in cities. Whether or not they were disproportionate participants in the wartime cotton trade cannot be determined, but contemporaries wrote as if they were. An 1863 investigation of cotton buying in the Mississippi Valley involved hundreds of soldiers and civilians, only four of them Jewish. Some ugly remarks about "Jew traders" may have been intended as insults to non-Jewish traders, but nonetheless had the effect of strengthening the impression that Jews dominated the cotton business.

Seeking the roots of this prejudice requires turning to the mass immigration of earlier years. In one decade, 1845–1854, 2,939,000 newcomers, largely from Germany and Ireland, added some 14.5 percent to the population of the United States. Such enormous numbers created social, economic, and political strains on Americans who called themselves natives, a group that always excluded the Indians. The sins of the Irish included voting Democratic and practicing Catholicism, the latter a source of outrage to many Protestants who found difficulty enough in tolerating each other. Between 1834 and the late 1850s, religious rioting erupted in many cities, and some twenty Catholic churches were burned in places ranging from Maine to Texas. Resentment of foreigners and their religions gave rise to political groups of nativists. This reached high tide in the Know-Nothing surge of 1854 and the American Party of 1856.[1] Before thinking better of it, Grant attended one meeting of a Know-Nothing lodge after his rejection for the post of county engineer in St. Louis in favor of a German immigrant.

Immigration ebbed and the slavery controversy grew as the Civil War approached, but nativism never disappeared. Tensions and animosities from the preceding decade provided tinder awaiting a spark. Ethnic and religious stereotypes remained a staple for newspaper articles. Cotton speculation, a risky and immoral enterprise, would naturally attract Jews and Yankees, some assumed, so the stereotypes and accusations circulated unencumbered.

Before the Civil War, American Jews lacked national organization, and generally those North or South followed regional politics and practices. Rabbis who took stands on slavery usually reflected their location, but one in New York City had defended slavery as sanctioned by the Bible, while another in slaveholding Baltimore acquired a reputation as an abolitionist.

When war began, Jews enlisted in local regiments much like their fellow citizens. Ultimately, an estimated ten thousand Jewish soldiers served North and South. But, especially in the North, many Jews enlisted in regiments in groups. When Grant issued General Orders No. 11, the highest-ranking Jewish officer in his command, Lieutenant Colonel Marcus M. Spiegel, 120th Ohio, son of a German rabbi, was with his regiment on Sherman's expedition to Vicksburg.

General Orders No. 11 was not the first major Civil War controversy involving Jews. The Volunteer Act of 1861 required that each chaplain be a "regularly ordained minister of some Christian denomination." This language excluded rabbis, but provided the first recognition of the right of Roman Catholic priests to serve as chaplains. Rabbi Arnold Fischel, representing the Board of Delegates of American Israelites, won the support of Lincoln, and after one year the law was amended to read "a regularly ordained minister of some religious denomination."

Although Jews were more numerous in the North, they were more prominent in the South, if only because Judah P. Benjamin, former U.S. senator from Louisiana, held (at various times) three different cabinet posts in the Confederate government. Confederates were not, however, immune to the anti-Semitism embodied in Grant's orders. Critics of Benjamin in the South as well as the North constantly harped on his ancestry. Confederates in Thomasville, Georgia, asserting that German

Jews passed counterfeit money and raised prices through speculation, demanded their expulsion from Thomasville. Prejudice pervaded both North and South; Grant hardly invented it.

Grant's imperial Department of the Tennessee stretched from northern Mississippi to Cairo, Illinois, and from the Mississippi River to the Tennessee River. Within this domain, he delegated administrative duties to subordinates while concentrating his attention on the armies moving southward. But he could not ignore the civil problems of his department. Both Grant and Sherman vehemently but fruitlessly protested current trade regulations as fostering fraud and corruption. Constantly vexed by the cotton trade, Grant fell prey to the pervasive anti-Semitism of the day.

On July 26, 1862, Grant telegraphed from Corinth, Mississippi, to his subordinate at Columbus, Kentucky. "Examine the baggage of all speculators coming South, and, when they have specie, turn them back. If medicine and other contraband articles, arrest them and confiscate the contraband articles. Jews should receive special attention." On November 9, he telegraphed to Major General Stephen A. Hurlbut at Memphis: "Refuse all permits to come south of Jackson for the present. The Isrealites especially should be kept out." The following day, Grant instructed his superintendent of military railroads: "Give orders to all the conductors . . . on the road that no Jews are to be permitted to travel on the Rail Road southward from any point[.] They may go north and be encouraged in it but they are such an intolerable nuisance. That the Department must be purged for them." Even so, when Colonel John Van Deusen Du Bois issued orders on December 8 expelling "Cotton-Speculators, Jews and other Vagrants" from Holly Springs, Grant immediately ordered them revoked as violating instructions from Washington encouraging cotton shipping from the South.

Grant's prompt revocation of Du Bois's order makes more puzzling his issuance of similar orders within a few days. The timing suggests that Grant's rage was ignited by the arrival of his father in Mississippi to buy cotton for a Jewish firm in Cincinnati in return for one-quarter of the profits. Jesse R. Grant was no simpleton ensnared by crafty speculators. A shrewd and aggressive businessman, he rose from poverty to affluence through attention to business. A neighbor remembered him as one willing "to follow a dollar to hell."

Jesse's relationship with his son was complex. It was the father who had arranged the son's appointment to West Point, but Ulysses said, "I won't go." Later, young Grant responded that "he thought I would, *and I thought so too, if he did.*" When Ulysses resigned from the army fifteen years later, his father-in-law rather than his father tried to help him establish a farm, and when necessity eventually drove him to his family's leather store in Galena, Illinois, he worked for a younger brother for a less-than-generous salary.

Jesse's efforts to defend his son in newspapers and to gain military appointments for friends embarrassed the general. But Ulysses never broke with his father and through his rise to fame during the Civil War frequently wrote to him, apparently seeking his approval. However, Jesse's attempt to use his paternity as a source of cotton profits was the last straw. On the eve of his father's arrival, Ulysses complained of "speculators whose patriotism is measured by dollars & cents. Country has no value with them compared to money." Suddenly he realized that his father fit this condemnation. Ulysses displaced his anger, lashing out at his father's Jewish partners.

Grant's anger appeared even more clearly in a letter written the day the orders were issued, addressed to Assistant Secretary of War Christopher P. Wolcott.

> I have long since believed that in spite of all the vigilance that can be infused into Post Commanders that the Specie regulations of the Treasury Dept. have been violated, and that mostly by Jews and other unprincipled traders. So well satisfied of this have I been that I instructed the Commdg Officer at Columbus to refuse all permits to Jews to come south, and frequently have had them expelled from the Dept. But they come in with their Carpet sacks in spite of all that can be done to prevent it. The Jews seem to be a privileged class that can travel any where. They will land at any wood yard or landing on the river and make their way through the country. If not permitted to buy Cotton themselves they will act as Agents for some one else who will be at a Military post, with a Treasury permit to receive Cotton and pay for it in Treasury notes which the Jew will buy up at an agreed rate, paying gold. There is but one way that I know of to reach this case. That is for Government to buy all the Cotton at a fixed rate and send it to Cairo, St Louis or some other point to be sold. Then all traders, they are a curse to the Army, might be expelled.

Grant's reference in his orders to Jews as a "class" made no sense and created considerable confusion in enforcement. Several officers asked whether the orders applied to Jewish sutlers, the licensed traders who accompanied regiments. At least one Jewish officer resigned. Captain Philip Trounstine, 5th Ohio Cavalry, writing from Moscow, Tennessee, explained that he was "either fortunately or unfortunately born of Jewish parents"; that he owed "filial affection to my parents, Devotion to my Religion, and a deep regard for the opinion of my friends" and could "no longer, bear the taunts and malice, of those to whom my religious opinions are known."

Information about enforcement within the Department of the Tennessee remains hazy, but the orders were zealously enforced at Paducah, Kentucky, where Jews were expelled on twenty-four-hour notice. Entire families were driven from their homes. Two women lying ill were exempt; two army veterans were not. In his inaugural address in 1869, President Grant stated: "I know no method to secure the repeal of bad or obnoxious laws so effective as their stringent execution." Nowhere had this been more effectively demonstrated than in Paducah, where Jewish leaders began a protest eventually heard in Washington.

Cesar F. Kaskel of Paducah, barred from telegraphing Grant under terms of the orders, telegraphed to Lincoln instead. Then he proceeded toward Washington, along the way visiting or writing to Jewish leaders to create pressure against the orders. Kaskel headed toward the right man. During the 1850s, Lincoln had flatly rejected any political advantage through harnessing nativism and in 1855 wrote:

I am not a Know-Nothing. That is certain. How could I be? How can any one who abhors the oppression of negroes, be in favor of degrading classes of white people? Our progress in degeneracy appears to me to be pretty rapid. As a nation, we began by declaring that "all men are created equal." We now practically read it "all men are created equal, except negroes." When the Know-Nothings get control, it will read "all men are created equal, except negroes, and foreigners, and catholics." When it comes to this I should prefer emigrating to some country where they make no pretence of loving liberty—to Russia, for instance, where despotism can be taken pure, and without the base alloy of hypocrasy.

Lincoln apparently knew nothing about Grant's orders until Kaskel arrived. After hearing Kaskel, Lincoln wrote a note—unfortunately lost—to Major General Henry W. Halleck. In response, on January 4, 1863, Halleck sent Grant a characteristically cautious telegram. "A paper purporting to be a Genl Order No. 11 issued by you Dec 17th had been presented here. By its term it expells all Jews from your Dept. If such an order has been issued, it will be immediately revoked." On the following day, Colonel John C. Kelton in Halleck's office wrote to Grant, "Permit me to inform you unofficially the objection taken to your Genl Order No 11. It excluded a whole class, insted of certain obnoxious individuals. Had the word 'pedler' been inserted after Jew I do not suppose any exception would have been taken to the order. Several officers and a number of enlisted men in your Dept are Jews. A Govr of one of the Western states is a Jew." Kelton presumably meant Governor Edward Salomon of Wisconsin, who was a Lutheran.

People of the period knew far more about stereotypes than they knew about Jews. Just how successfully Grant and his subordinates could identify Jews remains problematical; had Grant known more about Jews, he would have remembered those who fought in his army.

Halleck himself wrote to Grant on January 21: "It may be proper to give you some explanation of the revocation of your order expelling all Jews from your Dept. The President has no objection to your expelling traders & Jew pedlars, which I suppose was the object of your order, but as it in terms prescribed an entire religious class, some of whom are fighting in our ranks, the President deemed it necessary to revoke it."

After receiving Halleck's telegram, Grant revoked the orders. Consequently, Congress tabled censure resolutions introduced in the House and Senate. General Orders No. 11 might then have been forgotten. But its author entered politics.

General Orders No. 11 received more newspaper coverage in 1868 than when it first appeared. After Grant's 1868 presidential nomination, Democratic newspapers revived the issue, encouraging Jewish voters, then usually Republican, to switch party allegiance. Democratic attack inspired Republican counterattack. Had Grant acted on orders from Washington? This thought was first raised in 1863 by Jesse Grant and by newspapers. Accounts of Grant's instructions did contradict one another. However, no documentary evidence existed that would absolve Grant of responsibility.

Had Assistant Secretary of War Wolcott or someone else in

Washington expressed the anti-Semitism reflected in General Orders No. 11, giving Grant a sense of direction when he struck out at cotton traders? It is interesting to note that Grant, though not writing as one obeying orders, explained his actions to Wolcott in his December 17 letter. Wolcott was a man to whom Grant had never before addressed any communication.

Grant partisans tried other postwar political explanations for the embarrassing order, shifting blame to a staff officer or some other subordinate. Grant's other statements concerning Jews remained unpublicized, so this seemed a plausible tactic. But as election fever grew hot, this alibi failed. Grant did not disclaim personal responsibility. Instead, on September 17, 1868, he wrote to his old friend Isaac N. Morris, who had forwarded a letter from a concerned Jewish voter. The general replied:

> I do not pretend to sustain the order. At the time of its publication I was incensed by a reprimand received from Washington for permitting acts which Jews within my lines were engaged in. There were many other persons within my lines equally bad with the worst of them, but the difference was that the Jews could pass with impunity from one army to the other, and gold, in violation of orders, was being smuggled through the lines at least so it was reported. The order was issued and sent without any reflection and without thinking of the Jews as a sect or race to themselves, but simply as persons who had successfully (I say successfully, instead of persistently, because there were plenty of others within my lines who envied their success,) violated an order, which greatly inured to the help of the rebels. Give Mr. Moses assurance that I have no prejudice against sect or race, but want each individual to be judged by his own merit. Order No. 11 does not sustain this statement, I admit, but then I do not sustain that order. It never would have been issued if it had not been telegraphed the moment it was penned and without reflection.

Grant's assumption of responsibility, however, did not explain his earlier instructions concerning Jews. His somewhat defensive tone indicates Grant had not yet grasped the magnitude of his offense.

Presidential campaign pressures forced Grant to write something for publication on a topic he did not want to discuss, and through the remainder of his life he chose to maintain public silence about his expulsion of the Jews. The incident received no mention in the two volumes of his *Memoirs,* and even today is better known in American Jewish history than in Civil War history. Grant's wife, however, remembered his speaking of "that obnoxious order" and of the congressional resolutions he said were deserved, "as he had no right to make an order against any special sect."

13

The Road to Appomattox

The Generalship of Ulysses S. Grant

On May 4, 1864, Ulysses S. Grant crossed the Rapidan River in Virginia to attack the army of Confederate general Robert E. Lee. For the first time, Grant wore the regulation uniform of a lieutenant general, including vest, sash, sword, and a pair of fancy gloves. Almost immediately, Grant's forces were fiercely engaged in the Wilderness, a region of second-growth timber that would become synonymous with brutal bloodshed. Gradually, Grant shed the trappings of his dress uniform; a few days later, as he sat under a tree pondering the military situation and whittling absentmindedly, he forgot to take off his gloves and ruined them. For the rest of the campaign, he dressed in the uniform of a private, with only the three stars on his shoulder indicating his rank.

Following an unbroken string of successes in the Western theater, Grant had been called to Washington as general in chief in March 1864. He left his predecessor, Major General Henry W. Halleck, an able administrator, in the capital to issue orders while Grant himself accompanied the Army of the Potomac in the field without displacing Major General George G. Meade as its commander. These measures freed him from paperwork in Washington and military detail in Virginia while maintaining control of strategy, strengthening the morale of the Army of the Potomac, and implementing a modern command system.

Although he had thought full uniform appropriate to his new command, he had already acquired a reputation among Western troops for plain dress and lack of ostentation. Generals of the Army of the Potomac often wore sashes; military regalia always counted heavily. Spotting Meade's headquarters flag, Grant had asked whether imperial

Caesar was nearby. Grant's uniform was a minor reflection of an ambivalent relationship with the military that began when he entered the U.S. Military Academy only because his father insisted upon it. He remained in the army for eleven years after graduation largely because nothing better turned up, and he returned to the army when the Civil War began from a sense of obligation.

Once Grant grappled with Lee, he dressed for dirty work. Heavy losses in the Wilderness and beyond—at Spotsylvania, Cold Harbor, and Petersburg—justified Grant's skepticism toward military pomp. These bloody casualty figures have forever shadowed Grant's reputation, and he has been called a butcher who followed a strategy of annihilation and an inept commander who overwhelmed a foe possessing true military genius but not enough shoes and bacon. There is, of course, more to it than that.

As Grant took heavy losses in the Wilderness and yet pushed on, never disengaging from Lee except to move closer to Richmond, he implemented the Union's first coordinated strategic plan to defeat the Confederacy. The overwhelming numerical superiority of the Army of the Potomac had existed ever since General George B. McClellan had threatened Richmond in 1862, but this massive superiority had previously yielded only defeat in Virginia and angry frustration when the Confederates escaped intact after repulses at both Antietam and Gettysburg.

Grant intended to make all U.S. armies play a role in one campaign designed to crush or bisect the Confederacy. While Grant engaged Lee, General Benjamin F. Butler's Army of the James was ordered to close on Richmond from the south, and General Franz Sigel's forces would move up the Shenandoah Valley. In the West, General William Tecumseh Sherman's mighty hosts would advance into Georgia, while General Nathaniel P. Banks was expected to march from Louisiana to Mobile, Alabama, to close a key Southern seaport and to threaten the rear of the Confederate defenders of Georgia.

By midsummer nothing seemed to be working except Sherman's advance, and for Grant to pull back would allow Lee to detach troops to defend Georgia. Grant's dispatches leave no doubt about his intentions. "Lee's Army will be your objective point," he had written to Meade; "wherever Lee goes there you will go also." In effect, Grant was achieving more by bloody stalemate in the Virginia campaign than Meade had accomplished with victory at Gettysburg. The key to success lay in relentless coordinated pressure against the army and resources of the South.

The road to Richmond had led the Army of the Potomac through years of frustration and hardship, something Grant could understand. His last years in the old army had been spent on the Pacific Coast, separated from his wife and two children, one of whom he had never seen. Resigning from the army in 1854 to begin a new life as a farmer, he had failed in the Panic of 1857 and had held a variety of uncongenial jobs afterward, culminating with employment in his father's leather-goods store in Galena, Illinois, under the supervision of a younger brother. Upon his return to the army, after seven years of frustration, he showed no strong signs of ambition, but instead a workmanlike approach to military command.

When the war began, Grant wrote to his father that "we are now in the midst of trying times when evry one must be for or against his country. . . . Having been educated for such an emergency, at the expense of the Government, I feel that it has upon me superior claims, such claims as no ordinary motives of self-interest can surmount." At no point did the leather-store clerk suggest that the war represented an opportunity to better his station in life. In this he followed the pattern established at age seventeen when his father forced him to attend West Point. Later he recoiled from the battlefield horrors of the Mexican War, questioned the justification for the conflict, and hoped to leave the army to teach or to farm. Having resigned from the army in 1854 to reunite his family, only a profound sense of duty could call him back to service in 1861.

His military education was equal to that of all other aspirants to command, in fact, exactly the same. Graduating at almost precisely the midpoint of his class at West Point—twenty-first of thirty-nine—he had neither succumbed completely to the attractions of his courses nor neglected them. Reading his lessons over once rather than studying intently gave him more time to read novels, and his natural aptitude for mathematics compensated for deficiencies in French, a subject emphasized to prepare young officers to read the literature of Napoleon's campaigns, something Grant never did. Looking for an opportunity to serve his country in 1861, he attracted the attention of Illinois governor Richard Yates, not because he knew how Napoleon fought at Austerlitz, but because he understood the mysteries of army regulations and the duties of adjutant, quartermaster, and commissary officer. As Grant put it, "At present I am on duty with the Governer . . . occupation principally smoking and occationally giving advice as to how an order should be communicated &c."

When he assumed command of the Seventh Congressional District Regiment in Illinois, Grant's military style emerged. "Governor Yates's Hellions," an undisciplined bunch of farm boy rowdies, came to understand that their new colonel enforced military discipline. Unlike a previous colonel, who vacillated between Napoleonic bombast and willingness to accompany chicken-stealing expeditions, Grant established clear expectations of appropriate conduct, tempering the rigidity of the professional army with policy better suited to citizen volunteers. Building on years of army experience, Grant remained a learner. Sent against Confederate colonel Thomas Harris in Missouri, Grant felt his heart mount to his throat as he approached the enemy, but found that Harris had abandoned camp. "It occurred to me at once that Harris had been as much afraid of me as I had been of him. This was a view of the question I had never taken before; but it was one I never forgot afterwards." Grant began to study the celebrated tactics of William J. Hardee, then realized they embodied only "common sense and the progress of the age" applied to the older system of General Winfield Scott. Above all, Grant learned that "there are no fixed laws of war. . . . The laws of successful war in one generation would insure defeat in another."

In September 1861 he displayed initiative in occupying Paducah after the Confederates had been the first to violate the self-proclaimed neutrality of Kentucky by seizing Columbus. He had asked permission for his expedition from Major General John C. Frémont in St. Louis, but steamed from Cairo, Illinois, before orders arrived. His proclamation to the people of Paducah, stating "I have nothing to do with opinions," gave assurance of his purely military motives. Such lucid phrasing was characteristic: throughout the war his orders, reports, and correspondence nearly always reflected the clarity of his thought. His early-displayed aptitude for mathematics served him well in applying logic to the complex problems of command, detaching them from either the political or the emotional.

His first battle, at Belmont, Missouri, in November 1861, was a jumbled affair that brought him both praise and criticism. The capture of Fort Donelson, Tennessee, in February 1862, the first major Union victory of the war, won him both a commission as major general and universal acclaim that helped him survive a barrage of criticism when, two months later, he was surprised at Shiloh. When Grant demanded the unconditional surrender of Fort Donelson from Confederate general Simon B. Buckner, the phrase captured public attention because of both its succinctness and its echo of Grant's initials. Buckner labeled the demand "ungenerous and unchivalrous," but he was without alternatives. Closely examined, Buckner's complaint evaporates: McClellan may have lacked the aggressive drive to surround and besiege a Confederate army, but if he had, he too would have demanded its unconditional surrender. Grant's terms reflected the logical outcome of an overwhelming victory, and it was his repeated successes—the capture of two armies and near destruction of a third—that brought his appointment to overall command in 1864.

Understood in context, Grant's Fort Donelson terms represent only military mastery combined with clearheaded policy. He had no intention of humiliating or punishing his adversaries; he did intend to take direct action to suppress the rebellion. That he clearly distinguished between ascendancy and arrogance is seen in his order allowing captured Confederate officers to retain their sidearms—foreshadowing a similar provision at the final surrender at Appomattox—a gesture that proved unrealistic in Northern prison camps.

Nor is arguing that McClellan might have demanded the unconditional surrender of the Confederates at Fort Donelson the same as asserting that Grant's action represented only conventional military thinking. From his entrance into the Civil War, Grant exhibited both a high degree of standard professionalism and also something that set him apart from other commanders. The second set of qualities represents the essence of his generalship. He understood the strengths and limitations of his volunteer soldiers and proved an excellent judge of his principal subordinates. Both Sherman and Philip H. Sheridan, for all their prominence and responsibility before the end of the war, needed Grant's firm hand to bring out their strengths. Only Grant could have found the proper role for Halleck in Washington in 1864 that made use of his superb administrative strength without allowing his caution to interfere with strategy.

From start to finish of the war, Grant accepted responsibility for whatever command he held and used available resources, never asking for an increase of force or authority. Before launching the 1864 campaign, Grant wrote to Lincoln that "should my success be less than I desire, and expect, the least I can say is, the fault is not with you."

At no point did Grant, who had married into a Southern family and become, however briefly, a slaveholder himself, show a special animosity toward Confederates. On the contrary, he appeared sensitive to suffering on both sides. Grant reaffirmed his sympathy for the South late in life when a reporter introduced himself as a former Confederate soldier who had fought at Fort Donelson and Champion's Hill: "I was fighting not *against* the South, but *for* it. In every battle I felt a sympathy for you, and I felt that I was fighting for North and South—for the whole nation." How could such a man have developed a strategy of annihilation? The increasing bitterness of the conflict requires another explanation.

On January 1, 1863, what had been a rebellion that might conceivably end through negotiation became a struggle that could end only when the Confederacy collapsed. This change occurred not because Grant had demanded unconditional surrender but because the momentum of conflict had forced the North to assault slavery. Through the preceding year, Lincoln had explored every avenue of negotiation with the border states for peaceful emancipation and had been rebuffed by slaveholding loyalists and undermined by Northern Republicans. To Confederate leaders, any resolution without the preservation of slavery remained unacceptable, even unthinkable. Once emancipation became Northern policy, the war took on a new bitterness that increased as Southern suffering mounted.

As the war began, Grant had written of his apprehension of a slave insurrection, assuming that North and South would join forces to suppress it. Through the early days of the conflict, he carefully followed government policy regarding slaves, exhibiting a sure instinct in avoiding political issues. At midpoint, the war to preserve the Union changed, not through Grant's wishes and intentions but through the momentum of the struggle itself, into a war against slavery in which the slaves themselves fought to achieve their freedom. Grant's generalship in subsequent campaigns was influenced in several ways by the changed conditions that resulted.

Like other conventionally trained officers, and civilians also, Grant at first underestimated the fighting ability of former slaves. But their heroic defense of Milliken's Bend, Louisiana, in June 1863 converted him to a position, never abandoned, that this new resource, like the railroad and telegraph, should enter into military calculations. Grant's use of black troops, freemen and former slaves, received relatively little attention because of his avoidance of dramatics. Characteristically, he conscientiously followed orders from Washington when any reluctance might easily have hampered implementation of the new policy. By the close of the war, the large number of black troops available at Petersburg gave him the opportunity to launch the Appomattox campaign; finally, he had enough troops to hold the siege lines and also to break free on Lee's flank.

Southern intransigence concerning black troops caused the breakdown of prisoner exchanges in early 1864. Confederate insistence on returning captured blacks to their former masters and treating white officers of the U.S. Colored Troops as criminals exacerbated unresolved issues of accounting for troops by regular man-for-man exchange and influenced Grant to suspend negotiations for further exchanges. By midsummer Grant recognized that regular exchanges benefited the South more than the North, if only because he believed that released Confederates returned immediately to the ranks while Union troops more often went home to recuperate. By his grim arithmetic, imprisoned rebels "amount to no more than dead men." Exchanged, they would fight on until their metaphorical status became real.

Grant's calculations condemned thousands to the sufferings of Andersonville while bringing the end of war closer. Throughout the war, death from disease outstripped the loss in battle, and the humane path was never clear. By 1864, with all hope of negotiation extinguished, the only way to end the loss of life was to end the war. Hindsight convinces us that Gettysburg and Vicksburg turned the tide of war toward inevitable Northern victory, but only because Confederate armies won no smashing victories afterward, and leaves unfounded Lincoln's apprehension in the summer of 1864 that the Democrats would capture the White House and abandon the struggle to reclaim the South.

"This is essentially a People's contest," Lincoln had told Congress in July 1861, in a message explaining and justifying the coming of war. Here, as elsewhere, Lincoln repeatedly used the word "people" in a variety of contexts. For some historians, however, a people's contest means something quite different: a war of populations rather than armies, something the Civil War became as armies ceased to respect civilian rights and began to subsist on or to destroy civilian resources. Grant himself has become associated with a new strategy of annihilation and policy of unconditional surrender. He commented on the widening scope of war in his *Memoirs*.

Up to the battle of Shiloh I, as well as thousands of other citizens, believed that the rebellion against the Government would collapse suddenly and soon, if a decisive victory could he gained over any of its armies. . . . Then, indeed, I gave up all idea of saving the Union except by complete conquest. Up to that time it had been the policy of our army, certainly of that portion commanded by me, to protect the property of the citizens whose territory was invaded, without regard to their sentiments, whether Union or Secession. After this, however, I regarded it as humane to both sides to protect the persons of those found at their homes, but to consume everything that could be used to support or supply armies. . . . This policy I believe exercised a material influence in hastening the end.

This passage is somewhat misleading, for Grant did not implement these views immediately after Shiloh, and they had limited application through the Vicksburg campaign; indeed, this policy awaited his appointment to top command in spring 1864. By that time a broader concept of war had permeated both armies.

As Grant prepared to lead the Army of the Potomac toward Richmond in April 1864, Lincoln explained how he had come to war against slavery and to employ black troops. "I claim not to have controlled events, but confess plainly that events have controlled me." Lincoln and Grant shared this capacity to accept reality and alter course as required for ultimate victors; this was perhaps their strongest bond in the last year of the war. The victory they sought would bring vindication not of administration policy or military leadership, but of the popular will to reunite the nation.

Grant's reputation as a soldier callously willing to accept enormous casualties rests almost entirely on the spring campaign of the Army of the Potomac in 1864 from the Rapidan to Petersburg. And the casualties were enormous—an estimated fifty-five thousand, nearly equal to the initial size of Lee's entire army. Yet this campaign followed many others led by Grant, none spectacularly high in casualties. The only battle he had previously fought resulting in egregious losses was Shiloh, where he had been attacked, and the ferocity of the fighting reflected Confederate tactics, to which Grant could only react. Indeed, the May 1863 campaign in Mississippi leading to the encirclement of Vicksburg was remarkable for low Union losses.

The 1864 campaign should neither be minimized nor allowed to wrench Grant out of perspective. Casualties ran in a ratio of 5:3, overall perhaps more costly to Confederates with lower replacement capacity. The alternative to the heavy losses of the Wilderness and Spotsylvania, a regrouping near Washington, carried with it all the implications of future losses in Virginia, an opportunity for Lee as well as Grant to regroup, and an unacceptable blow to Northern morale. Further, as Grant planned an overall offensive, disengagement would have permitted Confederate deployment against other federal armies. Lincoln had expressed his appreciation of the strategy with a pithy phrase much to Grant's liking: "I see, those not skinning can hold a leg."

After the disastrous battle of Cold Harbor, Grant, displaying the indomitability and resilience that had brought him to top command, plunged into the maneuvering designed to carry the Army of the Potomac across the James River, free Butler's Army of the James from the bottleneck at Bermuda Hundred, and take U.S. forces into Petersburg, cutting the railroad lines to Richmond. He then would force Lee to fight on the offensive or suffer the loss of the Confederate capital. The movement across the James, a brilliantly executed flanking operation that left Lee guessing Grant's whereabouts, turned into a prelude to devastating disappointment when General William F. Smith inexplicably failed to take the thinly held lines of Petersburg on June 15, and overwhelming Union forces repeatedly botched the assault until Lee completed his full occupation of the Petersburg defenses on June 18. In retrospect, the failure to capture Petersburg in mid-June invalidated a strategy that brought the Army of the Potomac to Richmond's back door.

Grant's army then settled into a siege destined to last until the following April but without any realization of the magnitude of the stalemate. At the end of July, an innovative and resourceful plan to crack the Confederate line by exploding a mine led only to further disappointment, as once again Union command fumbles canceled strategic opportunity. The "miserable failure" actually made Grant ill.

What, then, of the strategy of annihilation and unconditional surrender? Strategic circumstance forced Grant to maintain the siege of Petersburg to immobilize Lee so that Confederates could not detach troops to operate against Sherman in Georgia or the Carolinas. The president controlled all political negotiations, and when Confederate emissaries arrived at City Point at the end of January 1865 to discuss peace, only Grant's encouragement brought Lincoln to the unproductive Hampton Roads conference. One month later Grant received explicit instructions to discuss no political matter with Lee, only the capitulation of his army. Grant, no less than the president, was circumscribed in his actions by the issues at stake in the contest. Walt Whitman, the soaring poet of democracy, sensed the greatness of this general who "went about his work, defied the rules, played the game his own way—did all the things the best generals told him he should not do—and won Out!" Whitman especially praised Grant's dress and manner. "Grant was the typical Western man: the plainest, the most efficient: was the least imposed upon by appearances, the most impressive in the severe simplicity of his flannel shirt and his utter disregard for formal military etiquette." Whitman concluded that Grant's "homely manners, dislike for military frippery—for every form of ostentation, in war and peace—amounted to genius." The true Grant was as unmilitary and unpolitical as he appeared to his countrymen; he looked and behaved like an ordinary American called from civilian life to save the nation.

The Civil War grew increasingly harsh as swords and roses gave way to rifles and bandages. Grant accepted the reality of that war, rejecting illusions of victory without fighting, or of a national conflict that left civilian life undisturbed. Grant represented the calm at the heart of the storm of battle, quietly and carefully thinking through problems without losing perspective, and he never lost sight of the ultimate goal of restoration of peace. The road that would take the nation to the end of the war in the shortest time with the smallest loss of life led through the Wilderness, Spotsylvania, and Cold Harbor. The alternative to what has been mislabeled a strategy of annihilation was a prolongation of killing. If Grant's realism is not mistaken for callousness and his logic not mistaken for cruelty, then we can understand the commander who moved so relentlessly to Appomattox and, once there, began immediately a campaign for peace.

Riding to meet Lee at Appomattox, Grant worried about his clothes. Not anticipating a formal interview, he had worn his customary private's uniform. His headquarters baggage was far in the rear, and the mud of Virginia spattered his boots. Grant's concern was accentuated as he stepped into the parlor of the McLean House. Lee wore a new uniform, clean shirt, and dress sword presented by a Maryland sympathizer. He wore a blood-red sash and gold spurs. While dressing that morning, Lee had remarked that he wanted to make his best appearance as Grant's prisoner of war. Perhaps he also realized that if he did not wear his new uniform that day he might never wear it.

Stripped of resources, the Confederacy sent a magnificently dressed officer to surrender to a slouchy man with muddy boots. Grant sought to put Lee at ease by speaking of happier times when both had served in the same victorious army. Grant said he remembered meeting Lee during the Mexican War when Lee, then on the staff of General Winfield Scott, had visited General Garland's brigade. Lee replied that he knew he had met Grant but had been unable to remember his features. Lee's commander, Scott, who had been Lee's patron, became known as Old Fuss and Feathers for his insistence on military etiquette and display. According to one story, Grant had reported to Scott's headquarters eighteen years earlier, after a reconnaissance in field dress, covered with Mexican dust. Scott had issued an order that all officers reporting to headquarters must do so in full uniform. It fell to Colonel Lee to tell Lieutenant Grant to return to his tent to change his clothes.

Grant had served also under Scott's rival, Zachary Taylor, whose attitude toward military formality had won him the name of Old Rough and Ready. Lee had clearly followed Scott while Grant clearly followed Taylor—followed him, in fact, into the White House. Beneath the superficial difference in attitude toward military display were more important questions involving attitudes toward war itself. In the moment of triumph at Fredericksburg, as he watched the shattered Union army scramble down Marye's Heights in the devastating fire, Lee had remarked, "It is well war is so terrible, or we should get too fond of it." For Grant, the concept was unthinkable. War was always a dirty business of death and destruction, justified only by the cause and never the conduct. "I never went into the army without regret and never retired without pleasure," he said. "My own feelings," Grant recalled of Appomattox, "were sad and depressed. I felt like anything rather than rejoicing at the downfall of a foe who had fought so long and valiantly, and had suffered so much for a cause, though that cause was, I believe, one of the worst for which a people ever fought."

Grant continued to speak of old days in Mexico for some time. "Our conversation grew so pleasant that I almost forgot the object of our meeting," he recalled. It was Lee who brought up the subject of terms of surrender and put the conference on a businesslike level by suggesting that Grant put his terms in writing. As Grant wrote, Lee's glittering sword caught his eye, and he thought that Lee might plan to surrender it. And so he wrote: "This will not embrace the side Arms of the officers, nor their private horses or baggage.—This done, each officer and man will be allowed to return to their homes not to be disturbed by United States Authority so long as they observe their paroles and the laws in force where they may reside."

Later, Grant explained to Lee the circumstances that brought him to Appomattox without a formal uniform and apologized for not wearing a sword.

Part 3

Lincoln and Grant

14

Lincoln, Grant,
and Kentucky in 1861

At the close of 1861, President Jefferson Davis of the Confederate States of America had reason for satisfaction. He had established a new nation with apparently secure frontiers. In the East, Confederate arms had triumphed in the first major encounter at Bull Run. Concerned about his capital's safety, President Abraham Lincoln had brought Major General George B. McClellan to command the Union forces. McClellan insisted upon training and disciplining his raw troops and demanded reinforcements to ensure any move southward. An impetuous attempt at quick victory by Colonel Edward D. Baker in October led to a disastrous Union repulse at Ball's Bluff in Virginia. Baker, killed in battle, was a special favorite of Lincoln, who had named a son in his honor. McClellan placed blame elsewhere and became even more cautious about advancing.

In Missouri, at the other end of the theater of war, secessionists were frustrated by Brigadier General Nathaniel Lyon in schemes to capture the U.S. Arsenal in St. Louis. But secessionist governor Claiborne Fox Jackson had rallied an army in Missouri that proved successful enough at Wilson's Creek, where Lyon was killed, and even more successful at Lexington, where a Union army was captured.

In Kentucky, General Albert Sidney Johnston, appraised by many as the ablest Confederate officer, commanded a Western army defending a strategic line from Columbus on the Mississippi River, through forts Henry and Donelson on the Tennessee and Cumberland rivers, to an anchor at Bowling Green, Kentucky. Union forces held Paducah, at the mouth of the Tennessee River, and Smithland, at the mouth of the Cumberland River, but little of Kentucky's interior.

From his capital at Richmond, President Davis surveyed a nation virtually unoccupied by Union forces. His government had "checked the wicked invasion which greed of gain and the unhallowed lust of power brought upon our soil, and has proved that numbers cease to avail when directed against a people fighting for the sacred right of self-government and the privileges of freemen."[1] Neither Missouri nor Kentucky, still contested by the Lincoln government, had formally joined the Confederacy. At the close of 1861, the Union warship *San Jacinto* had stopped the British vessel *Trent*, and Captain Charles Wilkes removed two Confederate emissaries to Europe, James Murray Mason and John Slidell. British protests provoked an international crisis that Davis hoped would end with British support of Southern independence, an outcome that he had tried to encourage with an embargo on shipments of Southern cotton to English mills. Diplomatic triumph for the Confederacy would appropriately follow a year of military success.

Dark clouds were less easily discerned. Confederate hopes rested upon Southern unity, defined as solidarity among people who lived in states in which law upheld the institution of slavery. Believing that Lincoln's election as president had posed an immediate danger to that institution, South Carolina rushed into secession, followed by six more states that had then organized a new federal government even before Lincoln had been inaugurated. Despite enthusiasm for this new nation in the black belt, eight more slaveholding states, including crucial Virginia, remained unaffiliated. Throughout the border slaveholding states, attention turned to Washington to determine if Lincoln's government would launch an assault on slavery that would unite the entire South.

Fully aware of the situation, Lincoln gave earnest assurances in his inaugural address that he would not attack slavery in any state. Instead, he pledged to maintain the property of the United States, a point which brought him into collision with Southern determination to seize Fort Sumter in Charleston Harbor, an inadequate fortification where the U.S. flag flew over a handful of men unprepared for battle or even the consequences of a blockade. When Lincoln resolved the tangled diplomacy of the incident by sending a fleet with food and supplies, assuring the South that no additional troops would land unless the fort were attacked, Davis and his cabinet rashly ordered a bombardment with tragic consequences for the attackers. Davis had begun a war by firing the first shot. He had initiated hostilities at the wrong place, at the wrong time, and for the wrong reasons. He had acted the part of bully, had fired on the flag, and had begun a war not tied directly to the institution of slavery. Throughout the border states, decisions quickly followed Lincoln's call for volunteers to suppress the rebellion; four states joined the Confederacy, four did not.

Of slaveholding states that did not secede, Kentucky was the most vital; Lincoln and Davis saw that from the outset. Both Lincoln and Davis had been born in Kentucky, not many miles apart. One had gone north, the other south. Lincoln had made Kentuckian Henry Clay his political idol. Like other Kentuckians, Lincoln had not forgotten Clay since his death in 1852 and retained Kentucky ties through his marriage into the Todd family of Lexington. Kentucky senator John Jordan Crittenden had inherited a portion of Clay's political power, which he used to further the principle of compromise. Both Democratic vice president John Cabell Breckinridge (president of the Senate) and Democratic governor Beriah Magoffin of Kentucky supported the Crittenden Compromise. Both Lincoln and Jefferson Davis, who rejected that compromise, accelerated the coming of war.

Clay's continuing power in Kentucky maintained his Whig Party long after its extinction elsewhere. Not until 1851 did Kentucky elect a Democratic governor. Elected in 1859, Magoffin proved to be one of the most enthusiastic secessionists in the state. In 1856, Breckinridge had been elected James Buchanan's vice president in the only antebellum presidential election carried by Democrats. In 1860, he represented the Southern wing of the Democratic Party in the presidential election. Despite having a native son on the ballot, Kentuckians gave their electoral votes to John Bell of Tennessee, representing the last gasp of the Whigs, now disguised as the Constitutional Union Party. Although only a handful of Kentuckians (1,362) cast votes for Lincoln, this fact was far less significant than the failure of Southern Democrats to carry the state.

For all his nationalism, Clay had represented a Southern state, as did Crittenden. Neither recognized a contradiction between support of the Union and support of slavery. Clay had championed the American Colonization Society, with its fantasy of returning emancipated American blacks to Africa. Clay's opposition to secession in 1850 was no less fervent than Lincoln's in 1861. Slaveholding, however, made Kentucky so Southern that Northerners feared that when war came, Kentucky would join the Confederacy.

Following Crittenden's lead, however, Kentuckians chose neutrality. After the firing on Fort Sumter, Lincoln called upon states for troops to put down the insurrection. Governor Magoffin, a rebel sympathizer, angrily refused to furnish "troops for the wicked purpose of subduing her sister Southern States."[2] Kentucky Unionists, however, sympathized with Magoffin, hoping that some path to restoration might yet be discerned and bloodshed averted. At a large and enthusiastic public meeting in Louisville, former senator Archibald Dixon urged Kentuckians to "stand firm with her sister Border States in the centre of the Republic, to calm the distracted sections." By doing this, "she saves the Union and frowns down Secession."[3] The meeting resolved that the "duty of Kentucky is to maintain her present independent position, taking sides not with the Administration, nor with the seceding States, but with the Union against them both."[4]

Ardent support for a policy of neutrality did not mean that Kentuckians were truly neutral. Instead, issues of the war divided families like those of the Breckinridges, Crittendens, and Todds. Neutrality represented an ideal or, in retrospect, a way-station between peace and war.

In the years closest to the Civil War, Kentucky had changed from a Southern to a border state. Twelve railroads connected Kentucky to the North, two to the South, altering older patterns of river trade. Patterns of immigration had changed Kentucky from a largely homogeneous Southern state to one of mixed population. As Kentucky grew, the proportion of slaves steadily diminished. Nor were such slaves evenly distributed across a domain that shared some seven hundred miles of border with Northern states. Circumstances of war forced Americans to regard states as more homogeneous than reality dictated. Stretching from Appalachia to the Mississippi River, Kentucky's wide economic and cultural diversity mirrored divisions between North and South.

Neutrality favored a lucrative trade policy involving both Union and Confederacy. Advocates of "free city" status in both New York City and Cairo, Illinois, foresaw promising economic windfalls. Businessmen recognized the advantages of an American Switzerland. When secession interrupted trade on the Mississippi River, the Louisville and Nashville Railroad became a major artery of commerce between North and South. Confederate policy forbidding trade in the great staples of the South eventually closed this avenue of prosperity. Characterizing the Confederacy as "too impatient to be tolerant and too impetuous to be tactful," one historian blamed trade policy for the loss of Kentucky to the Union.[5]

The role of Kentucky in the inevitable conflict depended on states-manship North and South. Both Lincoln and Davis knew that whatev-er the futility of neutrality, disrespect for that preposterous policy would cost them potential Kentucky allies. Lincoln had an added burden of continuing to dramatize the war as a struggle for the Union and not against slavery. In a meeting with Kentucky Unionist Garrett Davis, Lincoln again emphasized his intention to "make no attack, direct or in-direct, upon the institutions or property of any State," but rather to de-fend them. Further, that although he possessed the right to send troops wherever needed, "if Kentucky made no demonstration of force against the United States, he would not molest her."[6]

Both sides began to recruit in Kentucky, the South with the sup-port of Governor Magoffin, the North with less official sanction. Simon Bolivar Buckner, who headed the state guard, was generally understood to favor the South, but the legislature, Unionist in sentiment, autho-rized a rival home guard friendlier to the North. Working through naval officer Brigadier General William Nelson and old friends James and Joshua Speed, Lincoln secretly sent guns to Kentucky. Lincoln also sent to Kentucky a native Kentuckian, Robert Anderson, the honored hero of Fort Sumter. Originally sent to accept Union troops, Anderson re-mained across the Ohio to avoid provocation.

Elections for Congress held on June 20 sent a covey of Unionists to Washington. Unionists carried nine of ten districts with a total of 92,460 votes against 37,700 for State Rights candidates. Supporters of neutrality joined supporters of the North in opposition to Confederate sympathizers. Legislative elections in August gave Unionists a majority of seventy-six to twenty-four in the Kentucky House and twenty-seven to eleven in the Senate.

In his July 4 message to Congress, Lincoln reviewed the Fort Sumter crisis and steps taken since. Although denouncing secession, he avoided discussing slavery. Without mentioning Kentucky, Lincoln attacked armed neutrality as "disunion completed." This would benefit rebels by enabling them to trade freely with the North through intermediaries to avoid the blockade's consequences. As such, armed neutrality "rec-ognizes no fidelity to the Constitution, no obligation to maintain the Union; and while very many who have favored it are, doubtless, loyal citizens, it is, nevertheless, treason in effect."[7]

Magoffin had sent Buckner to negotiate with General McClellan in Ohio for a guarantee of Kentucky neutrality and later sent Buckner on a similar mission to Governor Isham Harris of Tennessee. Dissatisfied with the McClellan arrangement, Magoffin sent Buckner to Washington to confer with Lincoln. Buckner returned with a statement that Lincoln, determined to "suppress an insurrection," had "not sent an armed force into Kentucky; nor have I any present purpose to do so." Nonetheless, "I mean to say nothing which shall hereafter embarrass me in the performance of what may seem to be my duty."[8] Buckner also returned with an offer of a commission as brigadier general, something he would eventually accept only when it came from the Confederate government.

In August, Lincoln authorized the establishment of recruiting camps in Kentucky. General Nelson claimed that he was organizing Kentuckians to preserve neutrality, a thin excuse further weakened by his simultaneous recruiting and arming of East Tennessee loyalists. Within weeks, Union forces at Cairo, Illinois, had captured a rebel steamboat at Paducah, an action that produced a retaliatory local seizure of a steamboat from Evansville. After negotiating with Kentuckians, Lincoln concluded that "professed Unionists gave him more trouble than rebels." He believed that Magoffin hoped to maneuver the North into firing the first shot in Kentucky.[9] By the end of August, the Confederate government had also initiated recruiting within the borders of Kentucky and had passed a secret resolution appropriating funds for arms. Kentucky neutrality was doomed.

On August 24, Lincoln answered Magoffin's protest against camps established in Kentucky without his consent:

> I believe it is true that there is a military force in camp within Kentucky, acting by authority of the United States, which force is not very large, and is not now being augmented. I also believe that some arms have been furnished to this force by the United States. I also believe this force consists exclusively of Kentuckians, having their camp in the immediate vicinity of their own homes, and not assailing, or menacing, any of the good people of Kentucky. In all I have done in the premises, I have acted upon the urgent solicitation of many Kentuckians, and in accordance with what I believed, and still believe, to be the wish of a majority of all the Union-loving people of Kentucky. While I have conversed on this subject with many eminent men of Kentucky, including a large majority of her Members of Congress, I do

not remember that any one of them, or any other person, except your Excellency and the bearers of your Excellency's letter, has urged me to remove the military force from Kentucky, or to disband it. One other very worthy citizen of Kentucky did solicit me to have the augmenting of the force suspended for a time. Taking all the means within my reach to form a judgment, I do not believe it is the popular wish of Kentucky that this force shall be removed beyond her limits; and, with this impression, I must respectfully decline to so remove it. I most cordially sympathize with your Excellency, in the wish to preserve the peace of my own native State, Kentucky; but it is with regret I search, and can not find, in your not very short letter, any declaration, or intimation, that you entertain any desire for the preservation of the Federal Union.[10]

A few days later, Jefferson Davis replied to a similar request for reassurance from Magoffin with flat assurance that the Confederacy "neither intends nor desires to disturb the neutrality of Kentucky." He pledged to respect neutrality "so long as her people will maintain it themselves."[11]

How Kentucky was dragged into the war, by whom and under what circumstances, mattered much to fervent neutralists. Confederate brigadier general Gideon J. Pillow had insisted in May that the occupation of Columbus was essential to the defense of his native Tennessee.[12] Wiser heads prevailed—almost any head was wiser than Pillow's—but Pillow persisted in his determination to invade.

In what became Kentucky's decisive month of September, the chief commanders in the Western theater were Confederate major general Leonidas Polk and Union major general John C. Frémont. Neither, in retrospect, appeared suited for such weighty responsibilities. Polk proved arrogant, headstrong, and injudicious, behavior especially surprising in a former bishop. Trained at West Point, he had resigned a few months after graduation to pursue the ministry and had abandoned interest in military affairs before the Civil War. His ambitious subordinate, Gideon J. Pillow, untrained but unafraid, resented his secondary status in the Western armies and considered himself better qualified to lead. On August 28 he informed Polk that the Confederate position at New Madrid, Missouri, was inferior, that Columbus was the place to defend Tennessee. Kentucky neutrality, wrote Pillow, existed no longer.

Once the Federals took Columbus they could not be dislodged. Arguing that the time had come for decision, Pillow pushed the weaker Polk into action.[13]

Frémont was imperious, impetuous, and impatient. Frémont had dallied before going to headquarters in St. Louis to await fittings on his new uniform as major general, then rarely emerged from a St. Louis mansion rented from one of his wife's relatives. Inside, he played the role of "grand Monarque,"[14] surrounded by courtiers exiled from the armies of Europe. As military affairs in Missouri deteriorated, Frémont hoped to recoup with boldness elsewhere.

On August 28, Frémont ordered General Ulysses S. Grant to take command at Cape Girardeau, to cooperate with forces moving eastward from Ironton, and to be aware that Frémont had ordered forces at Cairo to prepare for a move southward. Colonel Gustav Waagner had been sent to Belmont, Missouri, opposite Columbus, Kentucky, to destroy Confederate works and to build his own. Frémont intended to occupy Columbus "as soon as possible."[15] Waagner's occupation of Belmont on September 2 triggered the end of Kentucky's neutrality.

Polk had already written to Magoffin that he considered it of "the greatest consequence" to the Confederacy that "I should be ahead of the enemy in occupying Columbus and Paducah."[16] Two days later a spy reported Union forces at Belmont. Under Polk's orders, Pillow embarked for Kentucky, occupying both Hickman and Columbus. Governor Harris of Tennessee immediately declared the incursion "unfortunate, as the President and myself are pledged to respect the neutrality of Kentucky."[17] Polk replied that Pillow had moved "under the plenary powers delegated to me by the President" and had occupied Hickman to avoid the cannon at Belmont.[18] Davis outlined a response on Harris's telegram: "Secty of War—Telegraph promptly to Genl. Polk to withdraw troops from Ky—& explain movement Ans—Gov. Harris inform him of action & that movement was unauthorized."[19] Secretary of War Leroy Walker immediately sent Polk orders for a "prompt withdrawal."[20] Polk then explained to Davis that the threat to Columbus justified the movement, vital also to the safety of western Tennessee. Davis replied fatuously but succinctly: "The necessity must justify the action."[21] Polk responded that his invasion was justified by information that a Union expedition to Paducah was already under way before he issued orders to seize Columbus.[22] Walker nonetheless again asked Polk the "reason for General Pillow's movement."[23] In response to yet another message from Harris, Walker responded that Polk had been "ordered to direct the prompt withdrawal of the forces under General Pillow from Kentucky. The movement was wholly unauthorized, and you will so inform Governor Magoffin."[24]

Confusion in Richmond originated through lack of communication between Walker and Davis, the former believing that he was secretary of war, an understandable mistake soon rectified by Walker's dismissal. Walker's instincts were correct, although he did not immediately recognize that the invasion of Kentucky could not be undone, repealed, or erased. Polk's argument that federal occupation of Belmont, across the river from Columbus, represented a threat to Kentucky was militarily correct, politically disastrous. Of course Frémont intended this move as a prelude to an occupation of Columbus but had not yet informed Washington, where Lincoln might well have intervened. Columbus occupied bluffs overlooking the river; Belmont sat on a flood plain. Once Polk and Pillow occupied Columbus, Waagner immediately evacuated Belmont. The issue remained one of respect for Kentucky's neutrality, not that of Missouri. Both Polk and Frémont represented an accident ready to happen; Polk proved the first to blunder. Justifying his action to a committee of the Kentucky legislature, Polk explained that he had infringed on Kentucky's neutrality only by seizing Columbus "and so much of the territory between it and the Tennessee line as was necessary for me to pass over to reach it."[25]

On September 2, Colonel Richard J. Oglesby, commander at Cairo, was surprised when an unprepossessing stranger, dressed as a civilian because his uniform had not yet arrived, handed him an order assuming command.[26] At Cape Girardeau, Missouri, Brigadier General Benjamin M. Prentiss had been similarly surprised a few days earlier when Grant arrived to assume command of the District of Southeast Missouri. Prentiss insisted that he was the senior officer, having held command while Grant vainly sought an opportunity to get into the war. Both had been nominated on the same day, but Grant held higher rank in the old army, and Grant preceded Prentiss on the army list. Prentiss, who eventually placed himself in arrest, may have accelerated Grant's move to Cairo, where he arrived the day before the Confederate advance into Kentucky. Without yet knowing that Polk had taken Columbus, Grant wrote that he wanted to occupy it the next day. "New Madrid will fall within five days after," he added.[27]

The next day word arrived of the Confederate incursion that Grant immediately telegraphed to the speaker of the Kentucky House of Representatives. "I regret to inform you," Grant began, but perhaps was more relieved than regretful. In reality Polk had spared Frémont and Grant the opprobrium of violating Kentucky neutrality.[28] By that afternoon, Grant was ready to start for Paducah, awaiting a telegram from Frémont either sanctioning or forbidding the expedition. Grant based his decision on information received from Charles de Arnaud, one of the more bizarre characters churned up by the war. Despite the name, de Arnaud was a Russian who had arrived in the United States in late 1860 and whom Frémont had commissioned as a spy. On September 5, de Arnaud arrived at Cairo to report that Confederate forces were advancing on Paducah.[29] Grant immediately began to prepare his expedition, which arrived in Paducah on the following morning. He found rebel flags flying and citizens abuzz with news that a Confederate force of thirty-eight hundred was sixteen miles away. He thought then and for the rest of his life that only his timely arrival had prevented the enemy from seizing the mouth of the Tennessee River.[30]

On Grant's approach, Lloyd Tilghman of Paducah, organizer of a local pro-Confederate force, fled the city and was later reported with his men at Columbus. As for Pillow's force, believed to be so close, there is no evidence that any troops had ever left Columbus. Initial confusion about nearby rebels and which direction they were heading, to which local sympathizers may have contributed, exaggerated the timeliness and boldness of Grant's expedition.[31] The Confederate occupation of Columbus benefited Grant by providing justification for occupying an even more vital site in Kentucky. Belief that Pillow was headed for Paducah rested upon a logical assumption that Confederates would make the most of their Kentucky invasion. Polk and Pillow did not, however, behave logically.

Grant landed at Paducah at 8:30 A.M. and left at noon. During the morning he ran up the U.S. flag, deployed his troops, occupied the post and telegraph offices, seized the railroad, disposed of rations and leather, and issued a proclamation remarkable for its measured tone of reassurance:

> I have come among you, not as an enemy, but as your friend and fellow-citizen, not to injure or annoy you, but to respect the rights, and to defend and enforce the rights of all loyal citizens. An enemy, in rebellion against our common Government,

has taken possession of, and planted its guns upon the soil of Kentucky and fired upon our flag. Hickman and Columbus are in his hands. He is moving upon your city. I am here to defend you against this enemy and to assert and maintain the authority and sovereignty of your Government and mine. I have nothing to do with opinions. I shall deal only with armed rebellion and its aiders and abetors. You can pursue your usual avocations without fear or hindrance. The strong arm of the Government is here to protect its friends, and to punish only its enemies. Whenever it is manifest that you are able to defend yourselves, to maintain the authority of your Government and protect the rights of all its loyal citizens, I shall withdraw the forces under my command from your city.[32]

Grant discovered Frémont's permission for the expedition to Paducah waiting back at Cairo. Actually, permission had arrived before Grant left Cairo—but in Hungarian![33] Frémont had surrounded himself in St. Louis with officers from many countries, including refugees of the Hungarian revolt of 1848. Their unusually impenetrable language was considered especially suitable for confidential messages. Apparently, nobody in Cairo could cope with Hungarian. Grant left for Paducah anyway. Rebuked for communicating with the Kentucky legislature, Grant received no censure for the Paducah expedition, since it had received advance official authorization from headquarters.

Grant continued to believe, however, that he had left for Paducah before receiving approval from his superior and he had gotten away with it. His belief that he could operate aggressively with impunity influenced his impetuous attack at Belmont in November. There he furnished a scare to the garrison at Columbus. Throughout the rest of 1861, Grant wanted to move south.

Frémont's plan to occupy Columbus imperiled the Union cause in Kentucky, as did his proclamation of August 30 declaring martial law in Missouri and threatening to enforce the Confiscation Act passed by Congress against slave property of Missouri rebels. Frémont's popularity in the Republican Party led Lincoln to caution in opposing the proclamation. He immediately pointed out, however, that the threat to liberate the slaves of traitors might "perhaps ruin our rather fair prospect for Kentucky."[34] In privately explaining his policy, Lincoln expanded on his concern for Kentucky:

The Kentucky Legislature would not budge till that proclamation was modified; and Gen. Anderson telegraphed me that
on the news of Gen. Fremont having actually issued deeds of
manumission, a whole company of our Volunteers threw down
their arms and disbanded. I was so assured, as to think it probable, that the very arms we had furnished Kentucky would be
turned against us. I think to lose Kentucky is nearly the same as
to lose the whole game. Kentucky gone, we can not hold Missouri, nor, as I think, Maryland. . . . You must not understand I
took my course on the proclamation *because* of Kentucky. I took
this same ground in a private letter to General Fremont before
I heard from Kentucky.[35]

Indeed, the day after Lincoln wrote to Frémont he heard from James
Speed of Louisville that Frémont's "foolish proclamation" would "crush
out" Kentucky Unionism.[36]

Lincoln's final response to Frémont was to remove him from command and ultimately replace him with Major General Henry W. Halleck, the epitome of military correctness and respect for procedure.
During the interval between Frémont's removal and Halleck's arrival,
Grant seized the opportunity for an adventitious expedition to Belmont,
possibly a prelude to an assault on Columbus. Grant's inconclusive tan-
gle with Pillow left both prepared to claim a victory that neither won.

In November, Davis explained his Kentucky policy:

Finding that the Confederate States were about to be invaded
through Kentucky, and that her people after being deceived
into a mistaken security, were unarmed, and in danger of being subjugated by the Federal forces, our armies were marched
into that State to repel the enemy and prevent their occupation
of certain strategic points which would have given them great
advantages in the contest—a step which was justified, not only
by the necessities of self-defense on the part of the Confederate
States, but, also, by a desire to aid the people of Kentucky. It was
never intended by the Confederate Government to conquer or
co-erce the people of that State; but, on the contrary, it was declared by our Generals that they would withdraw their troops if
the Federal Government would do likewise. Proclamation was
also made of the desire to respect the neutrality of Kentucky,

and the intention to abide by the wishes of her people as soon as they were free to express their opinions. These declarations were approved by me, and I should regard it as one of the best effects of the march of our troops into Kentucky if it should end in giving to her people liberty of choice and a free opportunity to decide their own destiny according to their own will.[37]

In his annual message of December 3, 1861, Lincoln declared that Kentucky, "for some time in doubt, is now decidedly, and, I think, unchangeably, ranged on the side of the Union." Maryland, Kentucky, and Missouri, "neither of which would promise a single soldier at first, have now an aggregate of not less than forty thousand in the field for the Union; while, of their citizens, certainly not more than a third of that number, and they of doubtful whereabouts, and doubtful existence, are in arms against it."[38]

Lincoln spoke accurately in December, and his remarks about Kentucky Unionism and about enlistment ratios north and south forecast the future. During the war, Kentucky furnished troops to North and South in a ratio of three to one. At the close of the year, despite a record that brought satisfaction in Richmond, the battle for Kentucky had turned into Confederate disaster. In January, rebel defeat at Mill Springs was followed by Halleck's reluctant permission to Grant to advance on Fort Henry. After the fall of Henry led Grant to attack and capture Fort Donelson, the entire Confederate line in Kentucky cracked. Confederate generals Albert Sidney Johnston and P. G. T. Beauregard united their forces at Corinth, Mississippi.

Lincoln had immediately recognized that the key to maintaining loyalty in Kentucky rested upon emphasis upon the Union, tolerance for slavery, and observation of neutrality. Kentucky's evasion of Civil War reality could not long endure. Confederates blundered by impetuously accepting the burden of invading Kentucky and then failing to make their occupation effective. Operating on false information and without proper authorization, Grant nevertheless made precisely the right move in occupying Paducah. Grant secured bases from which a superior U.S. Navy could operate on rivers that dominated western Kentucky. Fortification of Columbus confirmed an existing Confederate stranglehold on the Mississippi River without broader military advantages. At the end of 1861, the North harvested the fruits of Lincoln's patient policy of moderation.

Late in August 1861, commanders North and South had recognized that Kentucky neutrality was shattering. Both Frémont and Polk decided to risk the consequences of invading the state in exchange for the occupation of strategic positions. Polk won the race for Columbus with dire consequences. On the day that Polk crossed the border, Frémont wrote to Lincoln that the enemy was "creeping covertly forward into Kentucky lately, and I have been very anxious to anticipate him, but not quite able yet."[39] Had the North seized Columbus, as both Frémont and Grant intended, the outcome of the Civil War might have been different.

15

Grant, Lincoln, and Unconditional Surrender

Ulysses S. Grant first visited Washington to pursue a claim of one thousand dollars he lost during the Mexican War. As quartermaster, Grant was held liable for money stolen from the trunk of a brother officer in 1848. Cleared by a board of inquiry at the time, Grant remained responsible for repayment until relieved by act of Congress. In 1852, Lieutenant Grant, with a three-day leave, arrived in Washington to find the congressman from whom he expected help out of town for ten days and all offices closed for the funeral of Henry Clay. Frustrated in his business, Grant turned disappointed tourist, finding the city "small and scattering and the character of the buildings poor."[1] The debt hung over his head for another decade, until Congress rewarded the general who had captured Fort Donelson by relieving him of this unjust obligation.

Twelve years passed before Grant returned to Washington. On March 8, 1864, accompanied only by his teenage son, Grant registered at Willard's Hotel, where the clerk first assigned him an undesirable top-floor room and then fell all over himself when he looked at the registration book. Like almost everyone in Washington, the clerk knew that Grant had been promoted to lieutenant general, a rank held previously only by George Washington by right and Winfield Scott by brevet, and had come to take command of all the armies of the United States. When Grant and his son Fred tried to eat dinner at the hotel, other guests gave him a hero's welcome. Grant fled before finishing his meal.

Worse followed that evening at the White House, where Grant attended a public reception thronged with people eager to see the new commander. After meeting Abraham Lincoln for the first time, Grant stood on a crimson sofa in the East Room shaking hands and receiving congratulations. He might have been trampled had he not ascended the sofa.

Later that evening, Lincoln took Grant aside to explain the ceremony scheduled for the following day. In the presence of the entire cabinet, Lincoln intended to present Grant with his commission as lieutenant general and to make a brief speech, expecting Grant to reply. According to presidential secretary John Nicolay, Lincoln asked Grant to say something that would allay the jealousy of other generals and something to put him on "good terms" with the Army of the Potomac.[2] Grant's brief written remarks, three sentences to Lincoln's four, touched neither point directly, yet seemed entirely appropriate.

> I accept the commission with gratitude for the high honor conferred. With the aid of the noble armies that have fought on so many fields for our common country, it will be my earnest endeavor not to disappoint your expectations. I feel the full weight of the responsibilities now devolving on me and know that if they are met it will be due to those armies, and above all to the favor of that Providence which leads both Nations and men.[3]

The next day, Grant visited the Army of the Potomac and its commander, Major General George G. Meade, who had expected Grant to replace him with a veteran of the Western armies. When Meade said that he would willingly relinquish command to another, perhaps Major General William T. Sherman, and serve wherever placed, Grant promptly decided to retain Meade, a man who put service ahead of self. By the time he returned to Washington, Grant was ready to return west to confer with Sherman and to wind up affairs in Tennessee. To do so, he canceled dinner at the White House, an invitation he had already accepted, telling Lincoln that he had endured enough of "this show business."[4] Besides, he explained, "a dinner to me means a million dollars a day lost to the country."[5]

General in Chief Henry W. Halleck, now outranked by his former subordinate, had forced Grant's hand by requesting to be relieved. Higher rank required Grant to assume overall command. Grant resolved the problem by arranging Halleck's appointment as chief of staff, leaving him in Washington to coordinate orders, freeing Grant to establish headquarters wherever he wished. Halleck's new post separated strategic command from administration, a crucial innovation in modern warfare. Grant avoided the position of military adviser to Lincoln and Secretary of War Edwin M. Stanton, a role congenial to Halleck but intolerable to Grant, who intended to remain a commander rather than a courtier and to distance himself from politicians.

When he informed Sherman of his orders to report to Washington, Grant wrote that he would reject the promotion if required to stay there. As if unwilling to take Grant at his word, Sherman replied that Halleck was better able "to stand the buffets of Intrigue and Policy. . . . For Gods sake and for your Countrys sake come out of Washington."[6] But if Grant retained command in the West, as Sherman urged, he would supersede his most trusted lieutenant. Virtually without an alternative, Grant established headquarters with the Army of the Potomac, not displacing Meade but coordinating command from a point with the largest and most prominent of all armies, remaining close to Washington without becoming caught in its political eddies and entrusting Western command to Sherman.

Grant's visit to Washington lasted three days. During that time he conferred privately with Stanton and also with Halleck, dined with Secretary of State William H. Seward, and visited Meade. He spent little time with Lincoln and much of that in the presence of the cabinet. In their first private meeting, as Grant recalled it, Lincoln said that "he had never professed to be a military man or to know how campaigns should be conducted, and never wanted to interfere in them: but that procrastination on the part of commanders, and the pressure from the people at the North and Congress, *which was always with him*, forced him into issuing his series of 'Military Orders,'" some of which he conceded were mistaken. Lincoln added that "while armies were sitting down waiting for opportunities to turn up which might, perhaps, be more favorable from a strictly military point of view, the government was spending millions of dollars every day; that there was a limit to the sinews of war, and a time might be reached when the spirits and resources of the people would become exhausted." He simply wanted someone to "take the responsibility and act," something Grant assured him that he would do.[7] Lincoln said that he did not want to know what Grant proposed to do but brought out a plan of his own to use the Potomac as a base and advance between two streams that would protect the Union flanks. Grant realized, but did not mention to Lincoln, that these streams would also shield Lee. Thereafter, said Grant, he did not communicate his plans to Lincoln, Stanton, or Halleck.

Whether Lincoln abdicated his control of the war has since been disputed, but Grant thought that Lincoln did so. More likely, he gave this bulldog a longer leash than previous commanders, but a leash nonetheless. Facing the uncertainties of an election year, remembering that no incumbent had been reelected since Andrew Jackson, Lincoln dared not risk responsibility for military setbacks. Grant's spring campaign opened with an exchange of formal letters with Lincoln. "The particulars of your plan I neither know, or seek to know," wrote Lincoln. "Should my success be less than I desire, and expect," Grant responded, "the least I can say is, the fault is not with you."[8]

Although Lincoln wrote that he did not know the "particulars" of Grant's plan, Lincoln had heard overall strategy explained in some detail. Grant intended to use all armies in a coordinated offensive. The Army of the Potomac would advance against Richmond from the north while the Army of the James under Major General Benjamin F. Butler moved from Fort Monroe to threaten Richmond from the south. Major General Franz Sigel would move up the Shenandoah Valley to counter any Confederate threat to Washington and, if successful, drive against Richmond from the west. Sherman's thrust into Georgia would be supported by an expedition to Mobile led by Major General Edward R. S. Canby. Every army had orders to advance in early May. No longer could Confederates use interior lines to counter sporadic offensives. Every army would perform some role in the grand offensive. "Those not skinning can hold a leg," Lincoln observed to Grant, who repeated the same phrase, without attribution, in a letter to Sherman.[9] In devising this plan, Lincoln said privately, Grant implemented a strategy that Lincoln had always urged.

So Grant had a free hand not because Lincoln gave him one but because the president approved the strategy. Lincoln then led Grant to believe that he had more authority than he had in reality. By doing so, Lincoln enabled Grant to preserve the self-confidence that had brought victory in the West. At the same time, Lincoln separated himself from the carnage on the bloody road to Petersburg. He won unanimous renomination while bodies still lay on the field at Cold Harbor.

On May 4, Grant plunged across the Rapidan and led his armies into the Wilderness, suffering tremendous casualties. Moving on his left flank, he encountered Robert E. Lee again at Spotsylvania, at the North Anna, then at Cold Harbor, where the second assault proved singularly disastrous. Undaunted, Grant launched a brilliant flanking maneuver that bewildered Lee and took the Army of the Potomac south of the James River and Richmond to the thinly held Confederate lines at the vital rail center of Petersburg. Only then did Lincoln break six weeks of public silence about Grant's strategy and tactics. "I begin to see it. You will succeed—God bless you all."[10] Within a week, Lincoln visited Grant at his City Point headquarters.

Grant was the fourth man to command all the armies under Lincoln. The first, Winfield Scott, had filled the post since 1841. Despite age and infirmity he had served Lincoln well and retired on November 1, 1861, only because George B. McClellan insisted on holding the office himself. McClellan, in turn, lasted only four months, until March 11, 1862, when Lincoln, in effect, assumed the post himself on the eve of McClellan's ill-fated Peninsular campaign. McClellan's withdrawal from Richmond led to Halleck's arrival in Washington to restore shattered morale and to provide administrative control. Halleck's passive approach to strategy combined with his bureaucratic expertise suited Lincoln and Stanton. Eventually it suited Grant as well, for Halleck's role changed little when he moved from general in chief to chief of staff. Lincoln, however, had served as de facto general in chief for the past two years. He trusted some generals more than others, but trusted no general to see the war in the broad perspective afforded by the White House.

Grant had gone to Washington in March determined to return immediately to the West after accepting his commission. Once there, he changed his mind and decided to remain near Washington. Only the commanding general could "resist the pressure," he concluded, "to desist from his own plans and pursue others."[11] He proposed "to exercise actual command of all the armies, without any interference from the War Department." He did not intend to become "McClellanized."[12] The fall of McClellan was so much on his mind that one week after leaving the White House he discussed with Sherman restoring McClellan to a major command.

Early in the war, Grant had sought a position on McClellan's staff. Grant spent two days waiting in McClellan's outer office in Cincinnati before taking the hint to look elsewhere for a command. "I knew McClellan," he recalled, "and had great confidence in him. I have, for that matter, never lost my respect for McClellan's character, nor my confidence in his loyalty and ability." He remained, said Grant, "one of the mysteries of the war." As a military professional, Grant remained sympathetic to McClellan because the test which was applied to him would be terrible to any man, being made a major-general at the beginning of the war. It has always seemed to me that the critics of McClellan do not consider this vast and cruel responsibility—the war, a new thing to all of us, the army new, everything to do from the outset, with a restless people and Congress. McClellan was a young man when this devolved upon him, and if he did not succeed, it was because the conditions of success were so trying. If McClellan had gone into the war as Sherman, Thomas, or Meade, had fought his way along and up, I have no reason to suppose that he would not have won as high a distinction as any of us. McClellan's main blunder was in allowing himself political sympathies, and in permitting himself to become the critic of the President, and in time his rival.[13]

It is impossible to recapture precisely what Grant meant by his apprehension of becoming "McClellanized." In part it expressed unwillingness to follow strategy dictated by the president and secretary of war, subordinating military to political considerations. Grant's new command entitled him to put Meade out to pasture, along with McClellan, a move Grant immediately rejected. In their initial conference, Lincoln referred to his war orders of two years earlier, admitting that they were, at least in part, mistaken. By implication, Lincoln indicated that he would not treat Grant as he had treated McClellan.

Later generations lauded Lincoln's wartime leadership and even military genius, but Grant accepted command in 1864 with a degree of wariness that gradually dissipated and ultimately was forgotten. Although Lincoln had appointed Grant a brigadier general on July 31, 1861, even before the former captain, now a colonel, had encountered an armed enemy, he did so as a favor to Elihu B. Washburne, a political ally since 1843 and the ranking Republican in the House of Representatives. After a caucus of Illinois congressmen had decided how many of the thirty-four new brigadiers should come from Illinois, Washburne pushed Grant as the best-qualified soldier from his congressional district.

Grant's great victory at Fort Donelson, the North's first substantial victory, led to his promotion to major general and a similar promotion for a principal subordinate, John A. McClernand, who had entered the war as Democratic congressman from Lincoln's home district. Caught unprepared for the Confederate assault at Shiloh in April, Grant rallied his forces for a second day of battle that more than redeemed the field. Lincoln withstood demands for Grant's removal but did not intercede when Halleck took personal command of his army and shunted aside Grant to frustrating inaction. Only Halleck's call to Washington as general in chief gave Grant another opportunity to command independently.

In September 1862, McClernand arrived in Washington to intrigue for command of an expedition to open the Mississippi River. To gain Lincoln's support he used the promise of new regiments of loyal Democrats and the threat of disloyalty in the Northwest if its normal commerce remained blocked. Lincoln succumbed, but Halleck connived to send the new regiments to Grant at Memphis instead of holding them for McClernand's expedition. Grant sent Sherman on an ill-fated premature assault on Vicksburg designed to bag the Confederate citadel before McClernand arrived to claim command. Repulsed at Chickasaw Bayou, Sherman was superseded by McClernand. As quickly as possible, Grant arrived to supersede McClernand.

Grant ranked McClernand, but other corps commanders did not. Grant commanded a huge department; if he were called away to meet some threat elsewhere, McClernand would assume command of all forces before Vicksburg. At the suggestion of staff officer James Harrison Wilson, Grant wrote to Halleck proposing to merge the four departments in the Mississippi Valley under one senior commander, disclaiming any personal ambition for that post. As soon as Grant accepted that suggestion, Wilson began to scheme to bring the recently deposed McClellan west for a fresh start. Wilson recalled that Grant had no objection to serving under McClellan.[14] Lincoln, however, had no intention of giving McClellan further military opportunities, especially at Grant's expense.

In the early months of 1863, Grant endured the frustrations of flooded terrain that kept him from attacking Vicksburg and the presidential protection that kept him from sacking McClernand. Eventually Grant crossed the Mississippi River south of Vicksburg, launched a brilliant strike at Jackson, then drove the Confederates back to Vicksburg. Grant launched two assaults on Vicksburg before settling into a siege. Because of boastful misrepresentation by McClernand, the second assault proved more sanguinary than necessary. Constant friction between Grant and his ambitious subordinate ended with McClernand's removal two weeks before Vicksburg's surrender.

Lincoln had chosen McClernand as a fit partner for Rear Admiral David D. Porter, since both condemned West Pointers as arrogant and uncooperative. Stanton and Halleck concurred; neither had confidence in Grant.[15] After his removal, McClernand bombarded Washington with statements in his defense, claimed credit for Grant's victories, and argued that his removal had originated in a clerical oversight. Grant sent John A. Rawlins, his adjutant and a prewar lawyer, to argue his case. Rawlins made a successful two-hour presentation to the cabinet. Rejoicing over the imminent opening of the Mississippi River, Lincoln no longer needed to heed cries of potential Midwestern disaffection from a general who had demonstrated insubordination and incompetency.

So thoroughly had Lincoln changed that he wrote Grant a letter "of grateful acknowledgment for the almost inestimable service you have done." He had, he wrote, doubted Grant's strategy throughout and now wished "to make the personal acknowledgment that you were right, and I was wrong." This remarkable letter left Grant incapable of replying. Modesty halted his pen. Three weeks later Lincoln asked, "Did you receive a short letter from me, dated the 13th. of July?" "Your letter of the 13th of July was also duly received," Grant lamely responded.[16]

Presidential politics influenced the relationship between Lincoln and Grant. Democrats knew that the nomination of a successful general in 1864 represented their surest path to the White House. Like most professional soldiers of the prewar years, Grant had voted Democratic. The election of a Republican in 1856, Grant believed, would provoke secession and rebellion, so he had voted for James Buchanan. Besides, he explained, he knew John C. Frémont, the Republican candidate. Although uninvolved in politics, Grant had lost the post of county engineer of St. Louis in 1859 by a partisan vote of commissioners who believed him to be a Democrat. A recent move to Galena in 1860 cost Grant eligibility to vote; he favored Stephen A. Douglas. Grant's first military employment during the Civil War came from Republican governor Richard Yates of Illinois, who appointed him aide, mustering officer, then colonel, before Republican congressman Washburne arranged his appointment as brigadier general. From that time onward, Grant's political affiliation remained unclear, a lack of clarity he found beneficial.

Just when Grant became a Republican has no easy answer. His wartime policy stressed military professionalism and adherence to federal mandates. Of all divisive issues, the most important centered on emancipation and its military counterpart, the use of black troops. Here Grant gave model adherence to administration policy, strengthened by his admiration for black troops of his own command who had withstood a Confederate attack on Milliken's Bend in June 1863.

After Grant's smashing victory at Chattanooga in November 1863, politicians of both parties appraised him as a potential 1864 presidential candidate. He firmly rebuffed Democratic overtures, the more urgent because the party, divided and leaderless since the death of Douglas in June 1861, desperately needed a military hero to oppose Lincoln.

Nearly three years of Civil War, with the end beyond sight and even the outcome in doubt, gave Lincoln concern about his renomination and reelection. Republican radicals massed against him eventually nominated Frémont as a protest candidate. Other Republican dissidents already looked to Grant. At the Republican convention in Baltimore in June, every vote went to Lincoln on the first ballot except twenty-two Missouri votes for Grant, later switched to make the nomination unanimous. By the summer of 1864, Grant could almost certainly have received the Democratic nomination for president or could have mounted a strong threat to Lincoln as a Republican.

Yet as late as 1868, Grant still did not want to be elected president. He intensely disliked newspaper attention, public speaking, ceremony, and every aspect of politics. With four children still in school, he craved the security of lifetime tenure in the peacetime army. Only Andrew Johnson through a relentless assault on congressional Reconstruction and military authority could provoke Grant to action. Johnson first attempted to use Grant as a political pawn, then attacked him as faithless when he refused to comply. Even then, Grant referred to his enthusiastic supporters as "that awful Chicago Convention" and explained that he had been "forced into" accepting the nomination "in spite of myself."[17] Few have grasped his genuine reluctance to serve as president; little wonder that in 1864, Lincoln, a man supremely political, needed the most convincing evidence that Grant intended to remain in military command. Not until trusted political advisers like J. Russell Jones of Galena assured Lincoln that Grant harbored no presidential ambitions did Lincoln's concerns subside.

Congress created the rank of lieutenant general for Grant, but constitutional limitations prevented its naming him. Only Lincoln could nominate a lieutenant general—and he could have promoted Halleck without changing the command structure. Even after assembling all available evidence about Grant's lack of presidential ambition, Lincoln remained wary.

An interpretation of the relationship between Lincoln and Grant that argues their immediate rapport falls far short of reality. Lincoln saw Grant as a potential political rival, as possibly another McClellan, that former military savior headed toward the Democratic nomination for president. Grant saw Lincoln as the commander in chief who had burdened McClellan with advice and orders, given his army to John Pope, and destroyed his military career. Nor could he have forgotten that Lincoln had given Sherman's command to McClernand, whose ambitions included toppling Grant. Before Grant came east, Lincoln needed abundant reason to believe that Grant posed no political threat. Grant needed equal assurance that Lincoln posed no military threat. Once the deal was struck, both needed reassurance that it had been made sincerely.

Lincoln twice visited Grant in Virginia during the summer of 1864. On June 20, Lincoln left Washington at 5:00 P.M. and arrived slightly seasick at City Point the next day about noon. After reviewing troops, he spent the evening sitting outside Grant's tent telling stories to the general and his staff. Accompanied by his son Tad, Lincoln had apparently come to visit, to inspect, to strengthen a personal relationship, but hardly as commander in chief. Lincoln filled the following day with inspections and reviews before leaving for Washington. During the visit, the two had spent little time together; what they discussed and its effects on strategy remain unknown. Perhaps the meeting takes on significance largely through its lack of significance: Grant and Lincoln reassured each other of good intentions by maintaining separate spheres of authority.

Grant's brilliant movement across the James River to Petersburg had been followed by federal folly, incompetence, and timidity as thinly held Confederate lines stalled an assault of tenfold more troops. By the time Lincoln arrived on June 21, Grant had lost the momentum for a smashing victory and faced Lee's veterans in the Petersburg trenches. Furthermore, Jubal Early's corps, sent to stop David Hunter's threat to Lynchburg, had driven federal forces into West Virginia and could look down the Shenandoah Valley toward Washington. Gradually Grant grasped the dismal implications of those missed opportunities and settled into a siege. Meanwhile, he underestimated Early's threat, detaching troops only after Early reached Harpers Ferry. Lew Wallace, defeated at Monocacy, Maryland, on July 9, may have saved the capital by delaying Early's advance on Washington for a single day. By the time Confederate troops reached the outskirts of Washington, enough of Grant's tardily sent troops had reached the forts to discourage more than a skirmish. Yet Early's corps remained intact, threatening numerous important transportation and supply centers while weakening Northern morale. To coordinate the pursuit of Early, Grant first had suggested William B. Franklin. On July 25, he recommended placing Meade in charge, for reasons he did "not care to commit to paper."[18]

Smoldering animosities blazed in the Army of the Potomac, fanned by William F. Smith, the commander who deserved blame for the June 15 failure at Petersburg but who blamed everyone else. Relentless in charges against both Meade and Butler, Smith implicated Grant himself in failure. Both Meade and Butler reacted vigorously to criticism, Meade by loudly losing his temper, Butler by quietly plotting against his foes.

To break the Petersburg siege, coal miners of the 48th Pennsylvania dug a tunnel beneath Confederate lines, filled the end with explosives, and detonated a devastating blast. Union troops failed to exploit the opening and were repulsed with heavy losses, a battle Grant called the "saddest affair I have witnessed in this war. Such opportunity for carrying fortifications I have never seen and do not expect again to have."[19]

The day after the battle of the Crater, with Early still a threat to Northern cities, Lincoln arrived at Fort Monroe for a five-hour conference with Grant. So little is known of their discussion that the noted historian T. Harry Williams wondered if they had actually met; yet they did meet. This time, however, Lincoln came without Tad, Grant without his staff. Lincoln neither reviewed troops nor regaled an appreciative audience with stories. Grant omitted all mention of this meeting in his *Memoirs*.

Grant wrote his *Memoirs* with rare skill, modesty, balance, and candor. Desperately ill, he intended to leave a legacy for his impoverished family and a testament to his countrymen. Nonetheless, he summarized in six pages his six years in St. Louis from his resignation in 1854 until his move to Galena in 1860, years of struggle and hardship. These few pages contain more information about the politics of the period than of Grant's life. In an otherwise detailed Civil War narrative, he did not allude to General Orders No. 11, which he issued in December 1862. These orders, ostensibly designed to regulate trade, expelled all Jews from the Department of the Tennessee. Responding to vigorous protests, Lincoln revoked this outrageous act of bigotry. During the 1868 presidential campaign, Grant grudgingly admitted his error—the only Democratic charge against him that he answered—but chose not to revisit this painful incident in his *Memoirs*.

Grant's silence about the Fort Monroe meeting speaks eloquently of the pain of Lincoln's rebuke. Grant had been slow and ineffective in meeting Early's threat and had not yet coordinated a unified pursuit. After leading his army on the bloody road to Petersburg, he had not harvested the reward of his strategy. He had been vacillating and tentative in restructuring his command team and had ignored political realities tied to generalship. Although nothing is known of the actual content of the conference, its consequences were clear enough. If Grant had entered the Wilderness with any misconception that Lincoln had delegated management of the war, Grant received the necessary correction. Lincoln took control.

On the back of Grant's telegram arranging the meeting, Lincoln jotted a few words, presumably the agenda for the conference. "Meade & Franklin" represented Grant's suggestions for unified command to defend the capital; "Md. & Penna." indicated how broad that command might be. Between them Lincoln wrote the single word "McClellan."[20] Restoring McClellan to command had several advantages: enlisting the talents of the general who had twice before saved the capital, spurring Northern enlistments, and depriving Democrats of their most attractive potential presidential nominee. With Grant holding rank as lieutenant general and general in chief, McClellan would take the field as a subordinate. The Blair family had begun to negotiate with McClellan. The plan foundered because McClellan refused to take himself out of contention for the nomination or to ask Lincoln for command. While McClellan continued to sulk, however, Lincoln and Grant may well have discussed McClellan's military future. Such executive speculation reflected diminished faith in Grant.

As in 1862, when McClellan was as close to Richmond as Grant was two years later, the result of Early's raid might have been a detachment of troops from offensive to defensive deployment. Before Lincoln arrived, Grant had ordered a division of cavalry to Washington. After the conference, he sent Major General Philip H. Sheridan to take command of all troops in the area and "to put himself south of the enemy and follow him to the death."[21] When Lincoln read the telegram, he responded that such action would "neither be done nor attempted unless you watch it every day, and hour, and force it."[22] Grant hurried to Washington to organize the pursuit of Early, something he disliked doing since Butler was senior in command whenever Grant was absent.

In effect Lincoln had told Grant where to go and what to do, and had at least hinted what might happen if he failed the assignment. With twice as many troops as Lee, Grant had settled into a protracted siege and had allowed himself to become "McClellanized." Furthermore, Lincoln analyzed the military situation more clearly than did Grant. Lee had pinned Grant at Petersburg effectively enough to detach Early's corps for a major Northern campaign, with enough men to sweep down the Shenandoah Valley and to approach the defenses of Washington. If Lincoln's intervention had been unseemly, it was timely and necessary. Further, he had withheld intervention until the case for defending Washington was airtight. Even Grant recognized the necessity for an offensive in the Shenandoah Valley.

He also recognized that the president expected greater care in assigning generals. Of the commanders expected to lead major armies in the 1864 spring offensive, three owed their positions to political factors: Nathaniel P. Banks, Butler, and Sigel. None would survive Grant's drive for military professionalism; none would be easy to shelve. Banks's failure in the ill-conceived and badly executed Red River expedition led Grant to telegraph to Halleck that he had "been satisfied for the last nine months that to keep General Banks in command was to neutralize a large force and to support it most expensively." "Although I do not insist on it," he wrote, he wanted Major General Joseph J. Reynolds to replace Banks.[23] Halleck replied that Lincoln wanted to delay to assess the results of the expedition; furthermore, William B. Franklin would be the senior officer in the Department of the Gulf when Banks fell. If Banks could be ordered back to New Orleans, Grant conceded, placing the troops under the "senior officer" would suit him. Franklin had been "mixed up with misfortune," but was "much better than Gen Banks."[24] In response, Halleck explored the complexities.

> I submitted your telegram of 10.30 A.M. to the secty of War, who was of the opinion that, before asking the President for an order, I should obtain your views in regard to the extent of the proposed Division, the officer to command it, &c., and that I should write to you confidentially on the subject. Do you

propose to include Pope's Curtis' & Rosecrans' commands, or
only the present Depts of the Gulf and of Arkansas with the
Indian Territory? Is it proposed to give Banks the command
of the Division, or to leave him in the subordinate position of
his present Dept, or to remove him entirely? In either case, the
order must be definite. If Banks is superceded, Franklin will be
the ranking officer in the field, and Rosecrans, Curtis or Mc-
Clernand, in the Division. You have also heretofore spoken of
Steele and Reynolds in connexion with this command. I think
the President will consent to the order, if you insist upon Genl
Banks removal as a military necessity, but he will do so very
reluctantly, as it would give offence to many of his friends, &
would probably be opposed by a portion of his cabinet. Moreover, what could be done with Banks? He has many political
friends who would demand for him a command equal to the
one he now has. The result would probably be the same as in
the cases of Rosecrans, Curtis, Sigel, Butler & Lew. Wallace.
Before submitting the matter to the President, the Secty of War
wishes to have in definite form precisely the order you wish
issued.[25]

Grant countered with a suggestion that Halleck himself take command
of the "trans-Mississippi Division," at least temporarily turning over his
Washington office to Canby. Halleck responded that he would willingly serve "any where and every where," but Canby was quite ill.[26] The
president, fully aware of Grant's suggestions, had said nothing. When
Grant firmly insisted on Banks's removal, he learned that Canby had
already taken command. When Halleck contemplated leaving Washington for service in the field, Canby's health immediately improved.
Before Canby went to New Orleans, the extent of Banks's failure was
fully known. His removal, however, required more than an expression of
Grant's wishes; he had to take full responsibility. His first telegram was
unequivocal about the removal of Banks, however, and the president
required emphatic repetition of this request.

Appointed to command in the Shenandoah to please a German
constituency, Sigel soon demonstrated an inability even to hold a leg.
When Early appeared, Sigel disappeared. Grant urged Halleck to
relieve Sigel of command, "at least until present troubles are over."[27]
His replacement was another matter. Grant suggested Major General

Edward O. C. Ord, but through lack of response from Washington, Hunter took command, although Stanton considered him "far more incompetent than even Sigel."[28] Grant's recommendation that Franklin or Meade assume command brought Lincoln to the Fort Monroe conference and resulted in Sheridan's departure for the Shenandoah Valley.

From the time Grant took command he recognized the problem posed by Butler. A prominent prewar Democrat who had rushed to war and received the reward of the rank of major general of volunteers so early that he claimed to rank all other active generals except Grant, Butler had sedulously preserved political alliances while creating havoc throughout the army. Recognizing the necessity of maintaining Butler in the field in an election year, Grant had sent him two corps commanders for the Army of the James, William F. Smith and Quincy A. Gillmore, believed to represent the best military professionalism. During the campaign of May 1864, both Smith and Gillmore had failed Butler, with the resulting neutralization of thirty thousand troops "bottled up" at Bermuda Hundred. Once Grant crossed the James River, the Army of the Potomac and the Army of the James united, making Butler senior commander under Grant and commander by regulation whenever Grant was absent, as he rarely was for that very reason.

In this matter, Grant had strong allies in Washington. Both Stanton and Halleck so detested Butler that the former sent Assistant Secretary of War Charles A. Dana to City Point to suggest Butler's transfer. In a letter to Halleck, Grant danced daintily around the issue.

> Whilst I have no diff[i]culty with Gen. Butler, finding him always cle[ar] in his conception of orders, and prompt to obey, yet there is a want of knowledge how to execute, and particularly a prejudice against him, as a commander, that operates against his usefulness. . . . As an administrative officer Gen. Butler has no superior. In taking charge of a Dept.mt where there are no great battles to be fought, but a dissatisfied element to controll no one could manage it better than he. If a command could be cut out such as Mr Dana proposed, namely Ky. Ill. & I[ndian]a. or if the Depts. of the Mo. Kansas and the states of Ill. & Ia. could be merged together and Gen. Butler put over it I believe the good of the service would be subserved.[29]

Halleck answered with unusual frankness.

I will, as you propose, await further advices from you before I submit the matter officially to the Secty of War and the President. It was foreseen from the first that you would eventually find it necessary to relieve Genl. B. on account of his total unfitness to command in the field, and his generally quarrelsome character. What shall be done with him, has therefore already been, as I am informed; a matter of consultation. To send him to Kentucky would probably cause an insurrection in that state, and an immediate call for large reenforcements. Moreover, he would probably greatly embarras Sherman, or if he did not attempt to supersede him, by using against him all his talent at political intrigue and his facilities for newspaper abuse. If you send him to Missouri, nearly the same thing will occur there. Although it might not be objectionable to have a free fight between him and Rosecrans, the Government would be seriously embarrassed by the local difficulties, and calls for reinforcements likely to follow. Inveterate as is Rosecran's habit of continually calling for more troops, Butler differs only in demanding instead of *calling*. As things now stand in the west, I think we can keep the peace; but if Butler be thrown in as a disturbing element, I anticipate very serious results. Why not leave Genl Butler in the local command of his Dept, including N. C. Norfolk, Fort Monroe, Yorktown, &c, and make a new army corps of the part of the 18th under Smith? This would leave B. under your immediate control, and at the same time would relieve you of his presence in the field. Moreover, it would save the necessity of organizing a new Dept. If he must be relieved entirely, I think it would be best to make a new Dept. for him in New England. I make these remarks merely as suggestions. Whatever you may finally determine on, I will try to have done. As Genl. B. claims to rank me, I shall give him no orders wherever he may go, without the special direction of yourself or the Secty of War.[30]

Grant eagerly grasped Halleck's plan to shelve Butler, and Lincoln approved the orders; but Grant ultimately backed down for reasons that have remained controversial. Smith claimed that Butler blackmailed Grant after catching him drinking; others have argued that Grant realized that Smith's unrelenting criticism of other generals, including

Meade and perhaps Grant himself, led to recognition that Smith was a greater hazard than even Butler. Smith left, Butler stayed. Lincoln tried to avoid involvement; if Butler left, Grant would have to send him away.

In late June, Grant responded with disgust to a message that Major General William S. Rosecrans and Major General Samuel R. Curtis had called for reinforcements in Missouri. "I am satisfied you would hear the same call if they were stationed in Maine. The fact is the two Depts. should be merged into one and some officer, who does not govern so largely through a secret police system as Rosecrans does, put in command. I do think the best interests of the service demands that Rosecrans should be removed and some one else placed in that command. It makes but little difference who you assign it would be an improvement."[31] Nonetheless, it did make a difference who inherited Rosecrans's department. Furthermore, Rosecrans, a radical favorite, was the best-known Catholic general, hardly a factor to ignore in an election year.

Following the Fort Monroe conference, Grant no longer proposed to shuffle generals like a pack of cards. Rosecrans continued to mismanage Missouri until after the election. Meade remained in command of the Army of the Potomac, and Butler lost the Army of the James only after demonstrating clear incompetence at Fort Fisher—and after the election.

In August, despairing of both political and military victory, Lincoln prepared a memorandum for his cabinet to sign, sight unseen. "This morning, as for some days past, it seems exceedingly probable that this Administration will not be reelected. Then it will be my duty to so cooperate with the President elect, as to save the Union between the election and the inauguration; as he will have secured his election on such ground that he can not possibly save it afterwards."[32] Lincoln intended, he explained later, to call upon McClellan after his election victory to raise troops for one last desperate effort for victory. By implication at least, Lincoln had decided that Grant could not win the war; only McClellan could defeat the Confederates.

Within a few days, however, Lincoln learned that Sherman could finish the job. The fall of Atlanta came precisely in time to counter Democratic claims that the war was a failure. Sherman then planned a march to the sea, a move so daring that even Grant hesitated before giving approval. Rawlins vigorously opposed the expedition and, as Grant recalled, persuaded authorities in Washington to delay Grant's approval.

Stanton telegraphed on October 12 that the president expressed "much solicitude" about the plan and hoped that "it will be maturely considered."[33] Grant had already wired his approval. Sherman's celebrated Christmas gift of Savannah to Lincoln was equally Grant's triumph.

On February 16, 1862, Grant had demanded the "unconditional and immediate surrender" of Fort Donelson. Confederate brigadier general Simon B. Buckner accepted these "ungenerous and unchivalrous terms," which roused considerable enthusiasm in the North and gave Grant an enduring nickname since unconditional surrender matched the initials with which he signed official correspondence. Given the circumstances of a besieged fort from which two ranking commanders had fled with a portion of the garrison, Grant did not need to dicker with Buckner, to whom he showed considerable courtesy after the surrender. Under similar conditions, McClellan himself might have demanded unconditional surrender, though he had less aptitude for phraseology.

Capturing another Confederate army at Vicksburg, Grant again demanded unconditional surrender but in fact negotiated with Major General John C. Pemberton. Grant's decision to parole rather than imprison the garrison received some criticism despite logistical factors sustaining his judgment. Nonetheless, Grant came to Washington with his reputation intact for pushing for unconditional surrender.

By the end of 1864, after Lincoln's reelection, Sherman's capture of Savannah, and Major General George H. Thomas's smashing victory at Nashville, the end of the war loomed. Efforts to negotiate peace during 1864, sometimes bizarre and always doomed, at least uncovered the two basic Confederate demands: independence and slavery. When hope for independence waned, that for slavery persisted. Confederates thought that Northerners might sacrifice emancipation for peace and reunion. Under such circumstances, Lincoln stood for unconditional surrender and wondered whether Grant would stand firm.

During the summer of 1864, Grant had realized the importance of Lincoln's reelection. In a private letter to Washburne, clearly intended for public use, Grant unmistakably endorsed Lincoln without mentioning his name or his party.

> I state to all Citizens who visit me that all we want now to insure an early restoration of the Union is a determined unity of sentiment North. The rebels have now in their ranks their last man. The little boys and old men are guarding prisoners,

guarding rail-road bridges and forming a good part of their garrisons for intrenched positions. A man lost by them can not be replaced. They have robbed the cradle and the grave equally to get their present force. Besides what they lose in frequent skirmishes and battles they are now loosing from desertions and other causes at least one regiment per day. With this drain upon them the end is visible if we will but be true to ourselves. Their only hope now is in a divided North. This might give them reinforcements from Tenn. Ky. Maryland and Mo. whilst it would weaken us. With the draft quietly enforced the enemy would become dispondent and would make but little resistence. I have no doubt but the enemy are exceedingly anxious to hold out until after the Presidential election. They have many hopes from its effects. They hope a counter revolution. They hope the election of the peace candidate. In fact, like McCawber, they hope *something* to turn up. Our peace friends, if they expect peace from separation, are much mistaken. It would be but the begining of war with thousands of Northern men joining the South because of our disgrace allowing separatio[n.] To have peace "on any terms" the South would demand the restoration of their slaves already freed. They would demand indemnity for losses sustained, and they would demand a treaty which would make the North slave hunters for the South. They would demand pay or the restoration of every slave escaping to the North.[34]

This letter received wide circulation as Republican campaign material, including an appearance in a pamphlet entitled *Democratic Statesmen and Generals to the Loyal Sons of the Union*. Grant's status as a Democrat added strength to the Union ticket of 1864 on which Lincoln ran with Johnson, an unrepentant Democrat. In September, Washburne asked for permission to circulate the letter that Grant had written to Lincoln on the eve of the campaign. Grant replied, "I have no objection to the President using any thing I have ever written to him as he sees fit—I think however for him to attempt to answer all the charges the opposition will bring against him will be like setting a maiden to work to prove her chastity."[35] Grant also helped Lincoln by facilitating voting in the field. He congratulated Lincoln indirectly on reelection, emphasizing his relief that there had been no disorder at the polls.

Even after the election, Lincoln had no reason to forget that Grant was a prewar Democrat and slaveholder. As a professional soldier, Grant shared the conservatism of the peacetime army. Fifteen years in the army starting at West Point had provided him with close friends now commanding Rebel forces. Marriage into a family of border-state slaveholders strengthened his Southern ties, including those to his wife's cousin James Longstreet, previously Grant's old army friend. Grant had demanded unconditional surrender of armies when he had no practical alternative. How would he respond to peace initiatives and offers of negotiation?

The test came at the end of January 1865, when Confederate emissaries arrived at City Point requesting permission to visit Washington to confer with Lincoln about the "existing War" and "upon what terms it may be terminated." The impressive delegation consisted of Confederate vice president Alexander H. Stephens, once a Georgia Whig congressman admired by fellow Whig congressman Lincoln; Confederate assistant secretary of war John A. Campbell, former justice of the U.S. Supreme Court; and Robert M. T. Hunter, prewar U.S. senator from Virginia, late Confederate secretary of state. Lincoln sent Major Thomas T. Eckert to pose conditions: unless the commissioners discussed a "common country," no conference could take place. Grant, who had served dinner to the commissioners, now realized that he had blundered through cordiality. To underscore the point, Lincoln told Grant to allow "nothing which is transpiring, change, hinder, or delay, your Military movements, or plans."[36]

In a telegram to Stanton, Grant asserted that Stephens and Hunter had shown him "that their intentions were good and their desire sincere to restore peace and Union."[37] He regretted that Lincoln did not plan to meet at least these two. Grant forced Lincoln's hand. "Induced by a despatch of Gen. Grant," he wired Seward, "I Join you at Fort-Monroe so soon as I can come."[38] The conference itself, to which Grant was not invited, proved entirely unproductive. Lincoln demanded reunion and emancipation; Jefferson Davis had empowered his emissaries to concede neither but only to urge a hare-brained scheme to unite in an expedition to drive the French from Mexico. Although Lincoln suggested that he might favor compensation to slaveholders after rebellion ceased, Confederates characterized this policy as first demanding "unconditional submission." Indeed, the Confederates were correct. Lincoln gained nothing by conferring and would not have gone without Grant's urging, a point he emphasized in reporting to Congress.

Later in February, Grant was drawn into one of the silliest episodes of the war. Confederate commissioners at City Point had been favorably impressed by Grant's friendliness and that of Mrs. Grant, who hoped that the Confederates might be inveigled into releasing her brother John Dent, held prisoner in the South despite his ardent Rebel sympathies. Grant refused to exchange a soldier for his civilian brother-in-law, especially since Dent had foolishly thought that outspoken support of the Confederacy gave him license to travel freely in the South. Remembering Mrs. Grant's cordiality, and perhaps forgetting its cause, Julia's cousin Longstreet proposed to Ord that Mrs. Longstreet and Mrs. Grant exchange social visits as a first step toward conversations between officers of both sides that might end with Grant and Lee suspending hostilities to negotiate. Grant dismissed the proposal as "simply absurd."[39]

Conversations between Ord and Longstreet on political prisoners veered toward peace negotiations. Longstreet asserted, Ord recorded, that Lee believed the Southern cause to be hopeless while Davis insisted on continuing the war. Ord suggested that Lee threaten to resign so as to force Davis to negotiate for compensation for lost slaves "and an immediate share in the Gov't."[40] When Lee requested a meeting with Grant to discuss matters further, Grant forwarded the message to Washington and received an unequivocal reply from Stanton. "The President directs me to say to you that he wishes you to have no conference with Gen Lee unless it be for the capitulation of Lees army, or on solely minor and purely military matters[.] He instructs me to say that you are not to decide, discuss, or confer upon any political question: such questions the President holds in his own hands; and will submit them to no military conferences or conventions—mean time you are to press to the utmost, your military advantages." In his own name, Stanton elaborated.

I send you a telegram written by the President himself in answer to yours of this evening which I have signed by his order. I will add that General Ords conduct in holding intercourse with General Longstreet upon political questions not committed to his charge is not approved. The same thing was done in one instance by Major Key when the army was commanded by General McClellan and he was sent to meet Howell Cobb on the subject of exchanges, and it was in that instance as in this

disapproved. You will please in future instruct officers appointed to meet rebel officers to confine themselves to the matters
specially committed to them.[41]

Again, Lincoln rather than Grant pushed toward the goal of unconditional surrender.

In January, Grant had discussed with Lincoln the awkward status
of the president's son Robert, a student at Harvard College and Law
School during a war to which his father had sent so many other sons.
His father wrote that Robert "wishes to see something of the war before
it ends. I do not wish to put him in the ranks, nor yet to give him a commission, to which those who have already served long, are better entitled, and better qualified to hold. Could he, without embarrassment to
you, or detriment to the service, go into your Military family with some
nominal rank, I, and not the public, furnishing his necessary means?
If no, say so without the least hesitation, because I am as anxious, and
as deeply interested, that you shall not be encumbered as you can be
yourself."[42] Grant responded that he would "be most happy to have him
in my Military family." Rank, he continued, would be "immaterial but
I would suggest that of Capt. as I have three Staff officers now, of con-
ciderable service, in no higher grade. Indeed I have one officer with only
the rank of Lieut. who has been in the service from the begining of the
war. This however will make no difference and I would still say give the
rank of Capt."[43] The next day, Robert wrote that he needed to return
to Cambridge and then wanted to attend his father's second inauguration, so he asked Grant's "kind indulgence" before reporting.[44] Before
he did so, his father had formally nominated him for a commission as
captain. If Robert's princely status and aristocratic airs annoyed Grant,
he gave no indication of displeasure. Robert's staff appointment, so unwarranted a favor, cemented through an ignoble transaction a personal
relationship between Grant and Lincoln previously nonexistent.

Robert's prolonged civilian life and military sinecure probably owed
much to his mother's increasing emotional deterioration. She had never
recovered from her son Willie's death in February 1862, and her behavior grew steadily more irrational and intolerable. Perhaps unaware
of the extent of the problem, Grant invited Lincoln to visit in March,
thinking that he would want to see Robert but would not do so without a formal invitation. Besides, Robert had no staff role greater than
escorting his parents.

Accompanied by Mary and Tad, Lincoln arrived at City Point on March 24 for a visit that lasted a fortnight. Jealous of Grant's growing fame, Mary almost immediately insulted Julia. On a carriage ride to inspect Ord's division, Mary launched into a hysterical outburst that embarrassed everybody. For the remainder of the visit, Julia avoided Mary, who left for Washington on April 1, only to return on April 6.

Lincoln, Grant, Sherman, and Admiral Porter met on March 28 on the president's boat, the *River Queen*. With the end of the war finally in sight, the chieftains met to contemplate the future. What took place remains obscure. In his *Memoirs,* Grant omitted all mention of events during that part of the president's visit when Mary accompanied him. Sherman and Porter remembered that Lincoln was ready to recognize existing Southern governments whenever the war ended, with "liberal views" toward Rebels and "peace on almost any terms."[45] Both Sherman and Porter, however, sought to justify Sherman's overly generous terms to the Confederacy's General Joseph E. Johnston, given the day Lincoln died and quickly disavowed by Johnson and Stanton. Sherman had negotiated the surrender of all Confederate armies, had provided that their weapons could be taken to their state arsenals, and had stipulated that the United States would recognize the authority of these state governments and the political and property rights of their citizens. Had Sherman's terms received approval, slavery might well have survived the war when former Confederate states refused to ratify the Thirteenth Amendment.

If Sherman had been overwhelmed by the congratulatory and harmonious mood in the cabin of the *River Queen,* Grant remembered the harsh tone of the rebuke received when he proposed a military convention with Lee. He also remembered the two points made to the Confederate commissioners in February: that "the Union should be preserved" and that "slavery should be abolished."[46] These were preconditions for negotiation rather than negotiable. Porter, who unconvincingly claimed to remember the conversation on the *River Queen* in great detail, reported that Grant sat quietly smoking throughout, speaking only once, to ask about Sherman's destruction of railroads.

For that matter, Grant was absorbed in planning his final offensive, launched at the end of that month. When Petersburg fell on April 2, Grant invited Lincoln to meet him inside the town. Accompanied by Robert and Tad, Lincoln arrived the next day and strode to a house commandeered by Grant. As the president and Grant sat quietly on the porch, the yard filled with former slaves, staring worshipfully at their liberators. Again the two found little to say. Grant remembered only that Lincoln had the right to ask about campaign plans, something he refrained from doing, and Grant did not volunteer information. Yet Lincoln never took his eyes off the war. As he left for Washington, he telegraphed to Grant: "Gen. Sheridan says 'If the thing is pressed I think that Lee will surrender.' Let the *thing* be pressed."[47]

Lincoln left City Point on April 8 and arrived in Washington the next evening to find streets filled with people celebrating Lee's surrender at Appomattox. After the war, artist William Page, once hailed as "the American Titian," planned his masterpiece, a giant canvas of Grant entering Richmond in triumph. A request that Grant pose brought the response that Grant had never entered Richmond. In April 1865 he had hurried off to Washington to finish off the war. On April 13, he received a note from Mary Lincoln inviting him "to drive around with us to see the illumination."[48] During the drive, cheers for Grant so provoked Mary to abusive language that Grant decided against accompanying the Lincolns to the theater the following evening, deciding instead to visit his children in New Jersey. Aboard the train, the Grants learned of Lincoln's assassination.

Had Lincoln lived, Sherman insisted, the surrender terms to Johnston would have received presidential approval. Grant knew better. He made excuses for Sherman and embraced Sherman's quarrels with Stanton and Halleck without deviating from the central principle that Sherman had no executive warrant for terms beyond those given to Lee at Appomattox. Those terms, however tempered by graciousness and compassion, amounted to unconditional surrender. Lincoln had insisted upon that.

When all their meetings are summed up, Lincoln and Grant had spent little time together. Because of the problem of Mrs. Lincoln, Grant (and others) sometimes avoided the Lincolns. Grant remembered Lincoln's ready wit and storytelling ability better than some frustrations in implementing military policy. To interpret their relationship in terms of an immediate understanding that created an instantaneous partnership is to miss the point of Lincoln's leadership. He held the reins and taught Grant what was permitted and what was forbidden.

Lincoln's tragic death led to his enshrinement in the memories of those who had known him, even those who had clashed with him. A bitter quarrel with Johnson enhanced Grant's favorable opinion of

Lincoln. Grant's presidency as Lincoln's Republican successor provided additional reason for admiration. Finally, Grant's post-presidential role as party leader elicited further praise of Lincoln. In writing and speaking in later years, Grant succumbed to the sentimentality of the age. He created the impression that mutual harmony and respect had existed from their first meeting and persisted until Lincoln's death.

In reality, however, Grant and Lincoln forged an effective partnership in a turmoil of clashing authority. Amid the confusion of war, Lincoln redefined the concept of commander in chief, Stanton transformed the concept of secretary of war, and Halleck created the concept of chief of staff. Charged with vast responsibilities, General in Chief Grant had to act vigorously within the military sphere, tread softly in the political sphere, and understand as well the politics of command. Under Lincoln's guidance, sometimes oblique, sometimes imperious, Grant succeeded.

Acknowledgments

I am extremely grateful to Selina Langford, head of Western Kentucky University's Interlibrary Loan office, for helping me track down copies of essays that I lacked in my own files. A special thank you is due to two of my undergraduate students—Leigh-Anne St. Charles and Chelsea E. Kasten—who very ably and efficiently converted photocopies and PDF files of the essays into digital text files. Both of these young women performed these tasks as part of their duties as office assistants in the Department of History at Western Kentucky University, but actually they were two of my better students in class, so I was not surprised at how adept they were in quickly handling my technology requests—and always with a smile. David Lee, dean of the Potter College of Arts and Letters, and Robert Dietle, head of the Department of History, both at Western Kentucky University, supported this project from beginning to end and readily understood, as colleagues *and* as friends, how important this book is to me personally.

Mary-Jo Kline, a friend for three decades, commiserated with me about the project, Professor John Y. Simon's unique qualities as a scholar and a man, and our shared sadness over losing him. Sylvia Frank Rodrigue, another of John's good friends, suggested the collection and publication of these essays as a book, and I am grateful to her for sharing many creative ideas and helpful hints about how best to go about the project. At the University Press of Kentucky, Stephen M. Wrinn and Allison Webster guided the manuscript through the publication process with expert hands and exceptional enthusiasm. Carol Sickman-Garner copyedited the text with a sure eye.

Harriet Furst Simon, John's wife, shared memories and stories, helped me compile the bibliography of John's works, assisted in proofreading (as she had done with so many volumes of the *Grant Papers*), and offered words of support and loving kindness at a time when her own loss loomed large. She is a great lady.

My own wife, Donna, remained a constant source of inspiration, comfort, and love. While John always called her his favorite Saluki, she knew better. "I'll bet you say that to all the girls," she would repeatedly (and knowingly) reply.

Permissions

"House Divided: Lincoln and His Father" (Fort Wayne, Ind.: Louis A. Warren Lincoln Library and Museum, 1987). Published with the permission of the Lincoln National Life Foundation. Originally given as the tenth McMurtry Lecture at the Louis A. Warren Lincoln Library and Museum in Fort Wayne, Indiana, in 1987.

"Abraham Lincoln and Ann Rutledge," *Journal of the Abraham Lincoln Association* 11 (1990): 13–33. Used by permission.

"Abraham Lincoln, Jefferson Davis, and Fort Sumter," from *Abraham Lincoln and the Crucible of War: Papers from the Sixth Annual Lincoln Colloquium*, ed. George L. Painter (1993), 23–31. Used by permission.

"'Freeing Some and Leaving Others Alone': Lincoln's Emancipation Policy," from *Abraham Lincoln and a New Birth of Freedom: Papers from the Tenth Annual Lincoln Colloquium*, ed. Linda Norbut Suits and Timothy P. Townsend (1998), 21–35. Used by permission.

"Lincoln and 'Old Brains' Halleck," *North & South* 2 (November 1998): 38–45. Used by permission.

"Lincoln's Despair: The Crisis during the Summer of 1864," from *Abraham Lincoln and a Nation at War: Papers from the Ninth Annual Lincoln Colloquium*, ed. George L. Painter and Linda Norbut Suits (1996), 17–31.

"The Personal Sentiments of Mr. Lincoln," *Lincoln Herald*, 68 (1966): 89–92. Used by permission.

"Ulysses S. Grant One Hundred Years Later," *Illinois Historical Journal* 79, no. 4 (1986): 245–256; pamphlet reprint, Illinois State Historical Society, 1987. Published with the permission of the Illinois State Historical Society.

"The Paradox of Ulysses S. Grant," *Register of the Kentucky Historical Society* 81, no. 4 (1983): 366–382. Used with the permission of the Kentucky Historical Society.

"A Marriage Tested by War: Ulysses and Julia Grant," from *Intimate Strategies of the Civil War: Military Commanders and Their Wives,* ed. Carol K. Bleser and Lesley J. Gordon (New York: Oxford University Press, 2001), 123–137. Published with the permission of Oxford University Press, Inc.

"From Galena to Appomattox: Grant and Washburne," *Journal of the Illinois State Historical Society* 58, no. 2 (Summer 1965): 165–189. Published with the permission of the Illinois State Historical Society.

"That Obnoxious Order," *Civil War Times Illustrated* 23, no. 6 (Oct. 1984): 12–17. Used by permission.

"The Road to Appomattox: The Generalship of Ulysses S. Grant," *Ohio History* 8, no. 4 (August–September 1991): 2–19. Published with the permission of the Ohio Historical Society.

"Lincoln, Grant, and Kentucky in 1861," from *The Civil War in Kentucky,* ed. Kent Masterson Brown (Mason City, Iowa: Savas Publishing Company, 2000), 1–21. Published with the permission of Kent Masterson Brown.

"Grant, Lincoln and Unconditional Surrender," from *Lincoln's Generals,* ed. Gabor S. Boritt (New York: Oxford University Press, Inc., 1995): 163–198. Published with the permission of Oxford University Press, Inc.

Notes

Abbreviations

Butler, *Correspondence*	Benjamin F. Butler, *Private and Official Correspondence of Benjamin F. Butler,* 5 vols. (Norwood, Mass.: Plimpton Press, 1917)
CG	*Congressional Globe*
CW	*The Collected Works of Abraham Lincoln,* ed. Roy P. Basler, Marion Dolores Pratt, and Lloyd A. Dunlap, 8 vols. and supplement (New Brunswick, N.J.: Rutgers University Press, 1953–1955)
Hay, *Diaries and Letters*	John Hay, *Lincoln and the Civil War in the Diaries and Letters of John Hay,* ed. Tyler Dennett (New York: Dodd, Mead, 1939)
HMD	*House Miscellaneous Documents*
HRC	*House Reports of Committees*
ISHL	Illinois State Historical Library, Springfield, Ill.
JISHS	*Journal of the Illinois State Historical Society*
LC	Library of Congress, Washington, D.C.
LH	*Lincoln Herald*
NA	National Archives, Washington, D.C.
O.R.	U.S. War Department, *The War of the Rebellion: A Compilation of the Official Records of the Union and Confederate Armies,* 70 vols. in 128 parts (Washington, D.C.: Government Printing Office, 1880–1901)
PMJDG	Julia Dent Grant, *The Personal Memoirs of Julia Dent Grant,* ed. John Y. Simon (New York: G. P. Putnam's Sons, 1975)
PMUSG	Ulysses S. Grant, *Personal Memoirs of U. S. Grant,* 2 vols. (New York: Charles L. Webster and Co., 1885–1886)
PUSG	John Y. Simon et al., eds., *The Papers of Ulysses S. Grant* (Carbondale and Edwardsville: Southern Illinois University Press, 1967–)

Rice, *Reminiscences*   Allen Thorndike Rice, ed., *Reminiscences of*
                            Abraham Lincoln by Distinguished Men of His Time
                            (New York: North American Review, 1888)
Welles   Howard K. Beale, ed., *Diary of Gideon Welles:*
                            Secretary of the Navy under Lincoln and Johnson,
                            3 vols. (New York: W. W. Norton, 1960)

There are no source notes for Chapters 9 and 13.

Introduction

1. See Geoffrey Perret, *Ulysses S. Grant: Soldier and President* (New York: Random House, 1997), 172.

2. For the song's full lyrics, see Paul F. Boyer Jr., *Presidential Campaigns: From George Washington to George W. Bush* (New York: Oxford University Press, 2004), 112.

3. Professor Simon's informal presentation on selection standards was later shaped into a formal paper presented at a meeting of the Association for Documentary Editing in Providence, R.I., on Oct. 18, 1984, and later published as "The Canons of Selection," *Documentary Editing* 6 (Dec. 1984): 8–12, quotations at 11.

4. Simon, "Memorial to Ralph G. Newman," *Illinois Heritage* 3 (Fall–Winter 2000): 26.

5. For the Buck quotation, see Paul H. Buck, "The Years Ahead," *Journal of Higher Education* 28 (June 1957): 296. Simon never published his dissertation, perhaps because he became very quickly involved in—and totally consumed by—editing the Grant Papers after taking up his first teaching assignment at Ohio State, where, in something probably less than a coincidence, Buck had earned his bachelor of arts degree in 1921.

6. Marilyn Davis, "Listening to Grant," Southern Illinois University Carbondale *Perspectives* (Fall 2004): 10–15, quotation at 11.

7. Simon, "Editors and Critics," Association for Documentary Editing, *Newsletter* 3 (Dec. 1981): 1–4, quotations at 3.

8. R. J. Havlik, review, *Library Journal* 92 (1967): 3039.

9. Hal Bridges, review, *American Historical Review* 74 (Apr. 1968): 1243.

10. Warren W. Hassler Jr., review, *Journal of Southern History* 36 (Feb. 1970): 110.

11. Herbert Mitgang, "Grant at the Front," *New York Times,* July 13, 1985.

12. Michael Les Benedict, review, *Journal of Southern History* 72 (Feb. 2006): 201. Benedict, however, did criticize Simon and his fellow editors for not indicating "the comprehensiveness of the publication." He complained, too, that "the chronology in which Simon and his assistants place all this material is

often confusing," particularly the placement of incoming correspondence in the volumes' annotation. Benedict believed that "readers will often have to reconstruct the chronology for themselves." Ibid. Apart from this review, it is difficult to find any other criticism of the Grant Papers volumes in either scholarly journals or popular periodicals.

13. Davis, "Listening to Grant," 11.

14. See pp. 37–51, below.

15. See pp. 101–107, below.

16. Brooks D. Simpson, *Let Us Have Peace: Ulysses S. Grant and the Politics of War and Reconstruction* (Chapel Hill: University of North Carolina Press, 1991); Brooks D. Simpson, *Ulysses S. Grant: Triumph over Adversity, 1822–1865* (Boston: Houghton Mifflin, 2000); Jean Edward Smith, *Grant* (New York: Simon & Schuster, 2001); Joan Waugh, *U. S. Grant: American Hero, American Myth* (Chapel Hill: University of North Carolina Press, 2009). See also Ethan S. Rafuse, "Still a Mystery? General Grant and the Historians, 1981–2006," *Journal of Military History* 71 (July 2007): 849–874.

17. See pp. 123–134, below.

18. See pp. 89–99, below.

19. David Woodbury, "John Y. Simon: R. I. P.," Of Battlefields and Bibliophiles, http://obab.blogspot.com/2008/07/grant-project-consumed-him-though.html. On this webpage, Woodbury publishes for the first time an interview he conducted with Simon on Sept. 29, 2000, for the Civil War Forum (http://community.netscape.com/civilwar).

20. Simon, "Commentary at 10th Annual Lincoln Symposium," *Papers of the Abraham Lincoln Association* 6 (1984): 26.

21. Simon, interview with Woodbury, Sept. 29, 2000.

22. Simon, interview with Gerald Prokopowicz, Civil War Talk Radio, Dec. 17, 2004, http://www.voiceamerica.com/worldtalkradio/vepisode.aspx?aid =13017.

23. Simon, review of Wallace J. Schutz and Walter N. Trenerry, *Abandoned by Lincoln: A Military Biography of General John Pope* (1990), *Journal of American History* 78 (June 1991): 340.

24. Simon, interview with Woodbury, Sept. 29, 2000.

1. House Divided: Lincoln and His Father

1. George B. Forgie, *Patricide in the House Divided: A Psychological Interpretation of Lincoln and His Age* (New York: W. W. Norton and Company, 1979).

2. Dwight G. Anderson, *Abraham Lincoln: The Quest for Immortality* (New York: Alfred A. Knopf, 1982), 79.

3. Ibid., 7.

4. See Richard O. Curry, "Conscious or Subconscious Caesarism? A

Critique of Recent Scholarly Attempts to Put Abraham Lincoln on the Analyst's Couch," *JISHS* 77 (Spring 1984): 67–71; Major L. Wilson, "Lincoln and Van Buren in the Steps of the Fathers: Another Look at the Lyceum Address," *Civil War History* 29 (Sept. 1983): 197–211; Richard N. Current, "Lincoln after 175 Years: The Myth of the Jealous Son," *Papers of the Abraham Lincoln Association* 6 (1984): 15–24.

    5. William H. Herndon and Jesse William Weik, *Herndon's Lincoln: The True Story of a Great Life* (Chicago, New York, and San Francisco: Belford, Clarke and Company, 1889), 1: 3–4. Many years earlier, Herndon had shared with other biographers Lincoln's tribute to his mother. See J. G. Holland, *The Life of Abraham Lincoln* (Springfield, Mass.: Gurdon Bill, 1866), 23; Isaac N. Arnold, *The History of Abraham Lincoln, and the Overthrow of Slavery* (Chicago: Clarke and Company, 1866), 69; [Louis A. Warren], "The Lincoln Mother Controversy," *Lincoln Lore* 832 (Mar. 19, 1945). Herndon also placed the incident when Lincoln spoke of his mother's illegitimacy about 1851 and about 1852. Herndon to Ward Hill Lamon, Feb. 25 and Mar. 6, 1870, in Emanuel Hertz, *The Hidden Lincoln: From the Letters and Papers of William H. Herndon* (New York: Viking Press, 1938), 63, 73–74. Herndon also wrote that upon receiving news of his father's death, Lincoln praised his mother. *Herndon's Lincoln*, 1: 13. Since that event (Jan. 17, 1851) occurred about the middle of Herndon's recollected dates for Lincoln's other tribute to his mother, the two might be the same. The incident is undated in Herndon to Jesse W. Weik, June 19, 1887, Herndon-Weik Collection, LC. Herndon's undated manuscript "Lincoln in Ky." (ibid.) places the tribute to Lincoln's mother (without allusion to her illegitimacy) in 1846.

    Available evidence indicates that Lincoln spoke of his mother's illegitimacy only to Herndon, but in 1860 John Locke Scripps of the *Chicago Tribune* interviewed Lincoln in order to prepare a campaign biography. In later correspondence, Scripps revealed that "Mr. Lincoln communicated some facts to me concerning his ancestry which he did not wish to have published, and which I have never spoken of or alluded to before. I do not think, however, that Dennis Hanks, if he knows anything about these matters, would be very likely to say anything about them." Scripps to William H. Herndon, June 24, 1865, in Scripps, *Life of Abraham Lincoln*, ed. Roy P. Basler and Lloyd A. Dunlap (Bloomington: Indiana University Press, 1961), 13. Scripps never disclosed what Lincoln said concerning his ancestry, but Scripps wrote of Nancy Hanks Lincoln: "Facts in the possession of the writer have impressed him with the belief that, although of but limited education, she was a woman of great native strength of intellect and force of character; and he suspects that those admirable qualities of head and heart which characterize her distinguished son are inherited mostly from her." Ibid., 31. Modern editors added a snippy note. "The practice of belittling Thomas Lincoln continued for many years. Only recently has he been established as a man at least as industrious and successful as most of his neighbors." Ibid. They missed the point: Scripps had somewhere picked up a thought, most likely from Lincoln himself, that closely resembled Lincoln's reported statement to Herndon.

6. *Herndon's Lincoln*, 1: ix.

7. Benjamin P. Thomas, *Portrait for Posterity: Lincoln and His Biographers* (New Brunswick, N.J.: Rutgers University Press, 1947), 112–118.

8. Woodrow Wilson, *Division and Reunion 1829–1889* (New York: Longmans, Green, and Co., 1893), 216.

9. John T. Morse Jr., *Abraham Lincoln* (Boston and New York: Houghton, Mifflin and Company, 1893), 1: 9.

10. William E. Barton, *The Lineage of Lincoln* (Indianapolis: Bobbs-Merrill, 1929), 83. See Barton, *The Paternity of Abraham Lincoln: Was He the Son of Thomas Lincoln?* (New York: George H. Doran Company, 1924).

11. Louis Austin Warren, *Lincoln's Parentage and Childhood: A History of the Kentucky Lincolns Supported by Documentary Evidence* (New York and London: Century, 1926).

12. *CW*, 1: 456.

13. Ibid., 3: 511, 4: 61. A stray comma disappeared between the first and second use of the phrase, but the word "litterally" retained its double *t*.

14. Ibid.

15. Statement of Mrs. Thomas Lincoln, Sept. 8, 1865, in Hertz, *Hidden Lincoln*, 351.

16. *CW*, 3: 511. In the original document, the phrase about "second families" is interlineated, indicating that Lincoln may not have written it immediately after labeling the families "undistinguished." Facsimile in Ward Hill Lamon, *Recollections of Abraham Lincoln 1847–1865* (Chicago: A. C. McClurg and Company, 1895), between 10 and 11.

17. Barton, *Lineage of Lincoln*, 102, 127.

18. *CW*, 3: 511.

19. Copy of Dennis F. Hanks statement, 1877, Robert Todd Lincoln Papers, LC, 41699. "The Hanks were a peculiar people—not chaste—": David Turnham to Herndon, Sept. 15, 1865, Herndon-Weik Collection, LC. Herndon wrote that Lincoln said "that his relations were *lascivious, lecherous,* not to be trusted." Herndon to Ward Hill Lamon, Feb. 25, 1870, in Hertz, *Hidden Lincoln*, 63. Herndon later returned to this subject. "The Hanks family are or were a lecherous family—a family low even among the poor whites of the South. Lincoln as a matter of course knew all about them. This hurt Lincoln in the extreme being very sensitive. I was careful never to say Hanks in his presence. . . . I never dared to ask him any question about the Hanks family." Herndon to James H. Wilson, Oct. 1, Oct. 15, 1889, Herndon-Weik Collection, LC. See Reinhard H. Luthin, *The Real Abraham Lincoln* (Englewood

Cliffs, N.J.: Prentice-Hall, 1960), 142. Herndon's increasingly obsessive desire to prove Lincoln's illegitimacy as well as that of his mother undoubtedly influenced these remarks about the Hanks family. See David Donald, *Lincoln's Herndon* (New York: Alfred A. Knopf, 1948), 307–309.

20. Lincoln dated the death of his grandfather about 1784. *CW,* 1: 456, 3: 511, 4: 37, 61, 117. Other evidence places the event in 1786 or 1788. Albert J. Beveridge, *Abraham Lincoln 1809–1858* (Boston and New York: Houghton Mifflin Company, 1928), 1: 11; Warren, *Lincoln's Parentage and Childhood,* 11.

21. *CW,* 4: 61.

22. Thomas L. Purvis, "The Making of a Myth: Abraham Lincoln's Family Background in the Perspective of Jacksonian Politics," *JISHS* 75 (Summer 1982): 149–160, argues that Lincoln exaggerated his humble origins for political effect, ignoring prosperous and office-holding relatives. In this gentrification of the Lincoln family, the word "Hanks" does not appear.

23. Communication to the People of Sangamo County, Mar. 9, 1832, in *CW,* 1: 8–9.

24. Eulogy on Henry Clay, July 6, 1852, in ibid., 2: 121.

25. F. B. Carpenter, *Six Months at the White House with Abraham Lincoln* (New York: Hurd and Houghton, 1867), 123.

26. *CW,* 4: 61–62.

27. Dennis F. Hanks, in a statement of June 13, 1865, denied that the Lincolns moved to Indiana because of slavery. Hertz, *Hidden Lincoln,* 275.

28. O. M. Mather, "Thomas Lincoln's Accounts with Elizabethtown Merchants," *Register of the Kentucky State Historical Society* 28 (Jan. 1930): 92.

29. Charles H. Coleman, "The Half-Faced Camp in Indiana—Fact or Myth?" *Abraham Lincoln Quarterly* 7 (Sept. 1952): 138–146.

30. *CW,* 4: 62.

31. Beveridge, *Lincoln,* 1: 41, 61; Benjamin P. Thomas, *Abraham Lincoln: A Biography* (New York: Alfred A. Knopf, 1952), 9. This statement is emphatically denied in Louis A. Warren, *Lincoln's Youth: Indiana Years . . .* (Indianapolis: Indiana Historical Society, 1959), 21, 221–222.

32. Leonard Swett, "Mr. Lincoln's Story of His Own Life," in Rice, *Reminiscences,* 457.

33. Warren, *Lincoln's Youth,* 205.

34. *CW,* 4: 62. See ibid., 3: 463.

35. Leonard Swett to Josiah H. Drummond, May 27, 1860, typescript, Herndon-Weik Collection, LC; Swett, "Lincoln's Story," 458–459.

36. *CW,* 4: 62.

37. Henry C. Whitney, *Life of Lincoln: Lincoln the Citizen* (New York: Baker and Taylor Company, 1908), 1: 75.

38. Dennis F. Hanks quoted in Beveridge, *Lincoln,* 1: 68. See David Turnham statement, Sept. 15, 1865, Herndon-Weik Collection, LC.

39. Dennis F. Hanks statement, June 13, 1865, in Hertz, *Hidden Lincoln,* 280.

40. Beveridge, *Lincoln,* 1: 68.

41. Dennis F. Hanks statement, June 13, 1865, in Hertz, *Hidden Lincoln,* 278; Dennis Hanks interview, *Chicago Tribune,* May 30, 1885.

42. Mrs. Thomas Lincoln statement, Sept. 8, 1865, in Hertz, *Hidden Lincoln,* 351; Beveridge, *Lincoln,* 1: 81.

43. Beveridge, *Lincoln,* 1: 66. Hanks's son-in-law stated that "Abe's father habitually treated him with great barbarity." Ward H. Lamon, *The Life of Abraham Lincoln; From His Birth to His Inauguration as President* (Boston: James R. Osgood and Company, 1872), 40.

44. Ida M. Tarbell, *In the Footsteps of the Lincolns* (New York and London: Harper and Brothers, 1924), 143.

45. Hertz, *Hidden Lincoln,* 351; Beveridge, *Lincoln,* 1: 71.

46. *CW,* 4: 62.

47. The family record written by Lincoln is transcribed as "May [10]th. 18[15]." Ibid., 2: 94. Johnston was born in 1810, Lincoln recorded that date, and the information was so transcribed before the pages became worn, tattered, and partly illegible. *The History of Coles County, Illinois* (Chicago: Wm. Le Baron, Jr. and Co., 1879), 423. A facsimile in *Herndon's Lincoln,* vol. 1, between 4 and 5, indicates that the last digit of "1810" had flaked away in the nineteenth century. The date was also transcribed as 1810 when the page was sold at auction. Parke-Bernet Galleries Inc., Sale Number 1315, Feb. 19–20, 1952, 56. The 1830 U.S. Census for Macon County, Ill., had recorded two males between the ages of twenty and thirty (Johnston and Abraham Lincoln) in the household of Thomas Lincoln. Johnston gave his age as forty in 1850. U.S. Census, Coles County, Ill. See Marilyn O. Ames, "Lincoln's Stepbrother: John D. Johnston," *LH* 82 (Spring 1980): 302.

48. Beveridge, *Lincoln,* 1: 66.

49. Hertz, *Hidden Lincoln,* 352.

50. Francis F. Browne, *The Everyday Life of Abraham Lincoln* (New York and St. Louis: H. A. Thompson Publishing Co., 1886), 214.

51. Henry C. Whitney, *Life on the Circuit with Lincoln* (Boston: Estes and Lauriat, 1892), 476. See also ibid., 22–23.

52. *CW,* 4: 63, 64.

53. *Herndon's Lincoln,* 1: 22n–23n; Warren, *Lincoln's Youth,* 171; *CW,* 3: 16.

54. Beveridge, *Lincoln,* 1: 91–94.

55. Ibid., 1: 92–94; Hertz, *Hidden Lincoln,* 356, 362–363.

56. Ida M. Tarbell, *The Early Life of Abraham Lincoln . . .* (New York: S. S. McClure, 1896), 75.

57. Eleanor Gridley, *The Story of Abraham Lincoln . . .* (n.p.: Juvenile Publishing Company, 1900), 97–98. A daughter of Dennis Hanks remembered

her grandmother Lincoln saying that "John used to be the smartest when they were little fellows. But Abe passed him. Abe kept getting smarter all the time, and John he went just so far and stopped." Amanda Poorman in *St. Louis Post Dispatch*, May 26, 1901.

58. Gridley, *Lincoln*, 166. A similar statement quoted in Warren, *Lincoln's Youth*, 554, originates in the same source (Polly Richardson) discredited by Warren two pages later. See J. Edward Murr, "Lincoln in Indiana," *Indiana Magazine of History* 14 (Mar. 1918): 57.

59. Hertz, *Hidden Lincoln*, 347, 352, 363; Beveridge, *Lincoln*, 1: 80–81; Warren, *Lincoln's Youth*, 155. William E. Barton, *The Women Lincoln Loved* (Indianapolis: Bobbs-Merrill, 1927), 117–166, introduces a bevy of Indiana girlfriends for Lincoln, but these and others are summarily and effectively dismissed by Warren, *Lincoln's Youth*, 155–158.

60. *CW*, 1: 78.

61. Ibid., 1: 119.

62. A copy of a letter from Lincoln inviting John Hanks to the wedding was produced by a purported granddaughter of John Hanks. Jesse W. Weik, *The Real Lincoln: A Portrait* (Boston and New York: Houghton Mifflin Company, 1922), 58–59. John Hanks never mentioned an invitation in a lengthy statement prepared for Herndon. Hertz, *Hidden Lincoln*, 345–350. See *CW*, 8: 440.

63. *CW*, 5: 280.

64. H. A. Chapman to Herndon, Dec. 10, 1866, Herndon-Weik Collection, LC; Beveridge, *Lincoln*, 1: 509; Ruth Painter Randall, *Mary Lincoln: Biography of a Marriage* (Boston: Little, Brown and Company, 1953), 134–135.

65. Thomas L. D. Johnston interview, Herndon-Weik Collection, LC; *CW*, 2: 112; Weik, *Real Lincoln*, 50–51.

66. Hertz, *Hidden Lincoln*, 87.

67. William G. Greene quoted in David C. Mearns, *The Lincoln Papers* (Garden City, N.Y.: Doubleday and Company, 1948), 1: 153.

68. Carl Sandburg, *Lincoln Collector: The Story of Oliver R. Barrett's Great Private Collection* (New York: Harcourt, Brace and Company, 1949), 88.

69. Browne, *Everyday Life*, 84. See Gridley, *Abraham Lincoln*, 168.

70. *CW*, 1: 262–263.

71. Ibid., 2: 16.

72. Charles H. Coleman, *Abraham Lincoln and Coles County, Illinois* (New Brunswick, N.J.: Scarecrow Press, 1955), 30–31, 37–38, 54.

73. Sandburg, *Lincoln Collector*, 90, 92, 107.

74. Lamon, *Life of Lincoln*, 77; Coleman, *Abraham Lincoln*, 59.

75. Lamon, *Life of Lincoln*, 66, 73.

76. Weik, *Real Lincoln*, 161; Rufus Rockwell Wilson, ed., *Uncollected Works of Abraham Lincoln* (Elmira, N.Y.: Primavera Press, 1948), 2: 623–624.

77. Harry E. Pratt, *The Personal Finances of Abraham Lincoln* (Springfield, Ill.: Abraham Lincoln Association, 1943), 84–85.

78. Robert Todd Lincoln Collection, LC. Printed in Mearns, *Lincoln Papers,* 1: 179.

79. *CW,* 2: 96–97.

80. Hans J. Morgenthau and David Hein, *Essays on Lincoln's Faith and Politics* (Lanham, Md.: University Press of America, 1983), 4: 8.

81. Hertz, *Hidden Lincoln,* 352.

82. *CW,* 2: 108–109.

83. Ibid., 2: 111.

84. Ibid.

85. Ibid., 2: 113.

86. Sandburg, *Lincoln Collector,* 92–93.

87. Coleman, *Abraham Lincoln,* 145.

88. *CW,* 2: 112.

89. 31235, Robert Todd Lincoln Collection, LC.

90. John J. Hall to Lincoln, Oct. 18, 1864, 37368, ibid.

91. Coleman, *Abraham Lincoln,* 134–135.

92. Justin G. Turner and Linda Levitt Turner, *Mary Todd Lincoln: Her Life and Letters* (New York: Alfred A. Knopf, 1972), 465.

93. Coleman, *Abraham Lincoln,* 138–139.

94. J. W. Wartmann to William H. Herndon, July 21, 1865, Herndon-Weik Collection, LC.

95. *Herndon's Lincoln,* 1: 1.

96. Hertz, *Hidden Lincoln,* 44–45; Lamon, *Life of Lincoln,* 495; Weik, *Real Lincoln,* 50.

97. John Hanks statement, in Hertz, *Hidden Lincoln,* 345; Dennis F. Hanks statement, June 13, 1865, in ibid., 276; Beveridge, *Lincoln,* 1: 66.

98. Speech at Peoria, Oct. 16, 1854, in *CW,* 2: 267; debate at Alton, Oct. 15, 1858, in ibid., 3: 308. For a forty-item gathering under "Slavery, Policy of the Fathers," see Archer H. Shaw, ed., *The Lincoln Encyclopedia* (New York: Macmillan Company, 1950), 324–327.

99. Don E. Fehrenbacher, *Prelude to Greatness: Lincoln in the 1850's* (Stanford, Calif.: Stanford University Press, 1962), 71–72.

100. *CW,* 3: 7–8, 67–68, 178, 218–219, 265–266, 286–287.

101. Ibid., 2: 490–492, 512–514, 3: 17–18, 82, 86, 120–121, 305–309.

102. Ibid., 4: 195. See ibid., 4: 259.

103. Ibid., 4: 269.

104. Ibid., 7: 528. See ibid., 7: 512.

105. See James Hurt, "All the Living and the Dead: Lincoln's Imagery," *American Literature* 52 (Nov. 1980): 351–380; Charles B. Strozier, *Lincoln's Quest for Union: Public and Private Meanings* (New York: Basic Books, 1982),

50–65. Both argue that Lincoln's rejection of his father and his father's values found expression in the address to the Young Men's Lyceum, Jan. 27, 1838, but neither carries this argument to the White House, as do Forgie and Anderson.

106. *CW,* 1: 378. See ibid., 1: 367, for an earlier version with "gladden" for "sadden" in the second line, "sadness" for "pleasure" in the last line.

107. Ibid., 4: 191, 6: 392.

108. Carpenter, *Six Months at the White House,* 49–52.

109. Don E. Fehrenbacher, "Lincoln and the Weight of Responsibility," *JISHS* 48 (Feb. 1975): 45–56; Roy P. Basler, "Lincoln and Shakespeare," in *A Touchstone for Greatness* (Westport, Conn., and London: Greenwood Press, 1973), 206–227. See Forgie, *Patricide in the House Divided,* 244–250; Anderson, *Abraham Lincoln,* 195–202.

110. *CW,* 6: 392.

2. Abraham Lincoln and Ann Rutledge

1. Charles B. Strozier, *Lincoln's Quest for Union: Public and Private Meanings* (New York: Basic Books, 1982), 36.

2. William H. Herndon, *Lincoln and Ann Rutledge and the Pioneers of New Salem* (Herrin, Ill.: Trovillion Private Press, 1945).

3. *Chicago Tribune,* Nov. 28, 1866; *Boston Daily Advertiser,* Feb. 7, 1867; *New York Times,* Mar. 9, 10, 17, 1867; *Chicago Times,* Apr. 3, 1867.

4. Herndon, *Lincoln and Ann Rutledge,* 3–4.

5. R. T. Lincoln to David Davis, Nov. 19, 1866, quoted in David Donald, *Lincoln's Herndon* (New York: Alfred A. Knopf, 1948), 230.

6. Mary Lincoln to David Davis, Mar. 4, 6, 1867, and Mary Lincoln to James Smith, [June 8, 1870], in Justin G. Turner and Linda Levitt Turner, *Mary Todd Lincoln: Her Life and Letters* (New York: Alfred A. Knopf, 1972), 414–416, 567. See also Jean H. Baker, *Mary Todd Lincoln: A Biography* (New York: W. W. Norton, 1987), 270–271.

7. Ward H. Lamon, *The Life of Abraham Lincoln from His Birth to His Inauguration as President* (Boston: James R. Osgood, 1872), 171.

8. *New Salem: A Memorial to Abraham Lincoln,* 5th ed. (Springfield: State of Illinois, Department of Public Works and Buildings, 1940), 2–4.

9. Gary Erickson, "The Graves of Ann Rutledge and the Old Concord Burial Ground," *LH* 71 (Fall 1969): 90–107.

10. "New Monument over Grave of Ann Rutledge, Lincoln's Early Sweetheart," *JISHS* 13 (Jan. 1921): 567–568. As biographer, Masters reported "very little to be found to justify" the story of Ann Rutledge and that Lincoln was never "deeply attached" to any woman. *Lincoln the Man* (New York: Dodd, Mead, 1931), 45, 76.

11. William E. Barton, *The Life of Abraham Lincoln* (Indianapolis:

Bobbs-Merrill, 1925), 1: 214; Barton, *The Women Lincoln Loved* (Indianapolis: Bobbs-Merrill, 1927), 185; Barton, "The Little Sister of Lincoln's Sweetheart," *San Diego Sun,* Jan. 11, 1922. Other interviews with Sarah Rutledge Saunders late in life are among the clippings in the Rutledge file, Louis A. Warren Lincoln Library and Museum, Fort Wayne, Ind. Another sister, Nancy Rutledge Prewitt, in an interview ca. 1886, also confirmed the romance. Two printings of the same interview, both undated and unidentified, are in the same file.

12. Paul M. Angle, "Lincoln's First Love?" *Lincoln Centennial Association Bulletin* 9 (Dec. 1, 1927): 5. Angle, then executive secretary of the Abraham Lincoln Association, complained that "ninety-five per cent of the thousands who annually visit Springfield and New Salem on Lincoln pilgrimages are firmly convinced that Ann Rutledge was the only woman Lincoln ever loved." Ibid., 2. Nearly a generation later, Angle took a more temperate view: "Herndon's account of the Ann Rutledge romance is too highly colored. That there was a romance can hardly be doubted, but there is no good reason for believing that Ann Rutledge was the only woman Lincoln ever loved, as Herndon insisted, and that her death affected him throughout his life." Angle, *A Shelf of Lincoln Books: A Critical, Selective Bibliography of Lincolniana* (New Brunswick, N.J.: Rutgers University Press, 1946), 30.

13. Carl Sandburg, *Abraham Lincoln: The Prairie Years* (New York: Harcourt Brace, 1926), 1: 141.

14. Edmund Wilson, *Patriotic Gore: Studies in the Literature of the American Civil War* (New York: Oxford University Press, 1962), 116.

15. Don E. Fehrenbacher, "The Minor Affair: An Adventure in Forgery and Detection," in *Lincoln in Text and Context: Collected Essays* (Stanford: Stanford University Press, 1987), 246–269.

16. Jay Monaghan, "New Light on the Lincoln-Rutledge Romance," *Abraham Lincoln Quarterly* 3 (Sept. 1944): 138–145.

17. Lloyd Lewis, "New Light on Lincoln's Only Romance," *New York Times Book Review,* Feb. 11, 1945, 3, 27; Louis A. Warren, "The Rutledge Ghost Stalks Again," *Lincoln Lore* 830 (Mar. 5, 1945). Warren had already argued that Herndon's informants had confused Lincoln with John McNamar. "The Ann Rutledge Myth," *Lincoln Kinsman* 35 (May 1941): 1–8. Warren continued to assert that Lincoln's romance "took place only in Herndon's realm of imagination." "Herndon's Contribution to Lincoln Mythology," *Indiana Magazine of History* 41 (Sept. 1945): 223.

18. J. G. Randall, *Lincoln the President: Springfield to Gettysburg* (New York: Dodd, Mead, 1945), 1: ix, 2: 321–342; Ruth Painter Randall, *Mary Lincoln: Biography of a Marriage* (Boston: Little, Brown, 1953), [vii], 507n; Ruth Painter Randall, *I Ruth: Autobiography of a Marriage* (Boston: Little, Brown, 1968), 164–165, 178–179.

19. R. B. Rutledge statement, [Oct. 1866], Herndon-Weik Collection, LC. Printed in full in *The Hidden Lincoln: From the Letters and Papers of*

William H. Herndon, ed. Emanuel Hertz (New York: Viking Press, 1938), 312–313.

20. R. B. Rutledge statement, [Oct. 1866], Herndon-Weik Collection, LC. See also Rutledge to Herndon, Aug. 12, 1866, ibid.

21. R. B. Rutledge to Herndon, Aug. 5, 1866, ibid.

22. John M. Rutledge to Herndon, Nov. 4, 18, 1866, ibid.; R. B. Rutledge statement, [Oct. 1866], ibid.

23. *Illinois State Journal,* Oct. 15, 1874.

24. McNamar to George U. Miles, May 5, 1866, Lamon Collection, Henry E. Huntington Library, San Marino, Calif.

25. McNamar to Herndon, June 4, 1866, ibid.

26. Randall, *Lincoln the President,* 2: 340.

27. At New Salem, McNamar first used the name McNeil. *Sangamo Journal,* Jan. 12, 1833. He purchased land, however, as McNamar, something Lincoln knew through witnessing a deed. Thomas P. Reep, *Lincoln at New Salem* (New Salem, Ill.: Old Salem Lincoln League, 1927), 105, 107. As for his true name, his father's grave in Colesville, N.Y., is marked "John McNamarah," and the date of death, Apr. 10, 1833, conflicts with accounts that McNamar could not return to New Salem until late 1835 because of the illness and death of his father. Communication from Shirley L. Woodward, Apr. 27, 1988. In writing to Herndon, McNamar was evasive about his relationship with Ann, and "with regard to the crazy spell of Mr Lincoln, I had never heard of it[.] On application to my Brother in Law James Short who was quite intimate with Mr Lincoln in his younger Days and I think in Later years he frequently expressed a friendship for him[.] he informs me that there was such a report though not very publick and at a later period than you supposed and from a different source namely a lovers disappointment with regard to the Lady whom he afterwards married. he was in the Legislature at the time and resided in springfield[.] I am unable to give dates or particulars he thinks John T Stuart told him the circumstances[.]" McNamar to Herndon, Dec. 1, 1866, Herndon-Weik Collection, LC. McNamar closed this letter: "Note if you have any oil prospectors in springfield send them down I can show them oil floating on a small spring Branch for a quarter of a mile." Ibid. In his lecture, Herndon offered the opinion that McNamar had purchased the farm where Ann died "because of the sad memories that cluster over and around it." Herndon, *Lincoln and Ann Rutledge,* 9. In fact, McNamar had purchased the farm in 1831 and later placed the Rutledges on it as tenants. While answering Herndon's question about when he bought his farm, McNamar discovered a letter from Lincoln and "a small Braid or tress of Ann Rutleges Hair much worn and aparently Moth eaten." McNamar to Herndon, Jan. 26, 1867, Herndon-Weik Collection, LC. As for the "Aristocracy and Literary attainments of Miss Ann, undoubtedly she was about as Classic a Schollar as Mr Lincoln at that time[.] I think she attended

some Literary institution at Jacksonville a short time or was intending so to do in company with her Brother." Ibid. These two sentences appear as direct quotations in William H. Herndon and Jesse William Weik, *Herndon's Lincoln: The True Story of a Great Life* (Chicago, New York, and San Francisco: Belford, Clarke and Company, 1889), 1: 136, rewritten to eliminate the dismissive tone. Her brother David wrote to Ann shortly before her death that he was "glad to hear that you have a notion of comeing to school, and I earnestly recommend to you that you would spare no time from improving your education and mind." David H. Rutledge letter, July 27, 1835, photocopy, ISHL.

What McNamar remembered and what he forgot, what he revealed and what he concealed, were tied to his own interest, and his testimony is questionable. For a case against McNamar as a grasping man devoid of sentiment who changed his name to hide from his impoverished parents, then jilted Ann when her family's fortunes declined, turned the bereaved family off the farm, and forgot where Ann and his own mother were buried, see Barton, *Women Lincoln Loved*, 173–184. Barton's portrait, however speculative and overdrawn, contains enough substance to counterbalance arguments that McNamar's engagement to Ann precluded her romantic involvement with Lincoln.

28. Randall, *Lincoln the President,* 2: 330.

29. Ibid., 2: 331.

30. Herndon's ardent disciple Caroline W. H. Dall put it most succinctly. "Betrothed to two, both of whom she had loved, she had no choice but to die." "Pioneering," *Atlantic Monthly* 19 (Apr. 1867): 410.

31. Randall, *Lincoln the President,* 2: 333.

32. Ibid., 2: 334–335.

33. Lincoln was reminded of the Rutledge family and presumably their whereabouts shortly before his election, as shown by a secretarial acknowledgment: "He remembers Robert Rutledge very well indeed and sends him his regards." John G. Nicolay to R. L. Miller, Sept. 24, 1860, Abraham Lincoln Papers, LC. On May 8, 1863, Robert Rutledge received an executive appointment as provost marshal, First District of Iowa. U.S. Representative James F. Wilson of Iowa recommended Rutledge's appointment, and no evidence exists of Lincoln's direct involvement. Appointment Papers, Record Group 110, NA.

34. Farewell Address at Springfield, Feb. 11, 1861 [C. Version], in *CW,* 4: 191.

35. Randall, *Lincoln the President,* 2: 335; Mathew S. Marsh to George M. Marsh, Sept. 17, 1835, printed in William E. Barton, "Abraham Lincoln and New Salem," *JISHS* 19 (Oct. 1926–Jan. 1927): 88–93. The Randalls do not mention the unlocked office.

36. Lincoln to Mrs. Orville H. Browning, Apr. 1, 1838, in *CW,* 1: 117.

37. Mary S. [Owens Vineyard] to William H. Herndon, May 1, 1866, printed in Olive Carruthers and R. Gerald McMurtry, *Lincoln's Other Mary* (Chicago: Ziff-Davis Publishing, 1946), 201.

38. Randall, *Lincoln the President,* 2: 337.

39. Ibid., 2: 341.

40. Donald, *Lincoln's Herndon,* 184–241, 352–359; Donald, *Lincoln Reconsidered: Essays on the Civil War Era* (New York: Alfred A. Knopf, 1956), 156.

41. Randall, *Mary Lincoln,* 405–407.

42. Edward T. James, Janet Wilson James, and Paul S. Boyer, eds., *Notable American Women 1607–1950: A Biographical Dictionary* (Cambridge: Harvard University Press, 1971), 3: 216.

43. *CW,* 1: 60, 4: 104.

44. Benjamin P. Thomas, *Abraham Lincoln: A Biography* (New York: Alfred A. Knopf, 1952), 51.

45. Mark E. Neely Jr., *The Abraham Lincoln Encyclopedia* (New York: McGraw-Hill, 1982), 265.

46. Stephen B. Oates, *With Malice toward None: The Life of Abraham Lincoln* (New York: Harper and Row, 1977), 19, 29.

47. Lincoln to John T. Stuart, Jan. 20, 1841, in *CW,* 1: 228.

48. Lincoln to John T. Stuart, Jan. 23, 1841, in ibid., 1: 229–230.

49. Strozier, *Lincoln's Quest for Union,* 44.

50. *CW,* 1: 79, 228, 268.

51. Randall, *Lincoln the President,* 2: 326. According to her son, Arminda Rogers learned of the engagement from Ann. Henry B. Rankin, *Personal Recollections of Abraham Lincoln* (New York: G. P. Putnam's Sons, 1916), 71–72. Rankin's testimony eighty years after the fact deserves only a footnote; more valuable is his letter of rebuke to Herndon a half century earlier, asserting, on his mother's authority, "that Mr. Lincoln's grief, not 'insanity,'—was well known." Rankin to Herndon, Dec. 24, 1866, in ibid., 92.

52. Paul M. Angle, "More Light on Lincoln and Ann Rutledge," *Lincoln Centennial Association Bulletin* 12 (Sept. 1, 1928): 6–7; Carl Sandburg, *Lincoln Collector: The Story of Oliver R. Barrett's Great Private Collection* (New York: Harcourt, Brace, 1949), 133–134; Randall, *Lincoln the President,* 2: 338.

53. *Illinois State Journal,* May 5, 9, 1865. "Ann M. Rutledge is now learning grammar" on the title page, once but no longer believed to be written by Lincoln, may represent Ann's only surviving signature. Photocopy, Louis A. Warren Lincoln Library and Museum, Fort Wayne, Ind. In the family Bible, Ann's name is given as "Anney Mayes Rutledge" for her birth, "Anna Mayes Rutledge" for her death. Photocopies, ISHL. Her brother wrote to her as "Anna." David H. Rutledge letter, July 27, 1835, photocopy, ibid. Her brother Robert used "Ann." Rutledge to Herndon, Oct. 30, 1866, Herndon-Weik Collection, LC. A sister believed that she spelled her name "Anne" and was called "Annie." J. R. Saunders to Mary Saunders, May 14, 1919, ISHL. Herndon first lectured on "Ann" but used "Anne" in his 1889 biography of Lincoln. "Ann" has become standard, although not necessarily correct.

54. John G. Nicolay and John Hay, *Abraham Lincoln: A History* (New York:

Century, 1890), 1: 191–192; Benjamin P. Thomas, *Portrait for Posterity: Lincoln and His Biographers* (New Brunswick, N.J.: Rutgers University Press, 1947), 98, 110–119; David C. Mearns, *The Lincoln Papers* (Garden City, N.Y.: Doubleday, 1948), 1: 69–85.

3. Abraham Lincoln, Jefferson Davis, and Fort Sumter

1. Richard E. Beringer, Herman Hattaway, Archer Jones, and William N. Still Jr., *Why the South Lost the Civil War* (Athens and London: University of Georgia Press, 1986).
2. W. A. Swanberg, *First Blood: The Story of Fort Sumter* (New York: Charles Scribner's Sons, 1957).
3. Richard N. Current, *Lincoln and the First Shot* (Philadelphia and New York: J. B. Lippincott Company, 1963), 182–183.
4. Benjamin F. Butler, *Butler's Book* (Boston: A. M. Thayer and Co., 1892), 138–140.
5. *CW,* 1: 509–510.
6. Benjamin P. Thomas, *Abraham Lincoln: A Biography* (New York: Alfred A. Knopf, 1952), 97.
7. *CW,* 4: 263–271.
8. Ibid., 4: 261.
9. Ibid., 4: 271.
10. Davis to Governor Francis Pickens, Jan. 20, 1861, in *Jefferson Davis, Constitutionalist: His Letters, Papers and Speeches,* ed. Dunbar Rowland (Jackson: Mississippi Department of Archives and History, 1923), 5: 40. Davis had already turned the "point of pride" argument against the North. Ibid., 5: 11–12.
11. Leroy P. Walker letter quoted in Samuel W. Crawford, *The History of the Fall of Fort Sumter* (New York: S. F. McLean and Co., 1898), 421.
12. Pleasant A. Stovall, *Robert Toombs . . .* (New York: Cassell Publishing Company, 1887), 226. Toombs's prophecy was credited to a contemporary account in a New York City newspaper in Alvan F. Sanborn, ed., *Reminiscences of Richard Lathers* (New York: Grafton Press, 1907), 165. The *New York Journal of Commerce,* Apr. 10, 1861, which printed Lathers's letter of Apr. 3, does not include these remarks.
13. Apr. 3, 1861, quoted in Bruce Catton, *The Coming Fury* (Garden City, N.Y.: Doubleday and Company, 1961), 492. See Grady McWhiney, "The Confederacy's First Shot," in *Southerners and Other Americans* (New York: Basic Books, 1973), 72–82.
14. George H. Reese, ed., *Proceedings of the Virginia State Convention of 1861 . . .* (Richmond: Virginia State Library, 1965), 3: 722–723.
15. Douglas Southall Freeman, *R. E. Lee: A Biography* (New York: Charles Scribner's Sons, 1934–1935), 1: 432–447, 633–637.
16. Clifford Dowdey and Louis H. Manarin, eds., *The Wartime Papers of R. E. Lee* (Boston and Toronto: Little Brown and Company, 1961), 934.

17. Thomas L. Livermore, *Numbers and Losses in the Civil War in America, 1861–65* (Bloomington: Indiana University Press, 1957), 50, 61.

18. E. B. Long, *The Civil War Day by Day: An Almanac 1861–1865* (Garden City, N.Y.: Doubleday and Company, 1971), 705.

19. Edward Channing, *A History of the United States* (New York: Macmillan, 1936), 6: 431; James M. McPherson, *Battle Cry of Freedom* (New York: Oxford University Press, 1988), 306.

20. Long, *Civil War Day by Day*, 706.

21. Beringer et al., *Why the South Lost*, 249–250.

22. *O.R.*, ser. 4, 1: 256, 263.

23. Ibid., ser. 4, 1: 261.

24. Ibid., ser. 4, 1: 262.

25. Crawford, *History of the Fall*, 424.

26. O.R., ser. 1, 1: 301.

27. Ibid., ser. 1, 1: 14.

28. Rowland, *Jefferson Davis*, 6: 76.

29. Ibid.

30. P. G. T. Beauregard, "The First Battle of Bull Run," in *Battles and Leaders of the Civil War*, ed. Robert Underwood Johnson and Clarence Clough Buel (New York: Century, 1884–1888), 1: 222.

31. Ibid., 1: 226.

32. Ibid.

33. *CW*, 4: 425.

34. Message to Congress, July 20, 1861, in Rowland, *Jefferson Davis*, 4: 113. See Jefferson Davis, *The Rise and Fall of the Confederate Government* (New York: D. Appleton, 1881), 1: 292.

4. "Freeing Some and Leaving Others Alone": Lincoln's Emancipation Policy

1. Richard Hofstadter, *The American Political Tradition and the Men Who Made It* (New York: Alfred A. Knopf, 1948), 132.

2. *London Times*, Oct. 7, 1862.

3. Earl Russell to Lord Lyons, Jan. 17, 1863, in *American Annual Cyclopedia . . . of the Year 1863* (New York: D. Appleton and Company, 1866), 3: 834.

4. *CW*, 5: 433–436.

5. Sept. 22, 1862, in *Welles*, 1: 143; Sept. 22, 1862, in Salmon P. Chase, *Inside Lincoln's Cabinet: The Civil War Diaries of Salmon P. Chase*, ed. David Donald (New York: Longmans, Green and Co., 1954), 150.

6. *Chicago Tribune*, Sept. 3, 1862; William T. Sherman to Samuel R. Curtis, Nov. 6, 1862, in *O.R.*, ser. 1, 17, part 2: 859.

7. *New York Herald*, Sept. 26, 1862; Zachariah Chandler to Lyman

Trumbull, Sept. 10, 1862, Lyman Trumbull Papers, LC. John A. Andrew wrote that he was "trying to help organize some movement . . . to save the Prest. From the infamy of ruining his country." Andrew to Adam Gurowski, Sept. 6, 1862, in Henry Greenleaf Pearson, *The Life of John A. Andrew* (Boston and New York: Houghton, Mifflin and Co., 1904), 2: 48.

8. George Boutwell in Rice, *Reminiscences,* 125–126.

9. William B. Hesseltine, *Lincoln and the War Governors* (New York: Alfred A. Knopf, 1948), 249–272. The collective address is in *O.R.*, ser. 1, 3, part 2: 582–584.

10. Speech at Republican convention, Rome, N.Y., Sept. 26, 1862, in Alfred R. Conkling, *The Life and Letters of Roscoe Conkling* (New York: Charles L. Webster and Company, 1889), 182–183. See John Sherman, *Recollections of Forty Years in the House, Senate and Cabinet* (Chicago: Werner Company, 1895), 1: 330.

11. Ira Harris to Lincoln, Oct. 2, 1862, Lincoln Papers, LC. See George W. Curtis to C. E. Norton, Sept. 25, 1862, in Edward Cary, *George William Curtis* (Boston and New York: Houghton Mifflin Company, 1894), 158.

12. Benjamin F. Wade to George W. Julian, Sept. 29, 1862, Giddings-Julian Papers, LC.

13. *CW*, 5: 434.

14. *National Intelligencer,* Nov. 19, 1862.

15. Hay, *Diaries and Letters,* 17.

16. Fernando Wood to Lincoln, Jan. 15, Aug. 20, Sept. 12, 1862, Lincoln Papers, LC; Wood to William H. Seward, Nov. 30, 1862, ibid.; Samuel Augustus Pleasants, *Fernando Wood of New York* (New York: Columbia University Press, 1948), 128–129; *New York Herald,* Oct. 31, 1862.

17. Wood to Lincoln, Dec. 8, 1862, Lincoln Papers, LC; Jerome Mushkat, *Fernando Wood: A Political Biography* (Kent, Ohio: Kent State University Press, 1990), 131.

18. Lincoln to Wood, Dec. 12, 1862, *CW*, 5: 553–554; Feb. 17, 1863, in *Welles,* 1: 237.

19. Wood to Lincoln, Dec. 17, 1862, Lincoln Papers, LC.

20. Wood to Lincoln, Feb. 6, 1863, ibid. Governor John Letcher of Virginia published a letter denying that he had corresponded with Wood. *New York World,* Dec. 16, 1862.

21. Feb. 17, 1863, in *Welles,* 1: 237; Pleasants, *Fernando Wood,* 137–138.

22. Lincoln to Edward Stanly, Sept. 29, 1862, in *CW*, 5: 445.

23. *HMD*, 37th Cong., 3rd sess., Doc. 14; ibid., 37th Cong., 3rd sess., Doc. 13; *HRC*, 37th Cong., 3rd sess., Doc. 41; *HMD*, 38th Cong., 2nd sess., Doc. 57, 463–464. There was a small vote for Charles Henry Foster. *Cincinnati Gazette,* Jan. 14, 1863.

24. *HRC*, 37th Cong., 3rd sess., Doc. 33; *HMD*, 38th Cong., 2nd sess.,

Doc. 57, 460–462; Lewis McKenzie to Francis H. Pierpont, Jan. 27, Jan. 29, 1863, Francis Pierpont Papers, University of West Virginia, Morgantown.

25. *New York Tribune,* Dec. 26, 1862.

26. Lincoln to John A. Dix, Oct. 26, Nov. 20, Dec. 31, 1862, in *CW,* 5: 476–477, 502, 6: 26.

27. *HRC,* 37th Cong., 3rd sess., Doc. 23; *HMD,* 38th Cong., 2nd sess., Doc. 57, 455–459.

28. Christopher L. Grafflin to H. J. Samuels, May 14, 1862, and Grafflin to Francis H. Pierpont, July 18, 1862, in *Calendar of the Francis Harrison Pierpont Letters and Papers in West Virginia Depositories* (Charleston: West Virginia Historical Records Survey, 1940), 118, 145.

29. C. L. Grafflin to F. H. Pierpont, Nov. 21, Dec. 23, 1862, in ibid., 219, 228.

30. *HRC,* 37th Cong., 3rd sess., Doc. 43; *HMD,* 38th Cong., 2nd sess., Doc. 57, 464–465.

31. *HRC,* 37th Cong., 3rd sess., Doc. 46; *HMD,* 38th Cong., 2nd sess., Doc. 57, 466–468; Lincoln to W. W. Lowe, Nov. 7, 1862, in *CW,* 5: 489.

32. J. B. Rodgers to Lyman Trumbull, Mar. 27, 1861, Andrew Johnson Papers, LC; Samuel C. Pomeroy to Lincoln, June 29, 1861, Lincoln Papers, LC.

33. Johnson note, Mar. 18, 1862, and John B. Rodgers to Johnson, Apr. 7, 1862, both Andrew Johnson Papers, LC.

34. J. B. Rodgers to A. Johnson, May 4, May 31, 1862, ibid.

35. A. Johnson to Lincoln, July 6, 1862, Lincoln Papers, LC; A. Johnson to H. Maynard, July 6, 1862, Andrew Johnson Papers, LC.

36. Lincoln to E. M. Stanton, July 18, 1862, in *CW,* 5: 332–333.

37. J. B. Rodgers to A. A. Lawrence, Aug. 9, Aug. 26, Oct. 4, 1862, Lawrence Papers, Massachusetts Historical Society, Boston.

38. *HRC,* 37th Cong., 3rd sess., Doc. 32; *HMD,* 38th Cong., 2nd sess., Doc. 57, 462–463; Frederick W. Moore, "Representation in the National Congress from the Seceding States, 1861–1865," *American Historical Review* 2 (Jan. 1897): 293.

39. *Boston Advertiser,* May 26, 1862.

40. Lincoln to B. F. Butler, G. F. Shepley, et al., Oct. 14, 1862, in *CW,* 5: 462–463; Lincoln to J. E. Bouligny, Apr. 14, 1863, in ibid., 6: 172.

41. Lincoln to G. F. Shepley, Nov. 21, 1862, in ibid., 5: 504.

42. G. F. Shepley proclamation, Nov. 14, 1862, *New York World,* Nov. 26, 1862.

43. Lincoln to B. F. Butler, Nov. 6, 1862, in *CW,* 5: 487; B. F. Butler to Lincoln, Nov. 18, 1862, in Butler, *Correspondence,* 2: 447–450.

44. Hahn, Feb. 17, 1863, *CG,* 37th Cong., 3rd sess., 1031; Gov. Berry to B. F. Butler, Mar. 25, 1862, Flanders Papers, Louisiana State University, Baton Rouge.

45. George S. Denison to S. P. Chase, Nov. 19, 1862, in "Diary and Correspondence of Salmon P. Chase," *Annual Report of the American Historical*

Association for the Year 1902 (Washington, D.C.: Government Printing Office, 1903), 2: 335; S. P. Chase to B. F. Butler, Dec. 14, 1862, Jan. 20, 1863, in Butler, *Correspondence,* 2: 542–543.

46. B. F. Butler to Lincoln, Dec. 4, 1862, Lincoln Papers, LC; J. Wilson Shaffer to Ward H. Lamon, Dec. 3, 1862, ibid.

47. *HRC,* 37th Cong., 3rd sess., Doc. 22; *HMD,* 38th Cong., 2nd sess., Doc. 57, 438–447.

48. *CG,* 37th Cong., 3rd sess., Feb. 9, 1863, 835.

49. *CW,* 5: 537.

50. Lincoln remarks, Nov. 21, 1862, in ibid., 5: 503–504.

51. Dec. 1, 1862, in Orville Hickman Browning, *The Diary of Orville Hickman Browning,* ed. Theodore C. Pease and James G. Randall (Springfield: Illinois State Historical Library, 1925–1933), 1: 591.

52. H. L. Dawes to wife, Dec. 2, 1862, Dawes Papers, LC.

53. Lincoln remarks, Nov. 21, 1862, in *CW,* 5: 503.

54. C. Sumner to S. G. Howe, Dec. 28, 1862, in Edward L. Pierce, *Memoir and Letters of Charles Sumner* (London: Sampson Law, Marston and Company, 1893), 4: 113; C. Sumner to J. M. Forbes, Dec. 18, 1862, in Sarah Forbes Hughes, ed., *Letters and Recollections of John Murray Forbes* (Boston and New York: Houghton, Mifflin and Company, 1900), 1: 352–353.

55. Dec. 29, 1862, in *Welles,* 1: 209; John P. Usher in Rice, *Reminiscences,* 92–93. See Robert B. Warden, *An Account of the Private Life and Public Services of Salmon Portland Chase* (Cincinnati: Wilstach, Baldwin and Co., 1874), 538–539.

56. Dec. 31, 1862, in *Welles,* 1: 210–211; J. W. Schuckers, *The Life and Public Services of Salmon Portland Chase* (New York: D. Appleton and Company, 1874), 461–463; *CW,* 6: 23–26.

57. *Chicago Tribune,* Dec. 24, 1862; *New York Herald,* Dec. 26, 1862.

58. Clifton R. Hall, *Andrew Johnson: Military Governor of Tennessee* (Princeton, N.J., Princeton University Press, 1916), 91; A. Johnson to Lincoln, Jan. 11, 1863, in *O.R.,* ser. 1, 20, part 2: 317.

59. *CW,* 6: 28–30.

60. *Chicago Tribune,* Jan. 6, 1863.

61. T. Tilton to S. B. Anthony, Jan. 11, 1863, in Ida Husted Harper, *The Life and Work of Susan B. Anthony* (Indianapolis: Bowen-Merrill Company, 1899), 1: 226.

62. Lincoln to John A. McClernand, Jan. 8, 1863, in *CW,* 6: 48–49.

63. Lincoln to Horace Greeley, Aug. 22, 1862, in ibid., 5: 388.

5. Lincoln and "Old Brains" Halleck

1. George B. McClellan, *McClellan's Own Story* (New York: Charles L. Webster, 1887), 137.

2. July 15, 1863, in *Welles*, 1: 373.

3. Winfield Scott to Simon Cameron, Oct. 4, 1861, in *O.R.*, ser. 1, 51, part 1: 491–493; T. Harry Williams, *Lincoln and His Generals* (New York: Alfred A. Knopf, 1952), 43.

4. James Grant Wilson, "General Halleck—A Memoir," *Journal of the Military Service Institution of the United States* 36 (1905): 537–541; Stephen E. Ambrose, *Halleck: Lincoln's Chief of Staff* (Baton Rouge: Louisiana State University Press, 1962), 5–7.

5. Russell F. Weigley, *Towards an American Army: Military Thought from Washington to Marshall* (New York and London: Columbia University Press, 1974), 57–67.

6. George W. Cullum, *Biographical Register of the Officers and Graduates of the U.S. Military Academy . . .* , 3rd ed. (Boston and New York: Houghton, Mifflin, 1891), 1: 735; Lloyd Lewis, *Sherman: Fighting Prophet* (New York: Harcourt, Brace, 1932), 75.

7. Milton H. Shutes, "Henry Wager Halleck: Lincoln's Chief of Staff," *California Historical Society Quarterly* 16 (1937): 196–200; Ambrose, *Halleck*, 7–8.

8. McClellan to Mary Ellen McClellan, Aug. 8, 1861, in *The Civil War Papers of George B. McClellan: Selected Correspondence, 1860–65*, ed. Stephen W. Sears (New York: Ticknor and Fields, 1989), 81.

9. McClellan to Mary Ellen McClellan, Oct. 13, 1861, in ibid., 107.

10. Scott to Simon Cameron, Oct. 4, 1861, in *CG*, 37th Cong., 3rd Sess., 1263.

11. Dec. 3, 1861, in *CW*, 6: 31.

12. *PMUSG*, 1: 287.

13. John Y. Simon, *Grant and Halleck: Contrasts in Command* (Milwaukee: Marquette University Press, 1996), 14–20.

14. Gideon Welles, *Lincoln and Seward* (New York: Sheldon and Co., 1874), 197.

15. *O.R.*, ser. 1, 11, part 3: 311–312.

16. Grant to Julia Dent Grant, Apr. 30, 1862, in *PUSG*, 5: 102.

17. Grant to Elihu B. Washburne, July 22, 1862, in ibid., 226.

18. Halleck to McClellan, July 30, 1862, in *O.R.*, ser. 1, 11, part 3: 343; McClellan to Halleck, Aug. 1, 1862, in ibid., 345.

19. McClellan to Mary Ellen McClellan, July 20, 1862, and McClellan to Samuel L. M. Barlow, July 23, 1862, in Sears, *McClellan: Correspondence*, 368–369.

20. Halleck to Mrs. Halleck, July 5, July 28, Aug. 9, 1862, in J. G. Wilson, "Halleck," 556–557.

21. Halleck testimony, Mar. 7, 1863, in *Report of the Joint Committee on the Conduct of the War* (Washington, D.C.: Government Printing Office, 1863), 1: 451.

22. McClellan to Mary Ellen McClellan, Sept. 20, Oct. 2, 1862, in Sears, *McClellan: Correspondence*, 473, 488.

23. Ambrose, *Halleck*, 97.

24. Williams, *Lincoln and His Generals*, 203.

25. Lincoln to Halleck, Jan. 1, 1863, in *CW*, 6: 31.

26. Lincoln to Grant, July 13, 1863, in ibid., 326.

27. Mar. 24, Apr. 28, 1864, in Hay, *Diaries and Letters*, 167, 176.

28. John A. Rawlins to Elihu B. Washburne, Jan. 20, 1864, in James Harrison Wilson, *The Life of John A. Rawlins* (New York: Neale, 1916), 387.

29. Grant to Halleck, Aug. 1, 1864, in *PUSG*, 11: 358.

30. Grant to Edwin M. Stanton, Aug. 15, 1864, in ibid., 422.

31. Noah Brooks, *Washington in Lincoln's Time* (1895; New York: Rinehart and Co., 1958), 43.

32. Halleck to William T. Sherman, July 16, 1862, in *O.R.*, ser. 1, 17, part 2: 100.

33. Halleck to McClellan, Aug. 31, 1862, in ibid., ser. 1, 11, part 1: 103.

34. Apr. 28, 1864, in Hay, *Diaries and Letters*, 176.

35. *The Diary of Edward Bates*, ed. Howard K. Beale (Washington, D.C.: Government Printing Office, 1933), 293.

36. *Personal Memoirs of John H. Brinton* (New York: Neale, 1914), 166.

37. Dana to John A. Rawlins, July 12, 1864, in *PUSG*, 11: 231.

38. Sept. 24, 1862, in *Diary of George Templeton Strong*, ed. Allan Nevins and Milton Halsey Thomas (New York; Macmillan, 1952), 3: 258.

39. Jack D. Welsh, *Medical Histories of Union Generals* (Kent, Ohio: Kent State University Press, 1996), 146.

6. Lincoln's Despair: The Crisis during the Summer of 1864

1. *CW*, 7: 514.

2. *New York Tribune*, Aug. 5, 1864.

3. Francis P. Blair in *National Intelligencer*, Oct. 5, 1864.

4. George B. McClellan to Francis P. Blair, n.d., in *The Civil War Papers of George B. McClellan: Selected Correspondence, 1860–1865*, ed. Stephen W. Sears (New York: Ticknor and Fields, 1989), 584.

5. *CW*, 7: 470.

6. *National Intelligencer*, Oct. 3, 1864.

7. June 26, 1863, and Aug. 31, 1864, in *Welles*, 1: 345, 2: 130.

8. J. G. Randall and Richard N. Current, *Lincoln the President: Last Full Measure* (New York: Dodd, Mead, 1955), 209.

9. Thurlow Weed to William H. Seward, Aug. 22, 1864, Lincoln Papers, LC.

10. Henry J. Raymond to Lincoln, Aug. 22, 1864, ibid.

11. Lincoln to Raymond, Aug. 24, 1864, in *CW,* 7: 517; John G. Nicolay and John Hay, *Abraham Lincoln: A History,* 10 vols. (New York: Century, 1890), 9: 221.

12. Hay, *Diaries and Letters,* 238.

7. The Personal Sentiments of Mr. Lincoln

1. David Donald, *Lincoln Reconsidered* (New York: Alfred A. Knopf, 1956), 5–12.

2. Ida M. Tarbell, *The Life of Abraham Lincoln* (New York: Doubleday and McClure Company, 1900), 2: 73.

3. Benjamin P. Thomas, *Portrait for Posterity* (New Brunswick, N.J.: Rutgers University Press, 1947), 33.

4. Lamon to Johnson, June 23, 1866, Andrew Johnson Papers, LC.

5. The letter appeared in the *Crisis* (Columbus, Ohio), Apr. 25, 1866.

6. Hanks to Herndon, June 13, 1865, quoted in David C. Mearns, "Mr. Lincoln and the Books He Read," in *Three Presidents and Their Books* (Urbana: University of Illinois Press, 1955), 48.

7. *Crisis,* Oct. 17, 1866.

8. The letter originally appeared in the *Springfield Illinois State Register,* Oct. 4, 1866. It was reprinted in the *Crisis,* Oct. 17, 1866.

9. William H. Herndon and Jess William Weik, *Herndon's Lincoln: The True Story of a Great Life* (Chicago, New York, and San Francisco: Belford, Clarke and Company, 1889), 3: 517–520; Charles H. Coleman, *Abraham Lincoln and Cole County, Illinois* (New Brunswick, N.J.: Rutgers University Press, 1955), 230–233.

10. Albert J. Beveridge, *Abraham Lincoln: 1809–1858* (Boston and New York: Houghton Mifflin, 1928), 1: 5n.

11. John G. Nicolay and John Hay, *Abraham Lincoln: A History* (New York: Century, 1909), 1: 45.

8. Ulysses S. Grant One Hundred Years Later

1. *Chicago Tribune,* July 24, 1885; James P. Boyd, *Military and Civil Life of Gen. Ulysses S. Grant* (Philadelphia: P. W. Ziegler and Company, 1885), 677.

2. Quoted in Boyd, *Military and Civil Life,* 675.

3. Ibid.

4. *New York Times,* Aug. 9, 1885; *Chicago Tribune,* Aug. 9, 1885. See *Frank Leslie's Illustrated Newspaper,* Aug. 15, 1885.

5. *PMUSG,* 1: 100.

6. Ibid., 1: 102.

7. Ibid., 1: 32.

8. John Russell Young, *Around the World with General Grant . . .* (New York: American News Co., 1879), 2: 306, 447–448, 450–452.

9. Grant to Mrs. S. F. Bricker, Apr. 11, 1863, in *PUSG,* 7: 52.

10. Young, *Around the World,* 2: 625.

11. Halleck to Grant, Aug. 1, 1863, in *PUSG,* 8: 523n.

12. Young, *Around the World,* 2: 165.

13. Lincoln to Grant, July 13, 1863, in *CW,* 6: 326.

14. Lincoln to Grant, Aug. 9, 1863, in ibid., 6: 374; Grant to Lincoln, Aug. 23, 1863, in *PUSG,* 9: 195.

15. Alexander H. Stephens, *A Constitutional View of the Late War Between the States . . .* (Philadelphia: National Pub. Co., 1868–1870), 2: 598.

16. Meade to Henry A. Cram, Nov. 24, 1864, in George Meade, *Life and Letters of George Gordon Meade* (New York: Scribner's, 1913), 2: 246.

17. Young, *Around the World,* 2: 217.

18. Humphreys to Grant, July 15, 1864, in *PUSG,* 11: 260n.

19. Douglass, *Life and Times of Frederick Douglass Written by Himself* (1892; rpt., New York: Collier Books, 1962), 357.

20. Grant to Sherman, June 21, 1868, William T. Sherman Papers, LC.

21. Young, *Around the World,* 2: 452.

22. Grant to Julia Dent Grant, May 11, 1862, in *PUSG,* 5: 116.

23. Grant to Elihu B. Washburne, June 23, 1864, in ibid., 11: 122.

24. Garfield to Burke A. Hinsdale, Dec. 8, 1874, in *Garfield-Hinsdale Letters: Correspondence between James Abram Garfield and Burke Aaron Hinsdale,* ed. Mary L. Hinsdale (1949; rpt., New York: Kraus Reprint Co., 1969), 300. See Harry James Brown and Frederick D. Williams, eds., *The Diary of James A. Garfield* (East Lansing: Michigan State University Press, 1967–1981), 2: 399–400.

25. Eighth Annual Message to the Senate and House of Representatives, Dec. 5, 1876, in *Papers Relating to the Foreign Relations of the United States,* 44th Cong., 2nd sess. (1876), *House of Representative Executive Documents,* 1, part 1: [iii].

26. *PMUSG,* 1: 7.

27. Walt Whitman, "The Silent General," in *Prose Works 1892,* ed. Floyd Stovall (New York: New York University Press, 1963), 1: 226.

28. Sherman to Mrs. Hall, Nov. 18, 1879, in "Sherman's Estimate of Grant's Character," *Century Magazine* 70 (1905): 317.

29. Henry Adams, *The Education of Henry Adams: An Autobiography* (Boston: Houghton, 1918), 263.

30. William B. Hesseltine, *Ulysses S. Grant: Politician* (New York: Dodd, 1935), 1.

31. Ibid., viii, 304.

32. Edmund Wilson, "Homage to General Grant," *New Yorker,* Apr. 4, 1953, 117. Wilson expanded his essay in "Northern Soldiers: Ulysses S. Grant,"

in *Patriotic Gore: Studies in the Literature of the American Civil War* (New York: Oxford University Press, 1962), 131–173.

10. A Marriage Tested by War: Ulysses and Julia Grant

1. *PMJDG.*
2. For more on the Davis and Lee marriages, see Carol K. Bleser, "The Marriage of Varina Howell and Jefferson Davis: A Portrait of the President and First Lady of the Confederacy," in *Intimate Strategies of the Civil War: Military Commanders and Their Wives*, ed. Carol K. Bleser and Lesley J. Gordon (New York: Oxford University Press, 2001), 3–31; Emory M. Thomas, "The Lee Marriage," in ibid., 32–48. For more on the Lincoln marriage, see Ruth Painter Randall, *Mary Lincoln: Biography of a Marriage* (Boston: Little, Brown, 1953); and especially Jean H. Baker, *Mary Todd Lincoln: A Biography* (New York: W. W. Norton, 1987).
3. *PMJDG*, 38.
4. *PMUSG*, 2: 32.
5. Ibid., 1: 38.
6. Edward Chauncey Marshall, *The Ancestry of General Grant and Their Contemporaries* (New York: Sheldon, 1869), 72; Walter B. Stevens, *Grant in Saint Louis* (St. Louis: Franklin Club, 1916), 60–61; Lloyd Lewis, *Captain Sam Grant* (Boston: Little, Brown, 1950), 295, 333–334.
7. *PMJDG*, 59–60.
8. Ibid., 76.
9. *PMUSG*, 1: 247–248; *PMJDG*, 92; *PUSG*, 2: 70, 83.
10. Grant to Julia Grant, Apr. 30, 1863, *PUSG*, 5: 103.
11. Ibid., 4: 119.
12. *PMJDG*, 106.
13. Frederick Dent Grant, "At the Front with Dad," *Civil War Times Illustrated* 35, no. 6 (1996): 16–31 passim, 99–116.
14. *PMJDG*, 125–126; *PMUSG*, 2: 110–112.
15. Horace Porter, *Campaigning with Grant* (New York: Century, 1897), 22.
16. Albert D. Richardson, *A Personal History of Ulysses S. Grant* (Hartford: American Publishing Company, 1868), 388.
17. *PMJDG*, 130.
18. Ibid., 130–131.
19. John A. Rawlins to Mary Emma Rawlins, Apr. 25, 1864, in James Harrison Wilson, *The Life of John A. Rawlins* (New York: Neale Publishing Company, 1916), 425.
20. Grant to Julia Dent Grant, Apr. 27, 1864, in *PUSG*, 10: 363.
21. Porter, *Campaigning with Grant*, 283.
22. Julia Grant to Mrs. Charles Rogers, Feb. 7, 1865, Grant Papers, LC.

23. Grant to Lincoln, Jan. 31, 1865, in *PUSG,* 13: 333.
24. Lincoln to Grant, Feb. 1, 1865, in *CW,* 8: 252.
25. Grant to Stanton, Feb. 1, 1865, in *PUSG,* 8: 345.
26. Lincoln to Seward, Feb. 2, 1865, in *CW,* 8: 256.
27. *PMJDG,* 141.
28. *PUSG,* 14: 64.
29. Ibid., 14: 91.
30. Mar. 3, 1865, in ibid., 13: 281–282.
31. Adam Badeau, *Grant in Peace: From Appomattox to Mount McGregor* (Hartford: S. S. Scranton and Company, 1887), 362.
32. Ibid., 356–358.
33. Ibid., 358–359.
34. J. H. Wilson, *Rawlins,* 285–292, 303.
35. *PUSG,* 14: 366.
36. *PMJDG,* 157; John Russell Young, *Around the World with General Grant* (New York: American News Company, 1879), 2: 356.
37. *PMJDG,* 125.

11. From Galena to Appomattox: Grant and Washburne

1. Washburne's life before he reached Galena is treated in an autobiographical fragment printed in Gaillard Hunt, *Israel, Elihu and Cadwallader Washburn: A Chapter in American Biography* (New York: Macmillan Company, 1923), 155–171. Only Elihu added an *e* to the family name.
2. John S. Phelps, a Missouri Democrat, had served continuously since 1845. In July 1862, he resigned his seat to accept Lincoln's appointment as military governor of Arkansas. Thereafter Washburne had the longest consecutive service of any member of either party and the title "Father of the House."
3. Richard Nelson Current, *Old Thad Stevens: A Story of Ambition* (Madison: University of Wisconsin Press, 1942), 158–207.
4. *Welles,* 1: 234.
5. Albert D. Richardson, *A Personal History of Ulysses S. Grant* (Hartford: American Publishing Company, 1868), 178–179.
6. Augustus L. Chetlain, *Recollections of Seventy Years* (Galena, Ill.: Galena Publishing Co., 1899), 70; Augustus L. Chetlain, "Recollections of General U. S. Grant, Galena, Illinois, 1861–1863," in *Military Essays and Recollections; Papers Read before the Commandery of the State of Illinois, Military Order of the Loyal Legion of the United States* (Chicago: Dial Press, 1891), 1: 11–12. See also *PMUSG,* 1: 230–231.
7. E. B. Washburne in W. C. King and W. P. Derby, comps., *Camp Fire Sketches and Battle-Field Echoes of the Rebellion* (Springfield, Mass.: G. L.

Benjamin, 1886), 119; Richardson, *Personal History,* 181–182; Chetlain, "Recollections," 13.

8. Chetlain, *Recollections,* 71–72; Kenneth N. Owens, *Galena, Grant and the Fortunes of War* (DeKalb: Northern Illinois University Press, 1963), 38.

9. Thomas J. McCormack, ed., *Memoirs of Gustave Koerner, 1809–1896* (Cedar Rapids, Iowa: Torch Press, 1909), 2: 127.

10. Grant to his father, May 3, 1861, in *Letters of Ulysses S. Grant to His Father and Youngest Sister, 1857–78,* ed. Jesse Grant Cramer (New York: G. P. Putnam's Sons, 1912), 31–33.

11. *PMUSG,* 1: 239–241.

12. Elihu Washburne in Rice, *Reminiscences,* 12–13.

13. Ibid., 16.

14. Ibid., 17–19; Lincoln to Washburne, Apr. 30, 1848, in *CW,* 1: 467.

15. In 1858 Washburne believed that Republicans should stand by Douglas in his fight against the Lecompton Constitution. This brought a temporary coolness between Washburne and Lincoln. Washburne to William Herndon, Apr. 28, 1858, in Hunt, *Washburn,* 184–185.

16. *CW,* 4: 151, 159, 217. Both sides of the correspondence during the secession winter are in the Robert Todd Lincoln Papers, LC, or, more conveniently, in *CW* and in David C. Mearns, *The Lincoln Papers* (New York: Doubleday, 1948).

17. Washburne to his wife, Mar. 1861, in Hunt, *Washburn,* 186; Rice, *Reminiscences,* 38.

18. Allan Nevins, *The War for the Union* (New York: Charles Scribner's Sons, 1959), 1: 34.

19. Theodore Calvin Pease and James G. Randall, eds., *The Diary of Orville Hickman Browning,* Collections of the Illinois State Historical Library, 20 vols. (Springfield, 1925), 1: 487–488, 490; George W. Pepper, *Personal Recollections of Sherman's Campaigns in Georgia and the Carolinas* (Zanesville, Ohio: Hugh Dunne, 1866), 392–393; James Harrison Wilson, *The Life of John A. Rawlins* (New York: Neale, 1916), 52–53.

20. Washburne to his wife, July 22, 1861, in Hunt, *Washburn,* 203.

21. Bruce Catton, *Grant Moves South* (Boston: Little, Brown, 1960), 17. Another version is in Hamlin Garland, *Ulysses S. Grant: His Life and Character* (New York: Doubleday and McClure, 1898), 177–178.

22. Sept. 3, 1861, Ulysses S. Grant Papers, ISHL. The bulk of the letters from Grant to Washburne, with dubious editing, are in James Grant Wilson, ed., *General Grant's Letters to a Friend, 1861–1880* (New York: T. Y. Crowell and Company, 1897).

23. Frederick Phisterer, *Statistical Record of the Armies of the United States,* The Army in the Civil War no. 13 (New York: Charles Scribner's Sons, 1885), 247–261.

24. *PMUSG,* 1: 260–264.

25. Catton, *Grant Moves South,* 69; Washburne to Salmon P. Chase, Oct. 31, 1861, in American Historical Association, *Annual Report . . . 1902* (Washington, D.C.: Government Printing Office, 1903), 2: 507–508.

26. Dec. 30, 1861, in J. H. Wilson, *Rawlins,* 68–71.

27. Washburne to Lincoln, Oct. 17, Oct. 19, Oct. 21, Oct. 26, Oct. 29, 1861, all Robert Todd Lincoln Papers, LC; Lincoln to McClellan, Nov. 10, 1861, in *CW,* 5: 20. For the background of this letter, see Russell K. Nelson, "The Early Life and Congressional Career of Elihu B. Washburne" (PhD diss., University of North Dakota, 1953), 286.

28. *New-York Daily Tribune,* Feb. 18, 1862.

29. Feb. 18, 1862, *CG,* 37th Cong., 2nd sess., 1931–1932; Feb. 24, 1862, ibid., 930–931.

30. Arthur Charles Cole, *The Era of the Civil War,* Centennial History of Illinois, no. 3 (Springfield: Illinois Centennial Commission, 1919), 285–286.

31. C. C. Washburn to Washburne, Mar. 5, Mar. 7, Mar. 9, 1862, all Elihu B. Washburne Papers, LC.

32. M. Smith to Washburne, Apr. 22, 1862, J. Russell Jones to Washburne, May 1, 1862, and John E. Smith to Washburne, May 16, 1862, all Washburne Papers, LC; Cole, *Era of the Civil War,* 287.

33. May 2, 1862, *CG,* 37th Cong., 2nd sess., 1931–1932.

34. Ibid., 1932. Washburne received letters of thanks from Grant's wife (May 16, 1862, in Catton, *Grant Moves South,* 260–261) and his father (May 16, 1862, Washburne Papers, LC).

35. Clark B. Lagow to Washburne, May 22, 1862, Washburne Papers, LC.

36. May 9, 1862, *CG,* 37th Cong., 2nd sess., 2034.

37. Ibid., 2036–2037.

38. Grant to William T. Sherman, May 10, 1862, in *The Sherman Letters,* ed. Rachel Sherman Thorndike (New York: Charles Scribner's Sons, 1894), 147.

39. May 24, 1862, Washburne Papers, LC.

40. Catton, *Grant Moves South,* 273.

41. May 14, 1862, Grant Papers, ISHL. Washburne commented on Grant's letter in a letter to his wife (May 25, 1862, in Hunt, *Washburn,* 204).

42. July 22, 1862, Grant Papers, ISHL.

43. Sept. 1, 1862, Washburne Papers, LC.

44. Bertram Wallace Korn, *American Jewry and the Civil War* (Philadelphia: Atheneum, 1951), 121–144.

45. *CG,* 37th Cong., 3rd sess., 184, 222.

46. Jan. 6, 1863, Robert Todd Lincoln Papers, LC.

47. *CG,* 37th Cong., 3rd sess., 222, 245; J. H. Wilson, *Rawlins,* 96.

48. Feb. 24, 1863, and Washburne to John G. Nicolay, Mar. 8, 1863, both Robert Todd Lincoln Papers, LC.

49. Mar. 28, 1863, and Salmon P. Chase to Washburne, Apr. 3, 1863, both Washburne Papers, LC; Apr. 11, 1863, in Hunt, *Washburne*, 341–342; Wood Gray, *The Hidden War* (New York: Viking Press, 1942), 128; Nelson, "Washburne," 323.

50. J. Russell Jones to Washburne, Apr. 4, 1863, Washburne Papers, LC.

51. Mar. 29, 1863, in Madeleine Dahlgren, *Memoir of John A. Dahlgren* (Boston: James R. Osgood and Company, 1882), 389.

52. Dorothy Lamon Teillard, ed., *Recollections of Abraham Lincoln, 1847–1865, by Ward Hill Lamon* (Washington: Published by the editor, 1911), 184–185. Augustus Chetlain told a similar story with the characters reversed in "Recollections of General U. S. Grant," 29–30.

53. Donn Piatt, *General George H. Thomas: A Critical Biography* (Cincinnati: Robert Clarke and Co., 1893), 233–234; Adam Badeau, *Military History of Ulysses S. Grant* (New York: D. Appleton and Company, 1881), 1: 180.

54. Joseph Medill to Horace White, Mar. 5, 1863, Robert Todd Lincoln Papers, LC.

55. Grant to Salmon P. Chase, Apr. 1, 1863, and Chase to Lincoln, Apr. 4, 1863, both ibid.

56. William Butler to Lincoln, Apr. 9, 1863, and Butler to [John] G. Nicolay, Apr. 11, 1863, both ibid.

57. Feb. 9, 1863, ibid.

58. J. H. Wilson, *Rawlins*, 118–120.

59. Apr. 30, May 1, 1863, Robert Todd Lincoln Papers, LC.

60. Copies of some of these reports are in ibid., and Lincoln probably read others.

61. J. K. Herbert to Butler, July 27, 1863, in Butler, *Correspondence*, 3: 99.

62. *New-York Daily Tribune*, July 8, 1863, cited in Anna Maclay Green, "Civil War Public Opinion of General Grant," *JISHS* 22 (Apr. 1929): 36.

63. Washburne to Lincoln, Oct. 12, 1863, Robert Todd Lincoln Papers, LC; Lincoln to Washburne, Oct. 26, 1863, in *CW*, 6: 540.

64. Lincoln to Washburne, Dec. 18, 1863, in *CW*, 7: 79; Washburne to his wife, Dec. 20, 1863, in Hunt, *Washburn*, 231.

65. *CG*, 38th Cong., 1st sess., 21, 111–112, 429–431.

66. Feb. 1, 1864, ibid., 429–430.

67. Ibid., 431, 789–798, 842; William Pitt Fessenden to son, Mar. 12, 1864, Fessenden Papers, Bowdoin College, Brunswick, Me.

68. Dec. 24, 1863, in Hay, *Diaries and Letters*, 143–144.

69. Sept. 5, 1863, Feb. 21, Feb. 26, 1864, all in Hunt, *Washburn*, 342–344.

70. Richardson, *Personal History*, 380–381; Ida M. Tarbell, *The Life of Abraham Lincoln* (New York: Doubleday and McClure Company, 1900), 3: 187–189.

71. Washburne to E. B. [*sic*] Morgan, Oct. 18, 1864, owned by Robert Lewis Piper, Albion, Mich.

72. Feb. 26, 1864, in Hunt, *Washburn,* 344.

73. Rawlins to Washburne, Jan. 20, 1864, in J. H. Wilson, *Rawlins,* 387–389; Rawlins to his wife, Apr. 4, 1864, in ibid., 410–411, 416–417.

74. June 2, 1864, New-York Historical Society; John Y. Simon, "A Name for General Grant," *Echoes: A Publication of the Ohio Historical Society* 2 (Apr. 1963): 1.

75. Rawlins to James Harrison Wilson, Mar. 3, 1864, in J. H. Wilson, *Rawlins,* 184–187.

76. Hunt, *Washburn,* 179.

77. Horace Porter, *Campaigning with Grant* (New York: Century, 1897), 54–55.

78. *Letters from Lloyd Lewis* (Boston: Little, Brown, 1950), 71.

79. Porter, *Campaigning with Grant,* 42–43.

80. Ibid., 97–98; Richardson, *Personal History,* 404. Washburne's notes on his stay with the army are in Hunt, *Washburn,* 207–219. Grant had already used his famous phrase in a telegram to Stanton a half hour earlier.

81. Hay, *Diaries and Letters,* 198, 201; J. K. Herbert to B. F. Butler, Sept. 3, 1864, in Butler, *Correspondence,* 5: 120–121; *Welles,* 2: 157; William Frank Zornow, *Lincoln and the Party Divided* (Norman: University of Oklahoma Press, 1954), 63.

82. Henry J. Raymond to Lincoln, Aug. 22, 1864, in *CW,* 7: 518.

83. Washburne to Lincoln, Oct. 17, 1864, in ibid., 8: 563.

84. Washburne to his wife, Sept. 11, 1864, in Hunt, *Washburn,* 231; Sept. 20, 1864, in *O.R.,* ser. 1, 42, part 2: 934.

85. Sept. 21, 1864, Robert Todd Lincoln Papers, LC.

86. Chauncey M. Depew, *My Memories of Eighty Years* (New York: Charles Scribner's Sons, 1921), 54–55.

87. Richardson, *Personal History,* 430–431.

88. Grant to Lincoln, Dec. 9, 1864, and Grant to Nicolay, Jan. 23, 1865, both Robert Todd Lincoln Papers, LC; E. C. Coltrin to Washburne, June 7, 1862, Washburne Papers, LC.

89. Grant Papers, ISHL; Washburne to Grant, Feb. 1, 1865, in *O.R.,* ser. 1, 46, part 2: 343; Washburne to Grant and Grant to Washburne, Feb. 6, 1865, in ibid., 416; Ishbel Ross, *The General's Wife* (New York: Dodd, Mead and Co., 1959), 176.

90. Washburne to Grant, Feb. 20, 1865, in *O.R.,* ser. 1, 10, part 1: 746–747.

91. Washburne to Grant and Grant to Washburne, Mar. 3, 1865, in ibid., ser. 1, 46, part 2: 803; J. H. Wilson, *Rawlins,* 326.

92. Washburne in Rice, *Reminiscences,* 43–44; Hunt, *Washburn,* 220–227.

93. Hunt, *Washburn,* 222–223; Benjamin P. Thomas, ed., *Three Years with Grant as Recalled by War Correspondent Sylvanus Cadwallader* (New York: Alfred A. Knopf, 1955), 335; J. H. Wilson, *Rawlins,* 324.

94. Washburne to Stanton, Apr. 14, 1865, in *O.R.*, ser. 1, 46, part 3: 744.

95. Grant to Washburne, Apr. 15, 1865, in ibid., 758.

96. Alexis de Tocqueville, *Democracy in America* (New York: Alfred A. Knopf, 1945), 2: 293.

97. Grant to his father, Sept. 23, 1859, Missouri Historical Society, St. Louis.

98. Grant to his father, Aug. 3, 1861, ibid.

99. See Elmer Gertz, "Three Galena Generals," *JISHS* 50 (Spring 1957): 24–35.

12. That Obnoxious Order

1. White Anglo-Saxon Protestant reactionaries, colloquially known as Know-Nothings, took several seats in the congressional elections of 1854. Formally organized as the American Party in 1856, they performed poorly in that year's elections, sympathy for their aims having dwindled.

14. Lincoln, Grant, and Kentucky in 1861

1. Message to Congress, Nov. 18, 1861, in *The Papers of Jefferson Davis*, ed. Haskell M. Monroe et al. (Baton Rouge: Louisiana State University, 1971–), 7: 413.

2. Beriah Magoffin to Simon Cameron, Apr. 15, 1861, in *O.R.*, ser. 3, 1: 70.

3. Frank Moore, ed., *The Rebellion Record: A Diary of American Events* (New York: D. Van Nostrand, 1864–1868), 1 (documents): 76.

4. Ibid., 1: 74.

5. E. Merton Coulter, *The Civil War and Readjustment in Kentucky* (Chapel Hill: University of North Carolina Press, 1926; reprint, Gloucester, Mass.: Peter Smith, 1966), 80.

6. Garrett Davis to George D. Prentice, Apr. 28, 1861, *CG*, 37th Cong., 2nd sess., Appendix, 82–83.

7. *CW*, 4: 428.

8. Lincoln to Simon B. Buckner, July 10, 1861, in ibid., 4: 444.

9. Aug. 22, 1861, in Hay, *Diaries and Letters*, 25.

10. Lincoln to Beriah Magoffin, Aug. 24, 1861, in *CW*, 4: 497.

11. Jefferson Davis to Beriah Magoffin, Aug. 28, 1861, in *O.R.*, ser. 1, 4: 396–397.

12. Gideon J. Pillow to Jefferson Davis, May 16, 1861, in ibid., ser. 1, 52, part 2: 101.

13. Gideon J. Pillow to Leonidas Polk, Aug. 29, 1861, in ibid., ser. 1, 3: 685–687.

14. Andrew Rolle, *John Charles Frémont: Character as Destiny* (Norman: University of Oklahoma Press, 1991), 198.

15. John C. Frémont to Ulysses S. Grant, Aug. 28, 1861, in *PUSG*, 2: 151.

16. Leonidas Polk to Beriah Magoffin, Sept. 1, 1861, in *O.R.*, ser. 1, 4: 179.

17. Isham Harris to Leonidas Polk, Sept. 4, 1861, in ibid., ser. 1, 4: 180.

18. Leonidas Polk to Isham Harris, Sept. 1861, in ibid.

19. Monroe et al., *Davis Papers*, 7: 325; Steven E. Woodworth, *Jefferson Davis and His Generals: The Failure of Confederate Command in the West* (Lawrence: University Press of Kansas, 1990), 34–45; Steven E. Woodworth, "'The Indeterminate Quantities': Jefferson Davis, Leonidas Polk, and the End of Kentucky Neutrality, September 1861," *Civil War History* 38 (1992): 289–297.

20. Leroy P. Walker to Leonidas Polk, Sept. 4, 1861, in *O.R.*, ser. 1, 4: 180.

21. Jefferson Davis to Leonidas Polk, Sept. 5, 1861, in Monroe et al., *Davis Papers*, 7: 327. Printed as "The necessity justifies the action" in *O.R.*, ser. 1, 4: 181.

22. Leonidas Polk to Jefferson Davis, Sept. 6, 1861, in Monroe et al., *Davis Papers*, 7: 328.

23. Leroy P. Walker to Leonidas Polk, Sept. 5, 1861, in *O.R.*, ser. 1, 4: 181.

24. Leroy P. Walker to Isham Harris, Sept. 5, 1861, in ibid., ser. 1, 4: 189.

25. Leonidas Polk to John M. Johnston, Sept. 9, 1861, ibid., ser. 1, 4: 186.

26. *PMUSG*, 1: 264.

27. U. S. Grant to John C. Frémont, Sept. 4, 1861, in *PUSG*, 2: 186.

28. U. S. Grant to Speaker, Ky. House of Representatives, Sept. 5, 1861, in ibid., 2: 189.

29. U. S. Grant to John C. Frémont, Sept. 5, 1861, in ibid., 2: 193.

30. U. S. Grant to John C. Frémont, Sept. 6, 1861, in ibid., 2: 196–197; U. S. Grant to Julia Dent Grant, Sept. 8, 1861, in ibid., 2: 214; *PMUSG*, 1: 265–266.

31. On Sept. 7, the general commanding at Cairo in Grant's absence heard that Pillow, with four thousand men, would march on Paducah "in two days." John A. McClernand to John C. Frémont, Sept. 7, 1861, in *O.R.*, ser. 1, 3: 475.

32. Proclamation, Sept. 6, 1861, in *PUSG*, 2: 194–195.

33. Ibid., 2: 191–192.

34. Lincoln to John C. Frémont, Sept. 2, 1861, in *CW*, 4: 506.

35. Lincoln to Orville H. Browning, Sept. 22, 1861, in ibid., 4: 532.

36. James Speed to Lincoln, Sept. 3, 1861, in ibid., 4: 506–507.

37. Message to Congress, Nov. 18, 1861, in Monroe et al., *Davis Papers*, 7: 414.

38. *CW*, 5: 50.

39. John C. Frémont to Abraham Lincoln, Sept. 3, 1861, quoted in Allan Nevins, *The War for the Union: The Improvised War, 1861–1862* (New York: Scribner's, 1959), 1: 333.

15. Grant, Lincoln, and Unconditional Surrender

1. Ulysses S. Grant to Julia Dent Grant, July 1, 1852, in *PUSG*, 1: 243.

2. Helen Nicolay, *Lincoln's Secretary: A Biography of John G. Nicolay* (New York: Longmans, Green, 1949), 195–196.

3. *PUSG*, 10: 195.

4. Horace Porter, *Campaigning with Grant* (New York: Century, 1897), 22.

5. John Russell Young quoted in *Chicago Tribune*, Sept. 1, 1885.

6. Sherman to Grant, Mar. 10, 1864, in *PUSG*, 10: 188.

7. *PMUSG*, 2: 122; Porter, *Campaigning with Grant*, 26.

8. Lincoln to Grant, Apr. 30, 1864, and Grant to Lincoln, May 1, 1864, both in *PUSG*, 10: 380.

9. Hay, *Diaries and Letters*, 179; Grant to Sherman, Apr. 4, 1864, in *PUSG*, 10: 253; *PMUSG*, 2: 143.

10. Lincoln to Grant, June 15, 1864, in *PUSG*, 11: 45; *CW*, 7: 393.

11. *PMUSG*, 2: 116.

12. John M. Schofield, *Forty-Six Years in the Army* (New York: Century, 1897), 361–362.

13. John Russell Young, *Around the World with General Grant* (New York: American News Company, 1879), 2: 214, 216–217, 463.

14. Grant to Halleck, Jan. 20, 1863, in *PUSG*, 7: 234; James Harrison Wilson, *Under the Old Flag* (New York and London: D. Appleton, 1912), 1: 148–149; Adam Badeau to S. L. M. Barlow, Feb. 27, 1863, Barlow Papers, Henry E. Huntington Library, San Marino, Calif.

15. *Welles*, 1: 387.

16. Lincoln to Grant, July 13, Aug. 9, 1863, in *CW*, 6: 326, 374; Grant to Lincoln, Aug. 23, 1863, in *PUSG*, 9: 195.

17. Grant to David D. Porter, May 25, 1868, in *PUSG*, 18: 262; Grant to William T. Sherman, June 21, 1868, in ibid., 18: 292.

18. Grant to Lincoln, July 25, 1864, in ibid., 11: 309.

19. Grant to Halleck, Aug. 1, 1864, in ibid., 11: 361.

20. *CW*, 7: 470.

21. Grant to Halleck, Aug. 1, 1864, in *PUSG*, 11: 358.

22. Lincoln to Grant, Aug. 3, 1864, in *CW*, 7: 476.

23. Grant to Halleck, Apr. 22, 1864, in *PUSG*, 10: 340.

24. Grant to Halleck, Apr. 26, 1864, in ibid., 10: 356.

25. Halleck to Grant, Apr. 29, 1864, in ibid., 10: 369.

26. Halleck to Grant, May 2, 1864, in ibid., 10: 375.

27. Grant to Halleck, July 7, 1864, in ibid., 11: 185.

28. Charles A. Dana to Grant, July 12, 1864, in ibid., 11: 230.

29. Grant to Halleck, July 1, 1864, in ibid., 11: 155.

30. Halleck to Grant, July 3, 1864, in ibid., 11: 156.

31. Grant to Halleck, June 24, 1864, in ibid., 11: 124.

32. Memorandum, Aug. 23, 1864, in *CW*, 7: 514.

33. Stanton to Grant, Oct. 2, 1864, in *PUSG,* 12: 303. See *PMUSG,* 2: 375–376; Porter, *Campaigning with Grant,* 314–316.

34. Grant to Washburne, Aug. 16, 1864, in *PUSG,* 12: 16–17.

35. Grant to Washburne, Sept. 21, 1864, in ibid., 12: 185.

36. Grant to Lincoln, Jan. 31, 1864, in ibid., 13: 333–334; Lincoln to Grant, Feb. 1, 1865, in *CW,* 8: 252.

37. Grant to Stanton, Feb. 1, 1865, in *PUSG,* 13: 345.

38. Lincoln to Seward, Feb. 2, 1865, in *CW,* 8: 256.

39. *PMJDG,* 141.

40. *PUSG,* 14: 64.

41. Stanton to Grant, Mar. 3, 1865, in ibid. (cancellations omitted), 14: 91.

42. Lincoln to Grant, Jan. 19, 1865, in *CW,* 8: 223.

43. Grant to Lincoln, Jan. 21, 1865, in *PUSG,* 13: 281.

44. Ibid., 13: 282.

45. Porter to Sherman, 1866, in Sherman, *Memoirs of Gen. W. T. Sherman, Written by Himself,* 4th ed. (New York: Charles L. Webster, 1891), 2: 329.

46. *PMUSG,* 2: 514.

47. Lincoln to Grant, Apr. 7, 1865, in *CW,* 8: 392.

48. *PUSG,* 14: 484.

John Y. Simon

A Bibliography

Books

Ulysses S. Grant Chronology. Columbus: Ohio Historical Society for Ulysses S. Grant Association and Ohio Civil War Centennial Commission, 1963.

General Grant by Matthew Arnold with a Rejoinder by Mark Twain. Editor. Carbondale and Edwardsville: Southern Illinois University Press, 1966. Reprint, Kent, Ohio: Kent State University Press, 1995.

The Papers of Ulysses S. Grant. Editor. Carbondale and Edwardsville: Southern Illinois University Press.

Volume 1, 1837–1861. 1967
Volume 2, April–September 1861. 1969
Volume 3, October 1, 1861–January 7, 1862. 1970
Volume 4, January 8–March 31, 1862. 1972
Volume 5, April 1–August 31, 1862. 1973
Volume 6, September 1–December 8, 1862. 1977
Volume 7, December 9, 1862–March 31, 1863. 1979
Volume 8, April 1–July 6, 1863. 1979
Volume 9, July 7–December 31, 1863. 1982
Volume 10, January 1–May 31, 1864. 1982
Volume 11, June 1–August 15, 1864. 1984
Volume 12, August 16–November 15, 1864. 1984
Volume 13, November 16, 1864–February 20, 1865. 1985
Volume 14, February 21–April 30, 1865. 1985
Volume 15, May 1–December 31, 1865. 1988
Volume 16, 1866. 1988
Volume 17, January 1–September 30, 1867. 1991
Volume 18, October 1, 1867–June 30, 1868. 1991
Volume 19, July 1, 1868–October 31, 1869. 1995
Volume 20, November 1, 1869–October 31, 1870. 1995
Volume 21, November 1, 1870–May 31, 1871. 1998
Volume 22, June 1, 1871–January 31, 1872. 1998

Volume 23, February–December 31, 1872. 2000
Volume 24, 1873. 2000
Volume 25, 1874. 2003
Volume 26, 1875. 2003
Volume 27, January 1–October 31, 1876. 2005
Volume 28, November 1, 1876–September 30, 1878. 2005
Volume 29, October 1, 1878–September 30, 1880. 2008
Volume 30, October 1, 1880–December 31, 1882. 2008
Volume 31, January 1, 1883–July 23, 1885. 2009
The Personal Memoirs of Julia Dent Grant. Editor. New York: G. P. Putnam's Sons, 1975. Reprint, Carbondale and Edwardsville: Southern Illinois University Press, 1988.
Ulysses S. Grant: Essays and Documents. Editor, with David L. Wilson. Carbondale and Edwardsville: Southern Illinois University Press, 1981.
The Continuing Civil War: Essays in Honor of the Civil War Round Table of Chicago. Editor, with Barbara Hughett. Dayton, Ohio: Morningside, 1992.
Grant and Halleck: Contrasts in Command. Frank L. Clement Lecture. Milwaukee: Marquette University Press, 1996.
New Perspectives on the American Civil War: Myths and Realities of the National Conflict. Editor, with Michael Stevens. Madison, Wis.: Madison House, 1998. Reprint, Blue Ridge Summit, Pa.: Rowman and Littlefield Publishers, 2002.
The Lincoln Forum: Abraham Lincoln, Gettysburg and the Civil War. Editor, with Harold Holzer and William D. Pederson. Mason City, Iowa: Savas Publishing Company, 1999.
The Lincoln Forum: Rediscovering Abraham Lincoln. Editor, with Harold Holzer and Dawn Ruark. New York: Fordham University Press, 2002.
Lincoln Revisited: New Insights from the Lincoln Forum. Editor, with Harold Holzer and Dawn Vogel. New York: Fordham University Press, 2007.

Articles and Other Publications

"The Collected Writings of Ulysses S. Grant." In "Three Centennial Projects," special issue of *Civil War History* 9, no. 3 (1963): 277–279.
"The Collected Writings of Ulysses S. Grant 1822–1885." *Manuscripts* 15, no. 1 (1963): 33–34.
"A Name for General Grant." Ohio Historical Society, *Echoes* 2, no. 4 (1963).
"The Politics of the Morrill Act." *Agricultural History* 37, no. 1 (1963): 103–111.
"Hannah Fancher's Notes on Ohio Speech in 1824." *Ohio History* 73 (1964): 34–38.
"A Lieutenant's View of Shiloh." *Confederate Historical Society Journal* 2 (1964): 113–119.

"Lincoln and His Valet." Ohio Historical Society, *Echoes* 3 (1964). Reprinted in *Negro History Bulletin* 31 (1968): 14.

"Reminiscences of Isaac Jackson Allen." *Ohio History* 73 (1964): 207–238.

"From Galena to Appomattox: Grant and Washburne." *Journal of the Illinois State Historical Society* 58, no. 2 (1965): 165–189.

"Lincoln and Truman Smith." *Lincoln Herald* 67 (1965): 124–130. Reprinted in *The Many Faces of Lincoln: Selected Articles from the* Lincoln Herald, ed. Charles M. Hubbard, Thomas R. Turner, and Steven K. Rogstad. Mahomet, Ill.: Mayhaven Publishing, 1997. 196–206.

"Colonel Grant of the Illinois Volunteers." *Illinois Civil War Sketches, Civil War Centennial Commission of Illinois* 6 (1966).

"The Personal Sentiments of Mr. Lincoln." *Lincoln Herald* 68 (1966): 89–92.

"An Illinois Soldier at Vicksburg." *Manuscripts* 19 (1967): 23–31.

"Ralph G. Newman." *Manuscripts* 19 (1967): 25–29.

"An Incident at Fair Oaks." *Manuscripts* 20 (1968): 40–41.

"Jeb Stuart in Kansas." *Manuscripts* 20 (1968): 35–37.

"The Papers of Andrew Johnson." *Manuscripts* 20 (1968): 36–37.

"Confederate Recruiting in Washington: A Letter of Louis T. Wigfall." *Manuscripts* 21 (1969): 46–48.

Introduction to *The Sherman Letters: Correspondence between General and Senator Sherman from 1837 to 1891*, ed. Rachel Sherman Thorndike (1894). Reprint, New York: Da Capo Press, 1969. v–xi.

"The Remains of the Confederacy." *Manuscripts* 21 (1969): 121–122.

"The Ritzman Collection of Aurora College." *Manuscripts* 21 (1969): 211–213.

"Union County in 1858 and the Lincoln-Douglas Debate." *Journal of the Illinois State Historical Society* 62 (1969): 267–292.

"Autographs from Beyond." *Manuscripts* 22 (1970): 114–115.

"Grant, Ulysses S." *Encyclopedia Britannica*, beginning with 1970 edition.

"Letters of Admiral Samuel F. DuPont." *Manuscripts* 22 (1970): 209–211.

"Confederate Letters at Washington University." *Manuscripts* 23 (1971): 60–62.

"Grant, Ulysses S." *World Book Encyclopedia*, beginning with 1971 edition.

"Two Civil War Manuscripts at the Filson Club." *Manuscripts* 23 (1971): 280–283.

"The Facts of the Civil War." *Manuscripts* 24 (1972): 65–66.

"A Monument to Jefferson Davis." *Manuscripts* 24 (1972): 136–138.

Foreword to *The Captain Departs: Ulysses S. Grant's Last Campaign*, by Thomas M. Pitkin. Carbondale and Edwardsville: Southern Illinois University Press, 1973. xiii–xvi.

"Editorial Projects as Derivative Archives." *College and University Libraries* 35 (1974): 291–294.

"Lincoln Worship." *Lincoln Herald* 76 (1974): 117.

"The Rediscovery of Ulysses S. Grant." *Inland: The Magazine of the Middle West* 74 (1974): 8–14.

"General Grant and Mark Twain." *ICarbS* 2 (1975): 3–10.

"Andrew Johnson and the Freedmen." With Felix James. *Lincoln Herald* 79 (1977): 71–75.

"Ulysses S. Grant and the Ship Railway." *ICarbS* 4, no. 1 (1978): 3–9.

"Battle of the Crater." In *Encyclopedia of Southern History*. Baton Rouge: Louisiana State University Press, 1979. 308.

"Chattanooga Campaign." In *Encyclopedia of Southern History*. Baton Rouge: Louisiana State University Press, 1979. 201.

"Grant at Hardscrabble." *Bulletin of the Missouri Historical Society* 35, no. 4 (1979): 191–201.

"Hardscrabble." *Missouri Life* 7, nos. 2–3 (1979): 34–37.

Foreword to *They Died to Make Men Free: A History of the 19th Michigan Infantry in the Civil War,* by William M. Anderson. Berrien Springs, Mich.: Hardscrabble Books, 1980. ix–x.

"Editors and Critics." *Newsletter of the Association for Documentary Editing* 3 (1981): 1–4.

"Grant at Belmont." *Military Affairs* 45, no. 4 (1981): 161–166.

"Samuel H. Beckwith: 'Grant's Shadow.'" In *Ulysses S. Grant: Essays and Documents,* ed. John Y. Simon and David L. Wilson. Carbondale and Edwardsville: Southern Illinois University Press, 1981. 77–139.

"American Historical Editing Today." *AHA Perspectives* 20 (1982): 5–7.

"In Response." *Newsletter of the Association for Documentary Editing* 4 (1982): 5–6.

"In Search of Margaret Johnson Erwin: A Research Note." *Journal of American History* 69 (1983): 932–941. Comment on this article is available in ibid., 942–945, and in *Journal of American History* 70 (1984): 224–226.

"The Paradox of Ulysses S. Grant." *Register of the Kentucky Historical Society* 81, no. 4 (1983): 366–382.

"The Canons of Selection." *Documentary Editing* 6 (1984): 8–12. Reprinted in ibid. 25, no. 3 (2003): 135–143.

"Commentary at 10th Annual Lincoln Symposium." *Papers of the Abraham Lincoln Association* 6 (1984): 25–27.

"Daniel Harmon Brush and the Eighteenth Illinois Infantry." In *Selected Papers in Illinois History 1982.* Springfield: Illinois State Historical Society, 1984. 42–50.

"Lincoln and Grant." Lincoln Fellowship of Wisconsin, *Historical Bulletin No. 39* (1984): 2–9.

"Lincoln, Slavery, and Race Relations." In *Illinois: Its History and Legacy,* ed. Roger D. Bridges and Rodney O. Davis. St. Louis: River City Publishers, 1984. 80–89.

"Losses in War: A Sociological Approach." With Gunnar Boalt. In *Competing Belief Systems*, ed. Gunnar Boalt. Stockholm: Almqvist and Wiksell International, 1984. 151–156.

"That Obnoxious Order." *Civil War Times Illustrated* 23, no. 6 (October 1984): 12–17.

"Ulysses S. Grant." In *The Presidents: A Reference History*, ed. Henry F. Graff. New York: Charles Scribner's Sons, 1984. 289–307. 2nd ed., 1996. 245–260.

"Ulysses S. Grant and Civil Service Reform." *Hayes Historical Journal* 4, no. 3 (1984): 8–15.

"U. S. Grant: The Man and the Image." In *U. S. Grant: The Man and the Image*. National Portrait Gallery exhibition catalog. Carbondale and Edwardsville: Southern Illinois University Press, 1985. 13–26.

"Ulysses S. Grant One Hundred Years Later." *Illinois Historical Journal* 79, no. 4 (1986): 245–256. Pamphlet reprint, Springfield, Ill.: Illinois State Historical Society, 1987.

Foreword to *The Diary of Cyrus B. Comstock*, ed. Merlin E. Sumner. Dayton, Ohio: Morningside, 1987.

Foreword to *The Trial of U. S. Grant: The Pacific Coast Years 1852–1854*, by Charles G. Ellington. Glendale, Calif.: Arthur H. Clark Company, 1987. 15–19.

House Divided: Lincoln and His Father. Pamphlet. Fort Wayne, Ind.: Louis A. Warren Lincoln Library and Museum, 1987.

Introduction to *The Era of the Civil War 1848–1870*, by Arthur Charles Cole. Volume 3 of *The Sesquicentennial History of Illinois*. Urbana and Chicago: University of Illinois Press, 1987.

"Abraham Lincoln." In *Research Guide to American Historical Biography*, ed. Robert Muccigrosso. Washington, D.C.: Beacham Publishing, 1988. 3: 939–945.

"Lincoln's Navy." In *Christening and Launching of the Aircraft Carrier Abraham Lincoln*. Newport News, Va.: Newport News Shipbuilding and Dry Dock Company, 1988. Reprint, *USS Abraham Lincoln (CVN72)*, 1990.

"Ulysses S. Grant." In *Research Guide to American Historical Biography*, ed. Robert Muccigrosso. Washington, D.C.: Beacham Publishing, 1988. 3: 623–629.

"U.S. Colored Troops." In *Dictionary of Afro-American Slavery*, ed. Randall M. Miller and John David Smith. Westport, Conn.: Greenwood Press, 1988. 754–755.

"Boom and Bust in Grand Tower." In *Southern Illinois River Work*. Carbondale: Special Collections, Morris Library, Southern Illinois University, 1989.

"Abraham Lincoln and Ann Rutledge." *Journal of the Abraham Lincoln Association* 11 (1990): 13–33.

Foreword to *The Civil War Round Table: Fifty Years of Scholarship and Fellowship*, by Barbara Hughett. Chicago: Chicago Civil War Round Table, 1990.

"Fort Donelson." In *The Civil War Battlefield Guide*, ed. Frances H. Kennedy. Boston: Houghton Mifflin, 1990. 16–19.

"Mary Todd Lincoln 1818–1882." In *Research Guide to American Historical Biography*, ed. Suzanne Niemeyer. Washington, D.C.: Beacham Publishing, 1990.

"Civil War Comes to Williamson County." *Springhouse* 8 (1991): 33–34.

"The Era of the Civil War, 1848–70." In *A Guide to the History of Illinois*, ed. John Hoffmann. Westport, Conn.: Greenwood Press, 1991. 63–71.

Foreword to *Black Troops, White Commanders, and Freedmen during the Civil War*, by Howard C. Westwood. Carbondale and Edwardsville: Southern Illinois University Press, 1991. xvi–ix.

Foreword to *History, 31st Regiment Illinois Volunteers Organized by John A. Logan*, by W. S. Morris, L. D. Hartwell, and J. B. Kuykendall (1902). Reprint, Herrin, Ill.: Crossfire Press, 1991. Reprint, Carbondale and Edwardsville: Southern Illinois University Press, 1998. xi–xv.

"Lincoln and Charles L. Frost." *Lincoln Newsletter* 10 (1991): 5.

"The Road to Appomattox: The Generalship of Ulysses S. Grant." *Timeline* 8, no. 4 (1991): 2–19.

"Stephen A. Douglas and Isaac N. Morris." *The Little Giant: A Newsletter of the Stephen A. Douglas Association* 3 (1991): 3. Reprinted in ibid. 15 (2003): 1.

"The Civil War Years of Colonel Daniel H. Brush, 18th Illinois Infantry." In *Growing Up with Southern Illinois 1820 to 1861: From the Memoirs of Daniel Harmon Brush* (1944). Reprint, Herrin, Ill.: Crossfire Press, 1992. I–XXIII.

"Eighteenth President and the Press." *Media History Digest* 12 (Spring–Summer 1992): 27–31, 42.

"Fifty Years of the Civil War Round Table." In *The Continuing Civil War: Essays in Honor of the Civil War Round Table of Chicago*, ed. John Y. Simon and Barbara Hughett. Dayton, Ohio: Morningside, 1992. 19–23.

Introduction to *Bloody Williamson: A Chapter in American Lawlessness*, by Paul M. Angle (1952). Reprint, Urbana and Chicago: University of Illinois Press, 1992. ix–xxi.

"Lincoln and Father O'Hagan." *Lincoln Newsletter* 11 (1992): 1, 3.

"Abraham Lincoln in Southern Illinois." In *When Lincoln Came to Egypt*, by George W. Smith (1940). Reprint, Herrin, Ill.: Crossfire Press, 1993. xv–xlv.

"Abraham Lincoln, Jefferson Davis, and Fort Sumter." *Abraham Lincoln and the Crucible of War: Papers from the Sixth Annual Lincoln Colloquium*, ed. George L. Painter (1993): 23–31.

"Grant of Illinois." *Illinois History* 46 (February 1993): 21–22.

"Ulysses S. Grant: 'Mistakes Have Been Made.'" *Humanities* 14 (January–February 1993): 21. Reprinted in *Humanities* 18 (1997): 30.

"Doing Right by a Hero." *Newsday,* April 27, 1994.

"Grant, Lincoln, and Unconditional Surrender." In *Lincoln's Generals,* ed. Gabor S. Boritt. New York: Oxford University Press, 1994. 163–198.

"Lincoln's Decision to Issue the Emancipation Proclamation." *Abraham Lincoln and the Political Process: Papers from the Seventh Annual Lincoln Colloquium* (1994): 47–57.

"At the Battle of Shiloh." *Cobblestone* (October 1995): 27–29.

Foreword to *"Black Jack": John A. Logan and Southern Illinois in the Civil War Era,* by James Pickett Jones (1967). Reprint, Carbondale and Edwardsville: Southern Illinois University Press, 1995. xi–xix.

Foreword to *The Every-day Life of Abraham Lincoln,* by Francis Fisher Browne (1886). Reprint, Lincoln: University of Nebraska Press, 1995.

Foreword to *The Lincoln College Story 1865–1995,* by Barbara Hughett. Lincoln, Ill.: Lincoln College, 1995.

"Grant, Ulysses S." In *Biographical Dictionary of the Union: Northern Leaders of the Civil War,* ed. John T. Hubbell and James W. Geary. Westport, Conn.: Greenwood Press, 1995.

"Halleck, Henry Wager." In *Biographical Dictionary of the Union: Northern Leaders of the Civil War,* ed. John T. Hubbell and James W. Geary. Westport, Conn.: Greenwood Press, 1995. 228–229.

"Rawlins, John Aaron." In *Biographical Dictionary of the Union: Northern Leaders of the Civil War,* ed. John T. Hubbell and James W. Geary. Westport, Conn.: Greenwood Press, 1995. 428–429.

"Ulysses S. Grant and the Jews: An Unsolved Mystery." *The Record: Publication of the Jewish Historical Society of Greater Washington* 21 (1995): 25–33. Reprinted in *Jewish Life in Mr. Lincoln's City,* ed. Laura Cohen Apelbaum and Claire Uziel. Washington, D.C.: Jewish Historical Society of Greater Washington, 2009. 99–110.

Foreword to *Army Life of an Illinois Soldier,* by Charles W. Wills (1906). Reprint, Carbondale and Edwardsville: Southern Illinois University Press, 1996.

Foreword to *Personal Memoirs of John H. Brinton, Civil War Surgeon, 1861–1865* (1914). Reprint, Carbondale and Edwardsville: Southern Illinois University Press, 1996. ix–xiv.

"Julia (Dent) Grant." In *American First Ladies: Their Lives and Their Legacy,* ed. Lewis L. Gould. New York and London: Garland Publishing, 1996. 203–215.

"Lincoln's Despair: The Crisis during the Summer of 1864." *Abraham Lincoln and a Nation at War: Papers from the Ninth Annual Lincoln Colloquium,* ed. George L. Painter and Linda Norbut Suits (1996): 17–31.

Foreword to *A History of the Ninth Regiment Illinois Volunteer Infantry*, by Marion Morrison (1864). Reprint, Carbondale and Edwardsville: Southern Illinois University Press, 1997. ix–xii.

Foreword to *Reminiscences of a Soldier's Wife: An Autobiography*, by Mrs. John A. Logan (1913). Reprint, Carbondale and Edwardsville: Southern Illinois University Press, 1997. xvii–xxii.

"Grant's Tomb Deserves Respect." *New York Post*, April 23, 1997.

Foreword to *The Military Memoirs of General John Pope*, ed. Peter Cozzens and Robert L. Girardi. Chapel Hill: University of North Carolina Press, 1998. xi–xiii.

Foreword to *Mystic Chords of Memory: Civil War Battlefields and Historic Sites Recaptured*, by David Eicher. Baton Rouge: Louisiana University Press, 1998. ix–xi.

"Forging a Commander: Ulysses S. Grant Enters the Civil War." In *New Perspectives on the American Civil War: Myths and Realities of the National Conflict*, ed. John Y. Simon and Michael Stevens. Madison, Wis.: Madison House, 1998. Reprint, Blue Ridge Summit, Pa.: Rowman and Littlefield, 2002. 49–68.

"Forging a Commander: Ulysses S. Grant in the First Year of the Civil War." *Books at Brown* 40 (1998): 26–43.

"'Freeing Some and Leaving Others Alone': Lincoln's Emancipation Policy." *Abraham Lincoln and a New Birth of Freedom: Papers from the Tenth Annual Lincoln Colloquium*, ed. Linda Norbut Suits and Timothy P. Townsend (1998): 21–35.

"Judge Andrew D. Duff of Egypt." *Springhouse* 15 (August 1998): 8–9.

"Lincoln and 'Old Brains' Halleck." *North & South* 2 (November 1998): 38–45.

Reading about Grant. Pamphlet. Union League of Philadelphia, 1998.

"Elihu Benjamin Washburne." In *American National Biography*, ed. John A. Garraty and Mark C. Carnes. New York: Oxford University Press, 1999. 22: 750–751.

Foreword to *Don't Shoot That Boy! Abraham Lincoln and Military Justice*, by Thomas P. Lowry. Mason City, Iowa: Savas Publishing Company, 1999. i–iii.

"Grant, Ulysses S. (1822–1885)." In *Dictionary of Missouri Biography*, ed. Lawrence O. Christensen et al. Columbia: University of Missouri Press, 1999. 345–347.

"John Aaron Rawlins." In *American National Biography*, ed. John A. Garraty and Mark C. Carnes. New York: Oxford University Press, 1999. 18: 199.

"John Alexander Logan." In *American National Biography*, ed. John A. Garraty and Mark C. Carnes. New York: Oxford University Press, 1999. 13: 839–840.

"John Alexander McClernand." In *American National Biography*, ed. John A.

Garraty and Mark C. Carnes. New York: Oxford University Press, 1999. 14: 873–874.

"Lincoln and Halleck." In *Lincoln and His Contemporaries,* ed. Charles M. Hubbard. Macon: Mercer University Press, 1999. 69–85.

"Lincoln, Grant, and Meade: Vicksburg and Gettysburg in Retrospect." In *The Lincoln Forum: Abraham Lincoln, Gettysburg and the Civil War,* ed. John Y. Simon, Harold Holzer, and William D. Peterson. Mason City, Iowa: Savas Publishing Company, 1999. 65–81.

"Ralph G. Newman, 1911–1998." *Civil War History* 45 (March 1999): 61–63.

"Red River Radio Interview with Dr. John Y. Simon on Abraham Lincoln." *International Lincoln Association Newsletter* 11 (May–August 1999): 10–11.

"Skeptical." *North & South* 2, no. 4 (April 1999): 33–34.

"A Tribute to George L. Painter." *War, Politics, and the Lincoln Administration: Papers from the Eleventh Annual Lincoln Colloquium* (1999): 7–9.

"Winfield Scott Hancock." In *American National Biography,* ed. John A. Garraty and Mark C. Carnes. New York: Oxford University Press, 1999.

Foreword to *Life and Letters of General W. H. L. Wallace,* by Isabel Wallace. (1909). Reprint, Carbondale and Edwardsville: Southern Illinois University Press, 2000. v–xvi.

"Lincoln, Grant, and Kentucky in 1861." In *The Civil War in Kentucky,* ed. Kent Masterson Brown. Mason City, Iowa: Savas Publishing Company, 2000. 1–21.

"Memorial to Ralph G. Newman." *Illinois Heritage* 3, nos. 1–2 (2000): 26–27.

"'Rebellion Thus Sugar-Coated': The Case against Secession." *North & South* 3 (September 2000): 10–16.

"U. S. Grant Family Selling Artifact Collection." *Civil War Times Illustrated* 39, no. 1 (March 2000): 8.

Foreword to *Civil War High Commands,* by John H. Eicher and David J. Eicher. Stanford: Stanford University Press, 2001. xi–xii.

"Grant, Ulysses S." In *The Oxford Companion to United States History,* ed. Paul S. Boyer et al. New York: Oxford University Press, 2001. 318–319.

"Let's Bounce the Rubber Lincolns." *Chicago Tribune,* January 24, 2001. Reprinted in *White House Studies* 2, no. 1 (2002): 61–62.

"A Marriage Tested by War: Ulysses and Julia Grant." In *Intimate Strategies of the Civil War: Military Commanders and Their Wives,* ed. Carol K. Bleser and Lesley J. Gordon. New York: Oxford University Press, 2001. 123–137.

"The Other Illinois: How Egypt Lost Its Clout." *Chicago Tribune,* June 24, 2001. Reprinted in *Springhouse* 18, no. 4 (2001): 12–13.

"The Union Military Effort in the West: Grant Emerges." In *The Civil War in the Western Theater,* ed. John F. Marszalek. Starkville, Miss.: Mississippi State University Department of History, 2001. 48–60.

"What Was Wrong with the Army of the Potomac?" Panel discussion with several historians. *North & South* 4, no. 3 (March 2001): 12–18.

"The Civil War on the Internet." *Documentary Editing* 24, no. 1 (2002): 4–6.
"Commander in Chief and General Grant." In *The Lincoln Forum: Rediscovering Abraham Lincoln*, ed. John Y. Simon, Harold Holzer, and Dawn Ruark. New York: Fordham University Press, 2002. 16–33.
"Epilogue." In *Judging Lincoln*, by Frank J. Williams. Carbondale and Edwardsville: Southern Illinois University Press, 2002. 179–182.
"The Reluctant Cadet." *Humanities: The Magazine of the National Endowment for the Humanities* 23, no. 1 (2002): 18–19.
"Boom and Bust in Grand Tower." *Springhouse* 20, no. 2 (2003): 31–35.
"The Chancy Business We Call History." *Annotation* 31, no. 4 (2003): 6.
"John A. Logan and Education." Carterville, Ill.: John A. Logan College, [2003]. Reprinted in *Springhouse* 20, no. 1 (2003): 15–17.
"The Monuments." In *Gettysburg Battlefield*, ed. David J. Eicher. San Francisco: Chronicle Books, 2003. 276–277.
"Who Were the Top Ten Generals?" Panel discussion with several historians. *North & South* 6, no. 4 (May 2003): 12–22.
"Gettysburg Address." In *Americans at War: Society, Culture, and the Homefront*, ed. Jon P. Resch. Detroit: Thomson, Gale, and Macmillan Reference USA, 2004. 2: 73–74.
"Who Were the Worst Ten Generals?" Panel discussion with several historians. *North & South* 7, no. 3 (May 2004): 12–25.
"More Disney than Lincoln." *State Journal-Register* (Springfield, Ill.), April 14, 2005.
"The Ten Greatest Blunders of the Civil War." Panel discussion with several historians. *North & South* 8, no. 1 (January 2005): 12–23.
"Lincoln, Douglas, and Popular Sovereignty: The Mormon Dimension." In *Lincoln Revisited: New Insights from the Lincoln Forum*, ed. John Y. Simon, Harold Holzer, and Dawn Vogel. New York: Fordham University Press, 2007. 45–56.

Miscellaneous

"Congress under Lincoln." PhD diss., Harvard University, 1961.
Editor. Ulysses S. Grant Association *Newsletter*, 1963–1973.
Civil War editor. *Manuscripts*, 1967–1972.
Contributor to *Historical Times Illustrated Encyclopedia of the Civil War*, ed. Patricia L. Faust. New York: Harper and Row, 1986.
Historical consultant and commentator. *Abraham Lincoln: A New Birth of Freedom*. Judith Leonard Productions. Public Broadcasting Service, 1992.
Historical consultant and commentator. *Lincoln-Douglas Debates*. C-SPAN. Jonesboro, Ill., 1994.
Coauthor. "Grant Seen and Heard." Performed by Harold Holzer and Richard Dreyfuss. Metropolitan Museum of Art, November 13, 2003.

Content adviser. *Ulysses S. Grant: Union General and U.S. President,* by Brenda Haugen. Minneapolis: Compass Point Books, 2005.
Contributor to *Revisioning the Civil War: Historians on Counter-Factual Scenarios,* ed. James C. Bresnahan. Jefferson, N.C.: McFarland and Company, 2006.

Book Reviews

Reviews appeared in the following journals: *American Archivist, American Historical Review, Annals of Iowa, Choice, Civil War History, Civil War Times Illustrated, Claremont Review of Books, Columbiad, Illinois Historical Journal, Illinois Issues, Illinois Schools Journal, Journal of American History, Journal of Library History, Journal of Southern History, Journal of the Illinois State Historical Society, Lincoln Herald, Louisiana History, North & South, Ohio History, Old Northwest, Register of the Kentucky Historical Society, Virginia Magazine of History and Biography, Western Illinois Regional Studies, Wisconsin Magazine of History.*

Papers and Presentations at Professional Meetings

Mississippi Valley Historical Association, Milwaukee, 1962
Civil War Centennial Assemblies: Boston, 1963; Springfield, Ill., 1965
Civil War Round Tables: Columbus, Ohio, 1963; Chicago, 1964, 1970, 1975, 1976, 1979, 1980, 1983, 1985, 1986, 1989, 1990, 1995, 2000; Chillicothe, Ohio, 1964; Cleveland, 1964, 1970; Dayton, Ohio, 1964; Kansas City, Mo., 1964, 1967, 1973; Milwaukee, 1964, 1980, 1997, 2007; Fort Wayne, 1965, 1988; St. Louis, 1965, 1968, 1970, 1972, 1980, 1989, 2003; Madison, Wisc., 1966, 1968, 2003; Springfield, Ill., 1966, 1968, 1994, 1995; Glen Ellyn, Ill., 1967; Evansville, Ind., 1968, 2003; Minneapolis–St. Paul, 1969, 1977, 1982, 1984, 1992, 2002; Louisville, 1971, 2002; New York City, 1971, 1973, 1985, 1995; Harrisburg, Pa., 1979, 1994; Detroit, 1984; Madison County, Ky., 1987; Northern Illinois, 1987; Washington, D.C., 1988; Lexington, Ky., 1989; Boulder, 1992; Indianapolis, 1992; Seattle, 1992; Allentown, Pa., 1995; Knoxville, Tenn., 1995; Philadelphia, 1995; Greenwich, Conn., 1998; Torrington, Conn., 1998; Buena Park, Calif., 1999; Kankakee, Ill., 1999; Sarasota, Fla., 1999; Cape Girardeau, Mo., 2000, 2004; McHenry County, Ill., 2003; Houston, 2005
American Association for State and Local History, Harrisburg, Pa., 1966
Manuscript Society, Springfield, Ill., 1968; St. Louis, 1971
Ritzman Lecture, Aurora College, 1969
Illinois State Historical Society, 1970, 1973, 1974
Editing Institute, University of Virginia, 1972, 1974, 1975

Wright State University, 1972
American Library Association, Las Vegas, 1973
Calumet Campus, Purdue University, 1973
Military Order of the Loyal Legion, Philadelphia, 1973
Northern Illinois University, 1973
Abraham Lincoln Symposium, Springfield, Ill., 1974, 1978, 1984, 1988
Brigham Young University, 1974
University of Wyoming, 1974
Conference on the Bicentennial in Illinois, Springfield, 1975
Workshop for College Teachers of Illinois History, Springfield, 1975
Cairo Forum, Illinois Humanities Council, 1976
Stephen A. Douglas Association, 1976, 1986, 1995, 2003
Valparaiso University, 1976
St. John's University, Collegeville, Minn., 1977
Editing Conference, University of Kansas, 1978
Editing Institute, University of Wisconsin, Madison, 1978, 1979, 1980, 1983,
    1984, 1987, 1991, 1992, 2003
Illinois Humanities Council, Mount Vernon, Ill., 1978
Southern Historical Association, St. Louis, 1978
William L. Clements Library, University of Michigan, 1978
Rowfant Club, Cleveland, 1979
Southeast Missouri State University, 1979, 1984, 2003
Western Reserve Historical Society, Cleveland, 1979
Illinois History Symposium, Springfield, 1980, 1981, 1982, 1985
Missouri Conference on History, Southeast Missouri State University, 1980
Rice University, 1980
Association for Documentary Editing: Madison, Wisc., 1981; Providence,
    1984; Philadelphia, 1993; St. Louis, 1998; Charlottesville, Va., 1999; Ra-
    leigh, N.C., 2001; Chicago, 2003; Indianapolis, 2004
Midwest Archives Conference, St. Louis, 1981
Society of American Archivists: San Francisco, 1981; St. Louis, 1989
Union League of Philadelphia, 1981
Organization of American Historians: Philadelphia, 1982; St. Louis, 2000;
    Memphis, Tenn., 2003
Center for Military History, Washington, D.C., 1983
Hayes Presidential Center, Fremont, Ohio, 1983, 1991
Kentucky Historical Society, Frankfort, 1983
Lincoln College, Lincoln, Ill., 1983
Lincoln Fellowship of Wisconsin, 1983
National Forum on Lincoln and the Union, Springfield, Ill., 1983
Eastern Illinois University, 1984
Lincoln Group of Boston, 1984

Phi Alpha Theta Conference, Southeast Missouri State University, 1984
Wabash Valley Community College, 1984
Chicago Public Library, 1985
Grant Centenary, Galena, Ill., 1985
Grant Cottage, Mount McGregor, N.Y., 1985
Missouri Council on the Humanities, New Madrid, 1985
Mitchell Museum, Mount Vernon, Ill., 1985, 1998
National Archives, Washington, D.C., 1985
U.S. Army Command and General Staff College, Fort Leavenworth, 1985
U.S. Capitol Rotunda, 1985
Wheaton College, 1985
Evanston Historical Society, 1986
Lyndon B. Johnson Library and Museum, 1986
Midwest Civil War Round Table Conference: Cincinnati, 1986; Madison,
    Ind., 1990
Illinois Historic Preservation Agency Summer Institute, Springfield, 1987
Louis A. Warren Lincoln Library and Museum, Fort Wayne, 1987
Galena Historical Society, 1988, 1991
Georgetown University, 1989
Illinois College, 1989, 2000
Lincoln Group of the District of Columbia, 1989, 2002
MacMurray College, 1989
Marine Corps Command and Staff College, 1989, 1990
Morgan County Historical Society, Jacksonville, Ill., 1989
Petersburg Commemoration Seminar, 1989
Smithsonian Institution, Washington, D.C., 1989, 1993, 1994, 1995, 1996,
    1998, 2001
University of Tennessee, 1989
Wilderness and Spotsylvania Symposium, 1989
Filson Club, Louisville, 1990
South Carolina Department of History and Archives, 1990
Chicago Historical Society, 1991, 2003
Lincoln Boyhood National Memorial, Ind., 1991
Lincoln Colloquium, Springfield, Ill., 1991, 1992, 1994, 1995, 1996
Lincoln Legal Papers, Illinois Historic Preservation Agency, 1991
Anne S. K. Brown Memorial Lecture, Brown University, 1992
General Grant National Memorial, New York City, 1992, 1994, 2002
Illinois State University, Normal, 1992, 2001
John A. Logan Museum, Murphysboro, Ill., 1992, 2001
Lincoln-Douglas Debate Symposium, Ottawa, Ill., 1992
State Historical Society of Wisconsin, Madison, 1992, 1995
Travel America Seminar, Gettysburg, Pa., 1992

Civil War Institute, Gettysburg College, Gettysburg, Pa., 1993, 2001
Lincoln and Gettysburg Symposium, Gettysburg, Pa., 1993
Lincoln Seminar, Springfield, Ill., 1993, 1995, 1996, 1998
Southeast Civil War Conference, Vicksburg, Miss., 1993
Southern Illinois University School of Medicine, Springfield, Ill., 1993
Abraham Lincoln National Historic Site, Springfield, Ill., 1994, 1996
American Blue and Gray Association, Springfield, Ill., 1994
Center for Constructive Alternatives Seminar, Hillsdale College, Hillsdale, Mich., 1994
C-SPAN, Washington, D.C., 1994
E. B. "Pete" Long Memorial Lecture, University of Wyoming, Laramie, 1994
Civil War Conference, Corinth, Miss., 1995
Civil War Conference, San Diego, Calif., 1995
Civil War Conference, Washington, D.C., 1995
Fine Arts Building, Chicago, 1995
Jewish Historical Society, Washington, D.C., 1995, 2004
Missouri Historical Society, 1995
Pennsylvania State University, Mont Alto, 1995, 1996
Ulysses S. Grant Association: Richmond, Va., 1995; Washington, D.C., 1996, 2004; New York City, 1997, 2002; Providence, R.I., 1999; Georgetown, Ohio, 2000
University of California at Santa Barbara, 1995
University of Redlands, Redlands, Calif., 1995
World Affairs Forum, Mount Vernon, Ill., 1995
American Historical Association, Atlanta, 1996
Civil War Education Association: Sarasota, Fla., 1996, 1997, 1999, 2001, 2004, 2005; St. Louis, 2005
Civil War Seminar: *American Queen,* 1996, 1999, 2000; *Mississippi Queen,* 1997, 1998, 2005; *Delta Queen,* 2001, 2004, 2005
Civil War Symposium, Kankakee, Ill., 1996
Congress of Civil War Round Tables, Jackson, Miss., 1996
KFVS-TV, Cape Girardeau, Mo., 1996
Lincoln Forum, Gettysburg, Pa., 1996, 1999, 2001, 2003, 2004
Marquette University, Milwaukee, 1996
Model Editions Partnership, University of South Carolina, Columbia, 1996
Murray State University, Murray, Ky., 1996, 1997
Southeastern Louisiana University, Hammond, La., 1996
WLDS, Jacksonville, Ill., 1996
Annual Symposium, Ford's Theatre, Washington, D.C., 1997, 1998, 2000
Association for the Preservation of Civil War Sites, Hagerstown, Md., 1997
Civil War Institute: Campbellsville University, Campbellsville, Ky., 1997; Charleston, S.C., 1998
Grant's Tomb Rededication, C-SPAN, 1997

History Channel, 1997, 1999
Johns Hopkins University, 1997, 2003
Lincoln Memorial University, Harrogate, Tenn., 1997
National Public Radio: Chicago, 1997; Springfield, Ill., 2005
Ulysses S. Grant 175th Birthday Commemoration, Georgetown, Ohio, 1997
Blue and Gray Education Society, Corinth, Miss., 1998
C-SPAN, 1998
Hildene Conference on the Lincoln Women, Manchester, Vt., 1998
Historical Natchez Conference, 1998
Massachusetts Cultural Council, Springfield, Mass., 1998, 2000
Ralph G. Newman Memorial Service, Cultural Center, Chicago, 1998
St. Louis Mercantile Library, University of Missouri at St. Louis, 1998
Smithsonian Study Tours, Nashville, Tenn., 1998
Union League of Philadelphia, 1998
Brown University, Providence, R. I., 1999
Civil War Institute, Ohio Historical Society, Columbus, 1999
Lincoln Studies Institute, Knox College, Galesburg, Ill., 1999
Louisiana State University at Shreveport, 1999
Army and Navy Club, Washington, D.C., 2000
Chambersburg Civil War Seminar, Chambersburg, Pa., 2000
Civil War Society: Gettysburg, Pa., 2000; Richmond, Va., 2002, 2003
Clermont County History Symposium, Clermont College, Batavia, Ohio,
    2000
Governor French Academy, Belleville, Ill., 2000
Washington and Lee University, Lexington, Va., 2000
American Jewish Historical Society, New York City, 2001
Illinois Wesleyan University, Bloomington, Ill., 2001
Letitia Woods Brown Memorial Lecture, Historical Society of Washington,
    George Washington University, Washington, D.C., 2001
McLean County Historical Museum, Bloomington, Ill., 2001
Mississippi State University, Starkville, 2001
Pamplin Historical Park, 5th Annual Symposium, Richmond, Va., 2001
Wilson's Creek Symposium, Springfield, Mo., 2001
Fort Donelson 140th Anniversary Series, Dover, Tenn., 2002
General Benjamin H. Grierson Commemoration, Jacksonville, Ill., 2002
John A. Logan College, Carterville, Ill., 2002
Museum of the Confederacy, Richmond, Va., 2002
Pierre Menard Home, Ellis Grove, Ill., 2002
Vicksburg National Military Park, 140th Anniversary Seminar, Vicksburg,
    Miss., 2002
Centralia Historical Society, Centralia, Ill., 2003
Chester Public Library, Chester, Ill., 2003

Scholars in the Park Program, Ulysses S. Grant National Historic Site, White Haven, St. Louis, Mo., 2003

University of Missouri at St. Louis, 2003

University of Nevada at Las Vegas, 2003

University of the Air, Wisconsin Public Radio, 2003

Lincoln Prize Ceremony, Gilder Lehrman Foundation, Gettysburg College, New York City, 2004

Ponte Vedra Beach Public Library, Ponte Vedra, Fla., 2004

Roger Williams University, Bristol, R.I., 2004

South Atlantic Civil War Symposium, Hilton Head, S.C., 2004

Kentucky Wesleyan University, Owensboro, 2005

Lehrer Report, Public Broadcasting System, 2005

Missouri State Archives, Jefferson City, 2005

Ohio Valley History Conference, Murray, Ky., 2005

Ohio Wesleyan University, Delaware, 2005

Rochester Institute of Technology, Rochester, N.Y., 2005

World Talk Radio, 2005

Inauguration of W. E. B. Du Bois Center, Great Barrington, Mass., 2006

Address at Grand Opening of Visitor Center, Ulysses S. Grant National Historic Site, White Haven, St. Louis, Mo., 2007

Ohio Valley History Conference, Bowling Green, Ky., 2007

Index

family, 142; stays with Grant
family, 138; in St. Louis, 139,
143; in Vicksburg, 142; visits
Richmond, 148; in Washington,
143–144; and White Haven, 137
Grant, Orvil (USG's brother), 155
Grant, Peter (USG's uncle), 136
Grant, Simpson (USG's brother),
133, 140, 174, 181
Grant, Ulysses S.: accompanies
Army of the Potomac, 90,
115, 143, 164, 179, 186, 187,
209; alleged failure in office,
126; as American hero, 120,
124, 149; anti-Semitism,
169–178, 217–218; appearance,
112–113, 179–180, 188–189;
appointment of subordinates,
219–220, 222–224; appoints
relatives to office, 150–151;
Appomattox campaign, 116,
147, 185, 188–190; aptitude for
mathematics, 113, 128, 136, 137,
181; attends Know-Nothing
meeting, 172; attitude toward
enemy, 116, 189; attitude toward
slavery, 129, 184, as author,
120–121, 128, 133–134, 217;
at Belmont, 116, 182, 203, 204;
and Black Friday (1869), 118;
and black troops, 117, 129,
184–185, 215; as "butcher," 180;
in Cairo, Illinois, 140, 267n31;
captures Richmond, 116;
career, 114, 116, 117, 120, 123,
127–129, 132, 157, 181; and
casualties, 180, 186–187, 210;
character, 114–116, 119, 120,
123, 126, 130, 131–132, 162,
184, 188, 231; Chattanooga,
93, 162, 215; at City Point, 145,
165, 211, 221, 226; civilian life,

139, 155, 181, 214; on Civil
War, 126–127, 185–186; clarity
of communication, 115, 116,
133–134; Cold Harbor, 90, 115,
187; commands Department of
the Tennessee, 173; commands
District of Southeast Missouri,
201; commands postwar army,
117, 149–150; commands
regiment of Illinois volunteers,
116, 139, 157, 182; command
style, 114, 182; commissioned as
colonel, 139, 155, 214; concern
over cotton trade, 169–171,
173, 174, 177; on Confederacy
and Confederate soldiers, 129,
225; Confederate relatives, 128;
conversational style, 132, 133;
in Corinth, 141, 173; Crater,
115, 217; criticized, 118–121,
123, 130, 132, 141, 150–151, on
critics, 132, 158–159, 160–162;
crosses James River, 90, 187,
216, 221; crosses Mississippi
River, 213; crosses Rapidan
River, 179, 210; death and
funeral, 111–112, 123–124, 151;
decides not to enter Richmond,
165, 230; defends Orville E.
Babcock and William W.
Belknap, 119; as Democrat, 116,
129, 145, 154–155, 214, 225,
226; Depression of 1873, 119;
desire to annex Santo Domingo,
118; determination, 114, 115–
116, 120, 128, 144; dislike for
pageantry, 113, 188, 215; dislike
for politics, 117, 149–150, 155,
166, 215; distaste for publicity,
143, 215; drinking problem, 80,
130–132, 141, 158–159; early
life, 93, 113, 132, 136; eating

Grant, Ulysses S. *(cont.)*
 habits, 132; education, 113,
 116, 132, 136, 181; election of
 1868, 150, 176, 177–178, 218;
 election of 1872, 118; election
 of 1880, 117, 129; endorses AL's
 reelection, 224–225; employed
 in Illinois governor's office, 139,
 155, 214; facilitates voting in
 field, 225; farming in Missouri,
 128–129, 139, 181; Fifteenth
 Amendment, 118, 129; financial
 troubles, 120, 123, 128, 130,
 139, 151; foreign policy, 118;
 Fort Donelson, 113, 140,
 170, 182–183, 205, 212, 224;
 Fort Henry, 80, 205; at Fort
 Monroe, 217–218, 221, 223;
 friendships, 128, 130–131, 133,
 137, 145, 150, 226; in Galena,
 139, 141, 174, 181, 214; as
 general in chief, 85, 90, 115,
 143, 179, 183, 231; and General
 Orders No. 11, 160, 169–178,
 217–218; Grant and Ward silent
 partnership, 119–120, 123,
 128, 151; health, 120, 123, 131,
 138, 140, 151, 187; at Holly
 Springs, 142; hopes to become
 mathematics professor, 128,
 137; horsemanship, 113, 136;
 Indian policies, 118; inspires
 troops, 114; instincts, 119;
 institutes modern command
 system, 115, 208–209; invited
 to Ford's Theatre, 149, 230;
 keys to success, 113, 115, 127;
 letters of, 133–134, 137; as
 lieutenant general, 85, 90, 93,
 113, 115, 143, 162, 163, 179,
 207–208, 215–216; logic, 182,
 183, 188; at Long Branch,

150; love of family, 120,
 123, 132, 159; marches into
 Mississippi, 169–170; marriage
 to and relationship with Julia
 Dent, 128, 132, 135–151,
 181; meeting on *River Queen,*
 229; meets AL in Petersburg,
 229–230; *Memoirs,* 112, 120,
 121, 123–124, 126–127, 132,
 139, 151, 167, 178, 185–186,
 217–218, 229; Message to
 Congress (1874), 119; Message
 to Congress (1876), 119;
 Mexican Southern Railroad
 Company involvement, 128;
 Mexican War, 113, 114, 118,
 126–127, 128, 137, 181, 189;
 military orders, 133–134, 182;
 military principles, 127; military
 professionalism, 219; military
 staff, 129–131, 147–148,
 157–159, 163, 165, 167, 217,
 228; mistakes and failures, 116,
 117, 119, 128, 166, 181, 187,
 218; modesty, 114, 129, 149,
 214; moves into Kentucky,
 201–202; name change and
 middle initial, 118, 132–133,
 163; on Napoleon, 114; in
 New York City, 123, 128, 151;
 nominated by Republican Party,
 117; occupies Paducah, 182,
 202–203; opposes Ku Klux Klan,
 129; as ordinary American,
 120, 124, 125, 188; Overland
 campaign, 144–145, 179, 186,
 210–211; as paradox, 123–134;
 peacemaking authority restricted
 by AL, 146–147, 187, 227–228,
 229; peace terms, 227–230;
 Petersburg, 90, 115–116,
 185–187, 210–211, 216, 218,